Jennifer

THE UNAUTHORIZED BIOGRAPHY

Sean Smith is one of the UK's leading celebrity biographers, whose bestselling books have been translated throughout the world. Since his internationally acclaimed biography of J.K. Rowling, he has examined the world of the modern pop icon, writing biographies of Kylie Minogue, Robbie Williams, Justin Timberlake and Britney Spears. Described by the *Independent* as a 'fearless chronicler', he specializes in meticulous research, leaving his north London home to go 'on the road' to find the real person behind the star image. *Jennifer: The Unauthorized Biography* is Sean's eleventh book.

Also by Sean Smith

Britney: The Unauthorized Biography

Kylie: The Biography

Justin: The Biography

Robbie: The Biography

J.K. Rowling: A Biography

Royal Racing

The Union Game

Sophie's Kiss

Stone Me! (with Dale Lawrence)

Jennifer

THE UNAUTHORIZED BIOGRAPHY

Sean Smith

Pan Books

First published 2007 by Sidgwick & Jackson

First published in paperback 2008 by Pan Books
an imprint of Pan Macmillan, division of Macmillan Publishers Limited
Pan Macmillan, 20 New Wharf Road, London N1 9RR
Basingstoke and Oxford
Associated companies throughout the world
www.panmacmillan.com

ISBN 978-0-330-52231-1

1 3 5 7 9 8 6 4 2

A CIP catalogue record for this book is available from
the British Library.

Typeset by SetSystems Ltd, Saffron Walden, Essex
Printed and bound in the UK by
CPI Mackays, Chatham ME5 8TD

Contents

Part Three: A Soap Opera

Part One

92nd Street

When Jennifer was twenty-nine and with Brad Pitt, she was asked in an interview to name the best smell in the world. She replied, 'The best smell in the world is that man that you love.' The interviewer then asked, 'How is that smell?' and Jennifer sighed and replied, 'Oh, I don't know. It's like your dad. The smell of your dad.'

ONE

In The Footsteps Of Jennifer

Walking in Central Park at the start of autumn is a joy, especially if it's a sunny Saturday and New Yorkers are out cycling, running, singing, arguing or just sitting around watching their kids as they battle imaginary monsters. I had begun my day searching for brunch at a real-life 'Central Perk', the legendary coffee shop in *Friends*. Taking pot luck I try Alice's Tea Rooms for no better reason than the name reminds me of the film *Alice's Restaurant*, a hippyesque piece of whimsy starring Arlo Guthrie, son of the great American folk singer Woody Guthrie. The film was released in 1969, the year that Jennifer was born. I wonder if Jennifer could play Alice in the remake? She could certainly play a waitress, she is brilliant at it having portrayed waitresses in, it seems, every other thing she has ever appeared in, including as her most famous incarnation, Rachel Green. She was also a waitress in *Along Came Polly* and *Office Space*, and in the BAFTA award-winning animated film *The Iron Giant* she was the voice of a waitress. She isn't a waitress at Alice's Tea Rooms. Jennifer was a bit accident-prone when she worked as a waitress so my food would have ended up in my lap if she had brought it. My waitress seems in a happy mood as she brings my poached egg, hollandaise sauce on the side, with a home-made ham and cheese scone. The Aniston favourite – mayonnaise sandwich on white – is not on the menu.

At the next table three young women arrive for their weekly catch-up of all the news. This is more like Central Perk. They could be Rachel, Monica and Phoebe or, in real life, Jennifer and her best friends Andrea and Kristin. They order healthy drinks, a combination of smoothies and juices with some herbal tea and muesli to follow; I feel guilty as runny egg runs down my chin. This is how I imagine Jennifer liked to spend her time when she lived in New York, enjoying the company of her best friends, laughing and gossiping, making plans and telling secrets. As I get up to go, squeezing between the tables, the waitress arrives with the rest of their order – waffles with maple syrup, omelette with French fries, extra bacon and French toast. The healthy stuff was just the hors d'oeuvre.

I am in Central Park trying to walk off brunch. I decide to start at West 72nd Street next to Strawberry Fields, the monument to John Lennon, who was shot dead outside the Dakota Building in 1980 when Jennifer was eleven. In that year she was more concerned with her parents' divorce than the death of the former Beatle. She lived just twenty blocks away on West 92nd Street and would have walked around these paths a thousand times. Strawberry Fields itself is rather sombre and shady. I sit on one of the memorial benches, inscribed 'Our Hearts were Young and Gay', and watch the obligatory group of Japanese tourists take their holiday snaps. Not too far away I can hear a jazz band playing 'Over the Rainbow'. It should really be 'Imagine' to fit a poetic mood but *The Wizard of Oz* will have to do.

In the middle of this frenetic city of madness there is a little easy tranquillity about the place. Who would ever want to leave? Jennifer Aniston, for one.

The reality check occurs when I reach a fork in the pathway and go to ask a woman which way leads to Central Park West. She jumps out of her skin. Nobody asks for directions in New York. When I first came here in the late 1980s the atmosphere in this part of Manhattan was tenser. The so-called Preppie Murder hadn't helped. That was in 1986 when an eighteen-year-old girl, coincidentally also called Jennifer, had been killed by six-foot-five-inch Robert Chambers, with whom she had left a bar and crossed over into the park. Her body was found behind the Metropolitan Museum of Art, a couple of blocks from where Jennifer Aniston had gone to school. It was a notorious case that captured the headlines. Whenever a particularly nasty crime happens on your doorstep it sets everyone on edge, particularly parents of teenage girls. Jennifer Aniston was seventeen at the time.

I also recall the streets around where she lived being decidedly rough and not the sort of place to wander around in after dark. It all looks very clean and respectable outside her old building on West 92nd Street now although the doorman reminds me that there were drug dealers and addicts across the street when Jennifer lived here. This was her home for the major part of her childhood, on the twenty-third floor of a New York tower block with its large, cool and impersonal lobby. It's not dingy here. On the contrary it's quite bright and airy but I can understand why, after taking the lift to her home for more than ten years, Jennifer so prized her first house in the Hollywood Hills and, in particular, loved her garden. She left New York in

1989 although her mother Nancy stayed for a further two years until she too moved to California. Nobody here has a bad word to say about Nancy – 'a very nice lady' seems to be the gist of it. Funnily enough, one of the guys recalls Jennifer and Brad Pitt coming in one day, looking for her mother who was visiting old friends in the building. I am surprised because I didn't think there was any contact with her mother when she was with Brad.

'What do you think of Jennifer Aniston?' I ask my waitress at Big Nick's, at Broadway and 76th Street. 'I didn't like *Friends*,' says the waitress. 'I liked *Fresh Prince* and that one beginning with M.' And with that she is gone to take more orders, leaving me to ponder what sitcom begins with M.

Jennifer went to high school at LaGuardia Arts, an imposing, slightly scary-looking building which reminds me of the Barbican in London. On the outside wall is a list of famous alumni and Jennifer Aniston's is the first name on the list – proof indeed of the advantage of having a surname beginning with the first letter of the alphabet. I recognize many names including some favourites – Ellen Barkin, Adrien Brody, Liza Minnelli and Al Pacino. I don't see anyone who has worked on a movie with Jennifer. Every student has to use a picture ID on screen in order to get past security. Once past the soulless lobby, things really perk up. I am shown around all eight floors by Ed McCarthy, an English teacher and an illuminating companion. The cafeteria is huge, noisy and full of laughter and chatter. Jennifer used to love to laugh and gossip with her friends here between classes. I wonder if it's ok to describe Ms Aniston as a canteen girl; she seems to thrive in the company of a group of friends, not changing the world but just talking. I am struck by how many more girls than boys there seem to be. Ed confirms that the school is 73 per cent female which has me asking for an application form on my way out. Last academic year, however, there were 12,000 students competing for 700 places. There is a positive energy here; nobody is looking surly, confrontational or posing for adolescent effect. On the noticeboard outside the drama rooms is a picture of Adrian Grenier, the heart-throb star of *Entourage*, my favourite American comedy since *Friends*. I wonder, is it compulsory to come to this school to make it in US television?

Anthony Abeson, who taught Jennifer at high school, has invited me downtown to sit in on one of his drama classes in a studio on West 44th Street. Jennifer took one of these classes after she left school so I thought it might be valuable. Anthony, who clearly relishes his work, introduces me to the twenty-strong group of young actors and actresses, all of them relaxed and good-natured. 'Sean is a writer from England,' he begins, with a sly smile. 'Do you think he is here to interview me about my own research into the history and mythology of drama? Or is he perhaps interested in my methods of teaching you the finer points of acting? Or is he here, and this is pure conjecture, because I once taught Jennifer Aniston?' Everybody has a good laugh, including me, especially when I reveal it is the mythology of drama that most interests me.

I am lying of course. I am, in fact, at this particular class to watch how young people are taught acting. During this session a strikingly good-looking man and woman are developing a scene from Hemingway. They are sitting outside a bar in Mexico trying to order a beer while having a tense discussion about what to do about the baby she is expecting and the abortion she might have.

I am impressed with how quickly they snap in and out of character whenever Anthony chips in with a comment or direction. The principal bone of contention is how to order a beer in Spanish. The favoured approach is to shout the word '*cerveza*' as if the waiter has an IQ of ten. I comment that when I was in Spain I always shouted '*biero*' at the waiters, which is quickly ignored.

I leave full of vigour and the hope that Jennifer has not lost that enthusiasm which so pervaded the room. My last port of call for the day is the imposing St Mark's Church-in-the-Bowery, on the corner of Second Avenue and East 10th Street, a place of surprising peacefulness surrounded by the relentless noise of car horns and screeching brakes. The Bowery neighbourhood of Lower East Manhattan had a poor reputation when I first came to New York, much worse than where Jennifer was brought up. Crime and poverty went hand in hand here and it was not an area for an evening stroll. Like many other bad neighbourhoods in this city, however, the Bowery has seen a revival in the past twenty years, becoming a trendy and acceptable place to live. I remember coming to a nightclub here, one of the first 'new' ventures and chatting to Christopher Reeve who had popped in for a nightcap. It was before the tragic accident that left him paralysed in 1995. He was modest and likeable.

St Mark's is steeped in local history. The church itself was consecrated in 1799 but the original chapel on the site was built in 1660 by Peter Stuyvesant, who is buried in a tomb underneath. As the Governor of New Netherlands he surrendered New Amsterdam to the English fleet in 1664 when it was renamed New York. St Mark's today is just the sort of place that every local community needs, promoting fringe arts, theatre and dance.

These are the events that will never make Broadway but deserve an audience on your doorstep. Jennifer's first professional role was here when she played a lesbian high-school student. There's nothing showing when I visit but, outside among the pigeons and sparrows, two elderly gentleman are enjoying a pit stop on a bench in the courtyard. One is telling the story of when he was in Capri and went for lunch at Gracie Fields' villa. 'Why did she invite you?' asks his friend. 'Because I spoke English.'

TWO

Ouzo And Cigarettes

John Aniston was living proof that 'tall, dark and handsome' could exist in real life. At six foot three, he had jet-black hair, a chiselled jaw and strong features, with the tanned complexion that betrayed his Greek birthright. He wore a moustache that would have served Omar Sharif very well in *Doctor Zhivago* (1965). He may not exactly have been a Greek god but he was considerably better looking than his best friend, Telly Savalas. The man for ever associated with his role as lollipop-sucking New York detective Kojak was, however, a man of enormous charisma, and a genuine film star who was practically royalty within the Greek community. It was a great honour for the family when Telly agreed to be godfather to John's daughter Jennifer.

Jennifer was born in the Los Angeles suburb of Sherman Oaks on 11 February 1969. Her father was a well-liked member of Hollywood's Greek community but, as an actor, he was just a bit player despite an impressive stage pedigree. He may not have been a star but, aged thirty-five, he had come a very long way since he was born Ioannis Anastasakis on the Mediterranean island of Crete. His parents moved to the US when he was a young boy and settled in Eddytown, a small town in Pennsylvania, where they opened a diner. They were not the first immigrant family to work all hours – twenty hours a day – in the brave new country to try and improve the circumstances of their lives. Not long afterwards Ioannis Anastasakis became the more English-language-friendly John Aniston.

Growing up, Jennifer was always told that her grandfather decided on the new surname when driving through Anniston, Alabama, but this may just be the stuff of family legend. Certainly it is a made-up name and totally unique, but not everyone in the family chose to anglicize their name and there are still several entries under Anastasakis in the local phone book.

Jennifer's beloved grandmother Joanna was the matriarch of the family and lived in the same house in Eddytown until she died aged ninety-four. She was always very welcoming to her granddaughter who had been given the second name Joanna in her honour. Jennifer once described her as the 'godmother' of the family: 'She was amazingly strong and had the most beautiful skin, the softest thing that you ever felt.' Jennifer called her grandmother Yaya, a Greek term of endearment rather like Nana.

From an early age John had ambitions to act and graduated with a bachelor's degree in Theatre Arts at Pennsylvania State University before – perhaps realizing it would be a precarious existence – taking a postgraduate course in biology at California State University in Long Beach. After college he spent his national service in the United States Navy, first as an intelligence officer in Panama and later in the reserves, reaching the rank of Lieutenant Colonel. When he left the service he moved to New York to try and further his acting ambitions and, like his daughter would in the future, began his career in the theatre. He made his Broadway debut in 1959, aged twenty-six, at the Orpheum Theatre in the first production of *Little Mary Sunshine*, a popular musical of the day. John played the role of Chief Brown Bear, chief of the Kadota Indians, in what was an affectionate pastiche of the old Jeanette McDonald/Nelson Eddy musicals.

He moved to Los Angeles to try and make a breakthrough, along the well-worn path from Broadway to the major studios that his daughter would make twenty-five years later. The whole experience would prove supremely disappointing to John Aniston so it was little surprise that he later regarded his daughter's chosen path with great concern. His less than triumphant early screen career began in 1962 when he played an unnamed police officer in an episode of the television drama *87th Precinct*. He followed that a year later with an uncredited role in the film *Love With The Proper Stranger* (1963) which starred Steve McQueen and Natalie Wood. If he had received a credit, it would have read Birdman of Macy's, so perhaps it was just as well he was anonymous.

In real life, John Aniston fell in love. The object of his affection was a young mother and model called Nancy Dow, a pretty brunette from New England with the look of a young Jacqueline Bisset about her. Her father Gordon was a first-generation American. His parents had emigrated from Scotland and Nancy is proud to say that she is a relative of Mary Queen of Scots. Nancy's mother Louise was second-generation American. Her grandfather had arrived in New York from Melitto in Italy and become a successful businessman. Nancy was therefore half-Scottish and half-Italian, which makes Jennifer three-quarters Mediterranean. Gordon and Louise worked hard bringing up their large family during the Great Depression years. Nancy was the fourth of six sisters; one, Martha, was born with Down's Syndrome and died while still a young child. Times were so hard that like thousands of other families they made the long trip by car to California dreaming of a better life and settled in North Hollywood, not far from where Jennifer would be born.

Nancy's childhood was touched with a sadness similar to that which would so affect Jennifer's. The old maxim that history repeats itself has never been truer than when applied to the two Aniston women: in both cases one parent (for Nancy it was her mother) left the family home when they were young girls and Nancy's own story reveals a woman battling perceived rejection for most of her life. 'What a blow that must have been,' Jennifer once remarked with considerable understatement. Nancy and the three eldest sisters stayed in California where her father found work as a security guard at Universal Studios and life was a constant struggle with no mother and little money. When she was seventeen, Nancy met and married an older man but soon realized that she had made a mistake in her desperation for a normal family life. Unfortunately, by that time, she was already pregnant with her first son, Johnny. She divorced in 1961 when he was two and set about making her way in Hollywood. She has never revealed the identity of her first husband but in her memoir poignantly admits, 'The child who longed to be hugged felt she had married a man who was hugless.'

Nancy had lovely, well-defined features and beautiful cheekbones and was in demand for catalogue work, but the nearest she got to stardom as a fresh-faced youngster was to sign autographs for Rock Hudson, the epitome of a beefcake movie star. Superficially, Rock was probably the closest film star in looks and stature – tall, dark and handsome – to John Aniston.

She was a single mother with a three-year-old son when she first met John in 1962. At that time her own acting career was barely trumping the low levels reached by her Greek boyfriend.

For the great majority of his acting career, John Aniston was better known for his stage work than for television appearances which were distinctly unpromising. Not surprisingly, he was cast to play a Greek in a 1964 episode of *Combat* – he was billed as Greek Number 2 – a very popular Sixties' television series about a World War Two infantry platoon battling its way across Europe. The one bonus for John was that he was able to forge an on-set friendship with Telly Savalas who was the guest star of that particular episode. The two men really hit it off. Despite his tough-guy persona Savalas was a sensitive and cultured man whose mother had been a painter and friend of Picasso, while Aniston was reserved yet funny. Savalas was ten years older, also the son of Greek immigrants and immensely proud of his Greek heritage. He had also endured tough times before making it as an actor in his late thirties, working in a variety of jobs including selling newspapers and being a lifeguard. When John and Nancy married just before Christmas in 1965, Telly was best man.

After they were married neither Mr nor Mrs Aniston set the world of Hollywood alight. Both managed a very few television appearances. Nancy was on *The Red Skelton Show* and then one episode each of comedy *The Beverly Hillbillies* and adventure series *The Wild Wild West*. John's typecasting as a Greek character continued with an episode of *I Spy*, but at least this time he had a name, Economides. His only credit the year Jennifer was born was in an episode of *Mission Impossible* in which he played a pilot. This was really scratching around for scraps and John was forced to drive a taxi or work as a door-to-door salesman while 'resting' between engagements. It was an existence which Jennifer's half-brother Johnny Melick described as a 'struggle'.

Three years after they were married, Nancy discovered she was expecting a baby. It was the summer of 1968 and the prospects for the Aniston family were not getting any brighter. Nancy, however, made a decision which would have a profound effect on their future lives. She decided to give up work and devote herself to being a mother to her children. She had never been comfortable being promoted as a bikini-wearing sex kitten. Her final role before her very premature retirement reinforced her disquiet and brought an end to any serious acting pretensions. She was the victim of a strangler in a slice of soft-porn schlock horror called *The Ice House* (1969), also known as *Cold Blood*, *Love In Cold Blood* or *The Passion Pits* – take your pick.

The Ice House had the potential to become a cult classic. The 'hero', Fred Martin, played by David Story, is the manager of an ice house who is prone to blackouts during which he strangles any woman he is with at the time. His first victim is a girl called Venus De Marco played by Sabrina, the pneumatic British sex siren from Stockport who had been a fifties' pin-up in Britain, particularly after she had squeezed her 41-inch bust into a school uniform for one of the popular St Trinian's films.

Nancy was the strangler's second victim, Jan Wilson, who turns up at the ice house for some love action but gets more than she bargains for when she interrupts Story disposing of his first victim in the meat freezer. The only still from her truncated movie career available on the Internet is the one of poor Nancy, beautifully made up with not a hair out of place, eyes popping as two hairy hands grab her by the throat. The whole movie is magnificently sleazy with other highlights including a go-go club with totally nude dancers and the first screen appearance of John Holmes. The notorious porn star, whose life formed the basis of the Mark Wahlberg film *Boogie Nights*, was the proud owner of a foot-long penis. He only showed his rear view, however, in *The Ice House*.

Ironically *The Ice House* proved to be the only movie featuring its star, David Story. Holmes, however, made a grand total of 2,274 porn films including many after he had been diagnosed HIV-positive. He became even more notorious in the 1980s when he was implicated in the grisly Wonderland murders, named after the quiet street in Laurel Canyon where four bodies were discovered. In the movie *Wonderland* (2003) Holmes is played by Val Kilmer, while his estranged wife Sharon is played by Lisa Kudrow, Jennifer's co-star in *Friends*. Hollywood is truly a very small world: when she moved to Los Angeles Jennifer Aniston fell in love with Laurel Canyon and lived just around the corner from Wonderland Avenue.

Jennifer's own take on her mother's decision to forsake her career is that the acting business was too hard for her: 'You're unbelievably vulnerable and you get just ripped to shreds sometimes, and other times God knows what people say.'

Fresh from her decision to retire at the age of thirty-two, Nancy set about supporting her husband's search for success and finding a home big enough for what would soon be a family of four. The apartment they were living in was too small so they borrowed money from Nancy's father and managed to buy a small house in Sherman Oaks, an area of north LA generally referred to as the San Fernando Valley but more familiarly known as the Valley. The house had been on the market for a considerable time as a bank foreclosure. To the casual observer it was a 'dump' but the Anistons set about making it into a home for their new baby and now ten-year-old son.

Gradually they transformed the house into a home, although money was so tight Jennifer had to make do with hand-me-down baby clothes and an old black and white television. Nancy's best friend was Molly Reynolds, wife of successful television actor William Reynolds, star of the series *The FBI*. Some of Jennifer's happiest early memories are of trips to the Reynolds' luxury home where she and Johnny could splash around in the pool.

Nancy's other great friend was Lynn Savalas, wife of Telly. They forged a common bond, living with Greek husbands and indulging them in their passion for cards, which included the four of them playing bridge through the night at the Savalas home in Beverly Hills. In her fascinating book, tortuously titled *From Mother And Daughter To Friends*, Nancy describes the very real affection between the two families, culminating in Jennifer's baptism ceremony when she was nearly two years old. The arrangements were made over a rubber of bridge when Telly insisted that Greek tradition demanded the best man at the wedding be made godfather to the first child. Lynn, who like Nancy was brought up in New England, was nominated as the perfect godmother.

During the very orthodox Greek ceremony Telly Savalas, a big softie, held Jennifer, whispering reassuring nothings to keep her calm during all the excitement and helping the infant to a tot of holy wine. Part of the tradition involved Jennifer being taken to a dressing room where she was changed into a special baptism dress, a gift from her godparents. Afterwards Jennifer distinguished herself by throwing up all over Telly Savalas, making a proper mess of his black velvet dinner jacket. She followed up by vomiting over the back seat of his Rolls Royce. One of Jennifer's often-told stories from that day is how her Yaya scooped up the sick to preserve it because it contained holy water.

Despite his fame, Savalas took his role of godfather to Jennifer very seriously, spoiling her whenever he had the chance. She has always been very appreciative: 'He was one of the nicest people.' He gave her lollipops before they became his trademark prop in *Kojak* in which he used them as an aid to help him give up smoking. He also gave her a lovely pink bicycle with a big pink banana seat which little Jennifer thought was 'very cool'.

John's career meanwhile was going from bad to worse. He seemed to lurch from one disappointment to another. Later, he would always be set against Jennifer becoming an actress because of the number of let-downs she would have to face – wise words for the first part of her career. His biggest setback was when he was lined up for a major part in *The Mary Tyler Moore Show*. He was supposed to play Ted Baxter, the anchorman in the fictional television newsroom where the show was set. Eventually the key role went to another actor, Ted Knight, who ended up winning several Emmy awards during the show's seven-year run. John's career, meanwhile, reached a nadir when his own agent rejected him and refused to renew the contract they had. Without an agent, going to auditions and finding work was practically impossible, a situation made even more desperate by his age. He was nearly forty.

It was a far cry from the world of his friend Telly who

travelled to Britain the year Jennifer was born to film the new Bond film *On Her Majesty's Secret Service* (1969) in which he played the arch villain Ernst Blofeld. It would be the most successful of five films Savalas released that year. More significantly though, he was the first important man in Jennifer's life to leave his wife for another woman he met on location. In Telly's case, it was an English actress called Sally Adams, or, as she was known for that film, Dani Sheridan. Somewhat confusingly she played a minor character called The American Girl (the role of The English Girl had already gone to Joanna Lumley). She began an affair with Savalas which led to her becoming pregnant and giving birth to a son called Nick in 1973 – a year later Telly and Lynn divorced. When she met Savalas, Sally was already a single mother. Her daughter, Colette, would later find her own fame as Nicollette Sheridan, star of *Desperate Housewives*. Nicollette was six years older than Jennifer Aniston but they had several things in common, both being raised in a Greek culture. Besides being her stepfather (although he never officially married Sally Adams) Telly was also Nicollette's godfather and encouraged her to embrace Greek culture and learn the language. Rather touchingly Nicollette once said, 'Telly was my stepfather but I always thought of him as my daddy.' Somewhat surprisingly her mother keeps on turning up in minor roles on British television including episodes of *Coronation Street*, *Hollyoaks* and *Emmerdale*. These days she is usually credited as Sally Sheridan.

Telly's career, meanwhile, continued on an upward curve. In the 1970s his fame would spread even further when he played a New York cop called Kojak in a television film called *The Marcus-Nelson Murders* (1973). The role fitted him perfectly and led to one of the most popular television series of all time.

He also did his best to rescue his friend John's ailing career by making sure he had a couple of guest parts in *Kojak*, his only work in two years. He played a character called Albert Dancik in Season One and then returned in Season Two as a completely different person called Webster. The episodes did little to help and, by this time, John was thoroughly disillusioned with the acting business. More importantly, his family continued to struggle financially and, urged on by Nancy, he decided it was time to try for a more secure future by giving up acting in favour of going back to college to study medicine. This was not quite so much the shot in the dark that one might think because, in the US, a GI bill was in operation at the time through which John qualified for financial aid as a returning veteran.

For two years John studied for his pre-medical qualifications while the state paid the Aniston mortgage. He passed his exams but, now aged forty-one, found that his age was a barrier to being accepted into medical school. He and Nancy hit upon the idea of him studying abroad and the obvious solution was to go to live in Greece where they could stay, at least in the first instance, with Anastasakis relatives.

The young Jennifer was unaware of the family turmoil going on behind the scenes, immersing herself, as many little girls do, in games featuring her dolls and imaginary friends. She had a regulation Barbie doll but also one she dressed up to look like Cher, complete with long black hair and very high heels. She even built Cher a luxury apartment out of old shoeboxes. She would put her dolls into dramatic scenes and pretend they were acting the parts.

Jennifer, however, was not all dolls and pink ribbons. She could also be adventurous. On one occasion she had a very narrow escape when she rode her tricycle into a swimming pool and her pet poodle Dimitri leaped in after her, thinking it was a game. Fortunately her brother Johnny saw what happened and realized that the weight of the bike was dragging his sister under. He jumped in and rescued one small girl and her very wet dog.

The house in the Valley, which had been a happy first home for five-year-old Jennifer, was sold in the summer of 1974 and the Anistons flew east to stay with Yaya just outside Philadelphia. They had to sell the house to provide starter funds for their new life in Greece, especially as there would be no GI fund there to support John's studies. Leaving had been a huge wrench, especially for Nancy, but she was determined that the family should achieve a better life. Hearing Yaya's stories about life in the old country filled them with enthusiasm for the future. During her stay with Yaya, Nancy saw her own mother for the first time since she was a little girl. Louise was living in the neighbouring state of Connecticut. The two women had lunch and Louise met Jennifer for the first and only time. It was not a particularly satisfactory reconciliation but meant that Nancy was able to spend time with her mother when she was dying from cancer a year later. Neither of Jennifer's maternal grandparents played much of a part in her childhood. She was far more influenced by her Greek heritage, something she acknowledged, tongue in cheek, when she said, 'Greek families are like the Mafia except they're a lot friendlier'.

Nothing it seemed could thwart the Anistons' decision to embrace the country of John's birth – nothing that is except a cruel twist of political fate: Turkey invaded Cyprus and occupied about one third of the island including part of the capital of Nicosia. The situation in Cyprus had been volatile throughout the 1960s with the Greek Cypriots, more than three quarters of the population, favouring union with Greece. The Turkish minority were not at all keen on that idea and chose an unfortunate time to do something about it, at least as far as John's plans were concerned.

The military action resulted in the closure of the island's university and an enormous influx of displaced students arriving at the University of Athens where they were given preferential treatment. There was no place for a foreign resident like John Aniston for at least one academic year. Their new life was over before it began. They did take the opportunity to visit John's birthplace on Crete though, and to enjoy the hospitality of his many relations who still lived there. Jennifer, in particular, loved meeting her Greek cousins who were her own age which made a welcome change from being tormented by her big brother and his friends. The Greek sojourn which they had expected to be life-changing turned into nothing more than an extended holiday of jolly family meals and beautiful scenery.

Jennifer's mother Nancy was much struck by what she called the 'magic of Greece' and she and John vowed to return for more visits, little realizing that this nine-month trip would be the one and only time they would travel abroad as a family. The absurdity of red tape was never better illustrated than when it looked for a while as if John, still a Greek citizen, might be pressed into two years' national service in the Greek armed forces even though he had already done his bit for the US Navy. So, it was with some relief that the Anistons arrived back in Pennsylvania to stay with Yaya again, but this time with no home of their own and no prospects.

At this stage it was still John's intention to follow a career in medicine – perhaps the next academic year might bring more luck. In the meantime he travelled up to New York to look up some old friends and see if there was any temporary work there. Ironically it was not the 7,000-mile trip from LA to Athens that proved to be life changing but one of just a hundred miles from Philly to Manhattan. John returned with the news that he was going to be an actor again and that he was up for a part in the long-running daytime soap opera *Love Of Life*. The show was one of those American institutions like *I Love Lucy*, *Bilko* or *Days Of Our Lives*, which all started in the 1950s and just seemed to drift into national institutions. *Love of Life* had no particular pretensions. It started off as the day-to-day rivalry of two sisters in a fictional town in New York State. Then, when one sister was written out, it moved to another fictional town and there was more of the same. Nancy was overjoyed at the turn of events and that after such struggles fate was being kind to them at last. At first, John commuted from Philadelphia to New York while Nancy excitedly made preparations for the whole family to move to Manhattan where they eventually found the apartment which would be Jennifer's home for the rest of her childhood.

One year after leaving California, Jennifer Aniston became a New Yorker. While she had enjoyed her Greek adventure, as any child would, she was, in later years, less complimentary about the Greek community, particularly the men. She's forgotten all but a few words of the Greek she learnt as a small girl. She also hates the national drink, ouzo: 'There is nothing more disgusting to me. I used to hate Greek food. Basically it's awful food.'

Most tellingly, however, there will never be a big, fat Greek wedding for Jennifer. She told *FHM Magazine* that she could never marry a Greek man because she had grown up in a Greek family. 'Women are still second-class citizens, pregnant in the kitchen while the men sit around drinking ouzo and smoking cigarettes after dinner instead of helping with anything. And Greek men are well known for being philanderers. Greek men are all about moustaches, ouzo and dancing with women who aren't necessarily their wives. And also their moms tell them they're perfect so they think they can do no wrong. And there's nothing worse than a man who thinks he can do no wrong!'

Jennifer's remarks about Greek men may or may not have been influenced by her godfather Telly Savalas – six children by four different women – or by her own father, who was to break her heart when she was nine.

THREE

The Hard-Knock Life

Home for the Aniston family was a tower block on the Upper West Side of Manhattan. The building itself, just off Columbus, was clean and secure but the area was not the trendy, bistro-filled neighbourhood it is today. The Upper West Side was always a fun and lively area to live in but the nicer part was more than ten blocks down the street in the Sixties and Seventies. By the time you reached 80th it was necessary to quicken your step. Jennifer's area was home to many low-income and federal-assisted families living in 'the projects' which is the American description of government-assisted housing. Rightly or wrongly the projects are traditionally associated with higher crime, urban decay and a lack of prosperity. The nearest UK equivalent is council estates.

Gradually, thanks to a sense of purpose in City Hall and Mayor Rudy Giuliani in particular, a greater police presence started to clean up the neighbourhoods, literally block by block. Unfortunately Jennifer missed out on this when she was growing up in New York City. 'It was pretty seedy,' she admitted. Nancy instilled in her daughter from an early age the need to be careful in this urban jungle and always on the alert against possible muggers. Inevitably, during her dozen years in New York, Jennifer had her handbag snatched on more than one occasion. At least their apartment on the twenty-third floor had a balcony which meant they had an uplifting view of the Empire State Building.

In some ways that inspirational view represented the promise and excitement of the Anistons' new life. For the first time John had a steady income, although as a family they still had to be a little cautious over money. They were not in the Savalas league yet. Telly would come over to see them for cards whenever he was in New York for location work on *Kojak*. Watching Telly play in a fearless, cavalier way inspired a love of cards in Jennifer which she still has, but her game is poker, not bridge. The other legacy Telly bequeathed his god-daughter was a love of cigars, although smoking a stogie was not, perhaps, the most elegant pursuit for a female star in Hollywood so Jennifer kept this habit well out of the public gaze.

When the Anistons first settled in New York, they enjoyed the best times Jennifer had growing up. Laughter filled the apartment. It was as if an enormous black cloud had lifted and the family was transformed by the simple formula of a job and a regular income. She recalled, 'My dad had this laugh that made you want to laugh. The same with my mom. When one would start, the other would follow. There's nothing better than contagious laughter. It's the most peaceful feeling in the world.'

The apartment would also be filled with people. These happy memories of rooms filled with laughter and conversation when she was aged six and seven had a strong influence on Jennifer. When the good times left her family life, she longed to recapture those days and, since then, has always enjoyed being among large groups of people. She loves the camaraderie of a bunch of friends and enjoys being the centre of attention. As a child she would delight in singing or belly dancing for her parents' guests, saving her best performances for her Greek relatives. She was also accomplished at charades, the only indication at such a young age that she might have some talent for acting. She never, it seemed, suffered from performance nerves. She recalled, 'At seven I was completely fearless.' She was also a nightmare to try and put to bed, forever wanting to stay and enjoy the party until tiredness won through.

Jennifer's fearlessness was not just confined to the home. In the summer, the family would make the two-hour journey to the Hamptons, the fashionable beach resort for New York folk. Jennifer would play on the beach with boys and girls of her own age. A little boy she particularly liked called Michael would also go there on his holidays. One day, Michael's grandfather was encouraging the little boy to 'go and kiss Jennifer' but he was too shy to make the first move. Jennifer marched straight up to her friend, threw her arms around him and gave him a great big kiss.

The one cloud on this bright, new horizon was provided by elder brother Johnny who, as a growing teenager, found it much more difficult than the other three to settle in New York. At just seventeen he announced that he was heading back west to attend college in California and moved to Los Angeles to live with one of Nancy's sisters and her family. The young Jennifer always had trouble grasping the concept of a half-brother, particularly when Nancy explained to her that Johnny had another father: 'It never made sense to me. I mean, who is Johnny's other father? He must be my father too.' Johnny never returned to live in New York, staying on to live and work in LA after he graduated. Jennifer always loved to see him, however, even though he once made her sit through the classic horror *Friday The 13th* (1980). A frightened Jennifer went to the bathroom afterwards not realizing that Johnny had crept in first and hidden behind the shower curtain wearing a horrible mask with the eyeballs springing out on stalks. Surprise!

Johnny, being that much older, has never seemed to be one of Jennifer's innermost circle but they have always shared a strong family bond, a similar sense of humour and fun. Johnny now works in the movie business under the name of John T. Melick. He has been an assistant director and a set dresser on a variety of minor movies. He has worked on a couple of Jennifer's movies and they remain close, especially since she is Auntie Jen to his two children.

When Johnny left, Jennifer became, in effect, an only child at the age of nine. To cheer her up, Nancy took her to her first ever Broadway show, *Annie*, at the Alvin Theatre. This particular production of the favourite musical was a classic and had won seven prestigious Tony Awards the previous year. Surprisingly, considering her parents' acting credentials and not to mention those of her godfather, Jennifer was brought up in very unactressy surroundings. She may have wanted to join in charades with her parents' friends but she was never a precocious child performer in the way that Britney Spears or Kylie and Dannii Minogue had been. *Annie* did not inspire Jennifer to be an actress – or, for that matter, the next singing little orphan – but it did open the eyes of a young girl to the wonder of show business in a way that having a father on television had not. It was the feeling that she could reach out and touch the performers rather than stretching out and turning off the TV. One was real, the other was not.

If you asked Jennifer now to consign one year in her life to Room 101 then 1978 would be it. Back then Jennifer had no idea, at such a young age, of the drama and trauma that was unfolding behind closed doors, nor that her father had chosen to follow a path that would come back to haunt her in later life – John Aniston had fallen for his leading lady. Her name was Sherry Rooney and, ironically, her character Dory Patton was introduced in *Love Of Life* in 1977 as a love interest for Eddie Aleata played by John, who had been moaning that he was due a TV romance after two years in the show. Sherry, like Nancy, was a slim, elegant brunette whose acting career was less than inspiring. She also appeared in just one film, a minor role in a Dustin Hoffman vehicle entitled *Who Is Harry Kellerman And Why Is He Saying Those Terrible Things About Me* (1971) which may have seemed like a good title in the pub but must surely go down as one of the worst in movie history. Before *Love Of Life* she featured in another soap, *Search For Tomorrow*, which was also filmed at the CBS studios, although there is no suggestion that she had met John Aniston before they worked on the same programme.

Love Of Life, which had begun in 1951, was not as popular as it once was but was still a high-profile show for its actors. The biggest name to appear in its thirty-year run was probably Christopher Reeve, who joined the cast the year before John and stayed two years before going on to find fame as Superman. Jennifer was with Nancy one day when she saw Reeve in the street but was too shy to go over and say hello. She kicked herself when *Superman* (1978) opened the very next day and Reeve was temporarily the biggest star in the movie firmament. Her father, too, was soon getting recognized on the street, a massive change from the anonymity of the San Fernando Valley. He even opened a restaurant called the Fives, not far from the studios, at a time before celebrity diners became so fashionable. It was at the restaurant's opening night that Nancy first set eyes on Sherry. When she wrote her book twenty years later she could not bring herself to name her, preferring instead to call her 'John's leading lady', noting that she was wearing a brown silk dress costing eight hundred dollars. Nancy's account of the break-up reveals her shock to be just as great as her daughter's. The only clue perhaps was the amount of time John was spending at the restaurant. She thought they should be reaffirming their marriage vows, while he was thinking more in terms of a divorce.

It was autumn. Jennifer had been to a friend's birthday party when her mother arrived to pick her up, wearing sunglasses to hide a face puffed up with tears. When they got home, Nancy quietly explained that her father was not going to be around for a while. She was doing her best to spare her daughter the true agony of the situation by not revealing that he had gone for ever. Jennifer told *Rolling Stone* magazine, 'I don't know if I blocked it out, but I just remember sitting there, crying, not understanding that he was gone. I don't know what I did later that night or the next day.'

If Jennifer had looked in her father's wardrobe she would have seen just a few empty clothes hangers dangling there. The raw despair of the scene is movingly described by Nancy in her memoir: 'I watched a tear roll down Jenny's cheek as confidence faded from her once trusting eyes.'

Jennifer's and Nancy's recollections of subsequent events

differ. Jennifer says she did not see her father for a year. Nancy maintains that he joined them for a Thanksgiving dinner in November 1978, at a local restaurant where the atmosphere was distinctly cool despite Jennifer's efforts to be the best company a young girl could be – but perhaps Jennifer banished this painful evening from her memory. Certainly her father was not around that Christmas when Nancy decided to cheer them up with a dinner at the popular Tavern on the Green restaurant in Central Park. For once, they enjoyed an evening so much that they decided they would do it again the next year and it became a tradition in the depleted household for as long as they remained together in New York.

Her father was absent for Jennifer's tenth birthday in February and the months drifted by with Jennifer wondering when her father was coming home. Eventually she learned the bitter truth, although, once again, mother and daughter remember things differently. Nancy says she did not want Jennifer to know her father was with another woman in case it ruined her view of her father and, subsequently, of men in general. Jennifer, however, has said that one sunny summer's day, stuck as usual in New York traffic, her mother told her, 'Your father's not coming back. He's with another woman.' They can't both be right, but then it was a very emotional time.

Jennifer's next contact with her father was the following autumn when he just called her up one day and said, 'Let's go see *The Fantasticks*,' which was the longest-running stage show in America and the longest-running musical in the world. When it eventually closed on Broadway in 2002 it had played for 16,162 performances. *The Mousetrap*, the British equivalent of a theatrical chestnut, has managed more than 20,000 performances.

A film of *The Fantasticks* in 1995 was less successful but the show has been revived and was back on Broadway in 2006. Jennifer must have seen something like the 8,000th performance. She was, however, more interested in seeing her beloved father again.

That was the start of a pattern of seeing her father at weekends. He settled with Sherry in New Jersey, which sounds miles away, but is practically part of New York and was only just over the Hudson river and an easy car or train ride. Jennifer would go to their house on a Friday evening and return to her mother's apartment on Sunday night. After her parents had worked out the arrangements, it became a matter of routine. To begin with she would visit every weekend but then this was cut back to every other weekend, presumably because Sherry and John needed space to forge their own new relationship.

Perhaps unsurprisingly, Jennifer thought the whole saga of separation was her fault: 'I really felt it was because I wasn't a good enough kid.' Looking back, she told LA journalist Gill Pringle, 'Living through my own parents' separation when I was nine years old gave me a lesson in looking at life from a realistic point of view. When your parents split up, it's impossible to delude yourself about fairy-tale romance and happy endings. You have to be real. It taught me that life isn't always perfect.' Jennifer felt like she was a ball being bounced to and fro between two grown-ups: 'I found it incredibly difficult and my childhood memories are mainly about just going from place to place and taking care of adults.'

Her father left *Love Of Life* in that dreadful year of 1978, but nothing much changed because he went straight into the equally prominent show, *Search For Tomorrow*, which was filmed at the same studios. The formats were quite similar. Both shows were more than twenty-five years old and were a heady mixture of *Crossroads* and *Neighbours*. The central character in *Search For Tomorrow*, Joanne, played the entire time by actress Mary Stuart, one of the great soap stalwarts, ran an inn in the fictional midwestern town of Henderson. John, who, in real life was eight years younger than his co-star, was her new husband (her fourth) called Martin Tourneur for six years. As with all these shows the best fun is in spotting future stars and old favourites drifting in and out of the episodes. Larry Hagman, Susan Sarandon, Morgan Fairchild, Kevin Kline, Maureen O'Sullivan and Olympia Dukakis were just some of the well-known faces to pitch up in Henderson. During John's time on the show, the most famous name starting out was Kevin Bacon, who would later seduce Jennifer's character in her first starring movie, *Picture Perfect*.

Search For Tomorrow is significant because it provided Jennifer with her first experience of a television studio and gave her an early insight into the fickle nature of show business. Her father arranged for her to be an extra and she wore a pretty yellow dress, sat in make-up and generally had a thrilling day. When they were filming the scene she was in, a floor assistant came over and made her change places with another girl. Jennifer thought nothing of it until she was walking home with John and he told her that it was a good job she had swapped seats because in her original position she was not in the camera shot. Jennifer was mortified when she realized that the other girl had been 'bumped' because of her, the daughter of the soap star. It was a salutary initiation into the cut-throat world: 'I felt terrible, absolutely mortified and humiliated.'

John and Nancy Aniston were divorced in August 1980. John Aniston has always kept his own counsel about his divorce from Jennifer's mother. He has spoken very little about his family over the years, although he did acknowledge that the eventual divorce was very hard on his daughter: 'I'm sure I could have done a lot of things to make it easier,' he observed with candour. Jennifer also acknowledged that her father, who she has always adored, 'wasn't great with kids'.

John and Sherry married in 1984 and had a son, Alex, in 1989, who they have kept well away from the limelight. He could walk down Sunset in Los Angeles and nobody would have a clue that he was the half-brother of one of the most famous women in the world. John and Nancy were married for fifteen years. He will celebrate his silver wedding with Sherry in 2009, so he could hardly qualify as one of the world's great philanderers. Instead, the Anistons are pillars of the Los Angeles Greek community and regular guests at fundraisers and gala nights.

In many ways Jennifer's relationship with her father has been a less complex one than with her mother. Perhaps her father, taciturn by nature, is simply easier to handle than her more volatile mother. Page after page of Nancy's book reveals her hurt and pain. The book is like one long, confused and fascinating session on a therapist's couch. She conveys an impression of simmering anger at the injustice of it all. Jennifer witnessed her mother's private anguish which, for the most part, was kept well hidden from the outside world, although a close friend of Jennifer's remembers her mother crying all the time.

Together, Nancy and Jennifer set about creating a new life for themselves. Nancy had to take on some of the traditional paternal role, making sure that her daughter obeyed the house rules. She had, however, what today seems a thoroughly old-fashioned outlook of expecting respect as a parent and as an adult. Jennifer had an ambivalent attitude to this: 'It's good that she's got her rules, but you also want to go, "Mom, lighten up".' Nancy was very popular in the neighbourhood and, in particular within their building on 92nd Street. One of the building staff at the time recalls, 'She always called everyone by their name. She was a sweet person.' She enrolled in a course to become a therapeutic masseuse but decided it was not for her. Eventually she settled on a job as an office receptionist.

Money may have been tight but Nancy always made sure their home was clean and tidy. She also decided to redecorate Jennifer's bedroom to cheer her up during the difficult period after her father left. They chose yellow and white with pride of place going to a beautiful bed with a lace canopy.

Mother and daughter had to manage without the help of a man about the house, but at least they could call on the maintenance men if they needed someone to mend a table or fix a lamp. There was the occasional emergency as in the time when the power went off while Jennifer was drying her hair. The handyman raced up to the twenty-third floor to deal with the matter, quickly realized what was wrong, went over to the fuse box and flipped the trip switch. He was more than a little embarrassed when Nancy and Jennifer thanked him as if had just found a cure for smallpox.

FOUR

Steiner

The crackheads were on the corner every morning when Jennifer left the apartment building on West 92nd Street to go to school. They were still there when she got home. You knew that they were crackheads because they always looked as if they were about to fall over. One of the building employees at the time explains, 'It was a little rough around here. There were lots of kids breaking into cars and stealing radios and things. You couldn't leave anything lying about.'

If Jennifer Aniston had grown up in the United Kingdom, she probably would have had to suffer the media forever glibly referring to her as a public schoolgirl. Money was tight after her parents divorced. She and Nancy were not on the breadline but they had to be careful, constantly aware of what something cost. Jennifer described it as going out to dinner, ordering nothing on the side and telling the waiter, 'Yes, water will be fine.' Yet despite the caution over financial matters, one area of Jennifer's life was never short-changed – her education. She spent the majority of her educational life in a $15,000-a-year progressive private school – more than $20,000 today – which John always paid for from the proceeds of his soap-opera stardom. It was the one area which even Nancy could not really grumble about in her book.

Nancy Aniston had stumbled across the Waldorf method of education (also known as the Steiner method) while the family still lived in California. She was a devotee literally from the first time she picked up a brochure and discovered that this unusual teaching cultivated and nurtured a child's own, individual imagination. Like most mothers, Nancy believed her child to have a unique ability but, unusually, she was prepared to do something about it. At this stage all she knew was that she wanted something better than a regular kindergarten or pre-school for her four-year-old daughter. She persuaded a local clergyman that he should start a Waldorf group in the church hall. She even set about finding like-minded parents who would jump at the chance of showing that they considered their child special.

Jennifer's education – often skipped by writers in their haste to get to *Friends* and Brad Pitt – was distinctly unusual, first with Waldorf and later at a high school in which she could spend half her day studying acting. These schools had a profound effect on the person she became, especially as they formed the backdrop to the emotional trauma of her parents' divorce. Her very first taste of acting came not from watching her mother or father, but from acting out fairy tales in the back yard of her local church. This was a specific part of the early Waldorf curriculum. The teacher would read the class a fairy tale and then the children would perform the story together.

When the Aniston family left California, Jennifer would not come into contact again with the Waldorf method until they settled in New York, attending a regular school in Pennsylvania when they lived with Yaya. In Manhattan, however, Nancy was determined that Jennifer would again have the benefit of Waldorf. Her passion for this educational model undoubtedly stems from her feelings that the public- (state-) school system had not been the best option for her son Johnny and that he had suffered as a result. She was determined that Jennifer would not be one of the masses and was thrilled to discover that the Rudolf Steiner School, which taught this method, was just a short distance across Central Park on the Upper East Side. Johnny, who in any case was not impressed with New York, was less than enthusiastic because of the relative absence of any sporting activity and opted for a local 'regular' high school.

Nancy's devotion to and advocacy of the Waldorf method and support of the Steiner school would, ironically, indirectly lead to the massive rift between mother and daughter twenty years later.

Screenwriter Raven Metzner, a contemporary of Jennifer's at Steiner, crisply identifies the special quality of education at the school: 'All the students in my class, and in the school, were nurtured for their differences, not their sameness. In public school you are rewarded for your ability to conform. Steiner rewards you for taking different perspectives.'

The Rudolf Steiner Lower School on East 79th is in a tree-lined street between Fifth Avenue and Madison in an area populated by chocolatiers, galleries and expensive boutiques. The renowned Metropolitan Museum of Art (the Met) is just three blocks away and you could throw a stone into Central Park. The Upper School is around the corner with an entrance on East 78th Street. Across the street is a building housing the Permanent

Delegation of Iraq and another boasting the headquarters of the Greek Orthodox Archdiocese of America. The overall atmosphere is expensive and discreet. The Steiner building itself, a four-storey brownstone, must be one of the most desirable pieces of real estate in New York City. Unsurprisingly, there has never been a crackhead problem in these exclusive streets and, from the very outset, it must have seemed like travelling to the moon every day for Jennifer as she passed the drug dealers outside her own building.

Rudolf Steiner was arguably one of the great thinkers of the modern world – a philosopher and scientist who applied his beliefs to, among other things, the best way to educate and develop a child. He was born in 1861 in a small village in what was then Austria but is now part of Croatia. His father was the local station master. He was a prodigiously talented boy of formidable intellect, a mathematician, historian, classical scholar and master of languages. His great passion during his lifetime was the founding of the Anthroposophical Society in Germany, which promoted the development of spiritual science – discovering the spirit in ourselves so that we can understand the spirit in the universe.

One of the developments of anthroposophy Steiner devised, which became a cornerstone in his schools, was 'eurythmy'. This unique aspect of his educational model involved a series of movements with or without music that helps children – and adults – to understand their bodies and the space around them. To the untutored eye it would appear to be free dance in slow motion; Steiner, himself, called it 'the art of the soul'. For Steiner it was a performing art just as drama and music might be and featured in the curriculum at his very first schools. The concept is quite spiritual, almost in an oriental fashion, and children would carefully manipulate copper rods while keeping their main trunk completely still.

Little Jennifer Aniston was not too bothered about anthroposophy or eurythmy. She was more absorbed by the discovery that the Steiner School frowned on television. Steiner was very precise in devising his educational model. His prodigious energy was channelled into education when the owner of the Waldorf-Astoria cigarette factory in Stuttgart asked him to found a school for the children of the workers of the factory. This is the association that, somewhat confusingly, has led to the Steiner method being familiarly called Waldorf education.

Today, Steiner would have been described as a guru; those that follow him do so with great passion and belief. The New York school is the oldest Steiner facility in the US, established in 1928, just three years after the death of the man who inspired it. The Steiner philosophy of education is a patchwork quilt of ideas that come together to promulgate the overall goal of helping a child fulfil his or her full potential without pushing them towards aspirations that adults, or society in general, believe desirable or reflective of success. In lay terms, if Jennifer showed a talent – for instance a love of acting – then the Steiner intention would be to bring out that gift and help it to blossom.

Several aspects of the Steiner School stand out. Firstly, there were on average between eighteen and twenty-five children in Jennifer's class, a startling luxury modern schools can generally not afford. Each of the boys and girls, throughout their school career, was addressed by their first name. It was always Jennifer and never Aniston. Raven Metzner observes, 'Everyone knew everybody by name. It's such a lovely way to set up an educational system. It's not like a cold, unemotional school in any way. It's really warm.' That informality also extended to clothes. Jennifer never had to wear a school uniform, mostly preferring T-shirts and sneakers until she became a fashion-conscious teenager and a general fashion disaster.

Even today there is one teacher at Steiner for every eight pupils. Jennifer had the same main teacher every year. This is part of the process – one teacher to guide the child through seven or eight years, thereby promoting continuity, trust and engagement. For most of her time at Steiner, Jennifer's main teacher was Ms Jerelyn Everett, a tall, wholesome woman in her early thirties with long, curly dark hair and a temperate disposition. Every morning Jennifer's day would begin in the same way. She would walk into the class and be greeted by Ms Everett with her hand outstretched. The teacher would look Jennifer in the eye, benignly, and say, 'Good morning, Jennifer'. One of Jennifer's classmates, Thor Wasbotten recalls, 'Ms Everett always smiled and really made us feel important. You would never hear her swear or get upset. If she did get frustrated, or angry, her look would be enough. She was a great influence on us all.'

The first lesson of the day was perhaps the most important in the Steiner School. It would always be with Ms Everett and last for two hours. In the Lower School – encompassing grades 1–8 in the US (ages six to fourteen) – she would begin with a poem or a quote which in effect would be the thought for the day and which she would develop throughout the lessons. Occasionally there might be a painting on the wall or blackboard to provide a visual starting point. The Steiner method would be to concentrate on one subject at a time and explore it properly over a period of a couple of weeks, eschewing the more traditional scatter-gun method of teaching. Jennifer might have had botany for a couple of weeks, then geometry before going on to ancient history.

One of the most interesting subjects she had was Greek mythology. In the morning, Ms Everett would reveal the stories of the gods and in the afternoon the students would broaden that theoretical approach into more practical pursuits by designing costumes that the gods might have worn. Steiner encourages the things a child would naturally want to do, especially up to the age of seven. Jennifer first sampled that back in Los Angeles where storytelling, nature study and play acting were encouraged long before reading and writing. Art and music were given primary importance at Steiner. Mathematics is introduced to elementary-school children through rhythm and song.

One of the key themes is merging the cultural pursuits that require imagination with those that need careful practicality like woodwork and knitting. In fifth grade (age eleven) Jennifer and the other children made a salad spoon and fork, were encouraged to knit a pair of socks and to learn a musical instrument. Jennifer chose the flute and showed a natural aptitude, but hated to practise and never made much progress.

Another fundamental theme at Steiner was the careful use of implements for writing and drawing, with pupils only ever using the best materials and being carefully guided through what they should and should not use. Jennifer, for instance, was not allowed to use coloured pencils until the fourth grade (age ten). Raven Metzner explains, 'It's very well thought out. Every year you are given a different implement to write with, maybe a pencil, a regular pen or a coloured pencil until eventually they'd give you an ink fountain pen.' They use their writing implements to produce their main lesson book which is entirely devised by the student, complete with pictures and decorations from their own imagination. It is part of the Steiner philosophy of utilizing the whole person. The children also learn the art of proper writing and calligraphy. As a result, Jennifer has always had the most beautiful handwriting and a very elegant signature, even as a young teenager.

All this intellectual and well-reasoned education was played out while a rather confused and upset little girl tried to come to terms with emotional trauma. She was sent to a therapist to see if that might help. The original idea, according to Nancy, came from John and Sherry during one of Jennifer's visits. They thought it might help Jennifer to 'adjust' and make sense of her parents' break-up. The first session was 'worse than awful' and Jennifer vowed not to go again. Yet, despite that unpromising beginning Jennifer has said she has been in some sort of therapy ever since. She admits to having suffered from guilt a lot throughout her life. Therapy has obviously served a purpose for her and she was very upset twenty years later when her psychiatrist in Los Angeles died suddenly.

According to her mother, Jennifer ran the gamut of emotions when her parents divorced, from tears to tantrums, from anger to rebellion, the latter manifesting in misbehaviour at school. As she herself observed, 'I was rowdy'. Amusingly, Jennifer joked that there was a 'Teachers Who Hate Jennifer Aniston Anonymous Group'. The teacher who she recalled became most frustrated with her behaviour was the long-suffering English master Mr Ekkehard Piening, who spoke with a pronounced German accent. He taught in a classroom with two palm trees by the window. 'One day he got so mad at me, he shouted, "Jennifer, I want to tie a palm tree to each of your feet and throw you out of the window!"'

Getting into trouble to try and get her father's attention became a favoured pursuit for Jennifer for a while, making sure that her parents would both be called to the Head of School's office for a discussion about their wayward daughter. Naturally it did not have the desired effect: 'It's hard to impress your dad when you're in the principal's office for being stupid.' Jennifer may have missed out on the complete extent of the Steiner education because her attention-seeking meant she failed to absorb as much as she should.

Her efforts to attract attention were no more successful away from school. When she was twelve, and staying for the weekend with her father, she was sent from the dinner table where he was entertaining guests because she 'didn't have anything interesting to say'.

Jennifer is not particularly enthusiastic about her school achievements but Steiner had far more effect on her than perhaps she credits. She is still immensely proud of the occasion when, at the age of nine, a painting she had done at school was part of a special exhibit of ten Steiner students at the Met. At the time Jennifer was not overly impressed, but the love of painting which Steiner inspired in her and her classmates has remained and is something she still enjoys on quiet days. The school's approach was, as with all pursuits, to encourage creativity within a careful framework: 'I used to paint with shading, colours and dimension but now it's just freehand and whatever comes to mind.'

At eleven, Jennifer joined the Drama Club under the guidance of the redoubtable Michael Ridenhour, who also taught English and, like her father, boasted an impressive 'Zapata' moustache. Mr Ridenhour was a popular eccentric at the school with a long gait and big glasses. Thor Wasbotten describes him as the 'consummate Steiner teacher'. The most telling contribution the Drama Club made to Jennifer Aniston's career was that her ambition grew under its umbrella, while her natural acting instincts prospered. Later, when she went to a much more drama-intensive high school, the coaches there did not have to 'unteach' her.

Drama always played some part at Steiner with classes preparing plays every year. Her very first public performance as an actress came in her 8th-grade class nativity play in which she was an angel. Thor, who is convinced Jennifer the actress benefited from her time at Steiner, recalls, 'It was fitting for her. She was beautiful.' Jennifer has always claimed she was a bit of an ugly duckling as a girl but that does not appear to be how her young male friends saw her at all. Her own self-image is more indicative of her brittle relationship with her mother, a former model who was very precise with make-up and clothes and tried to encourage her daughter to be the same. Jennifer was much more natural, which teenage boys found 'cute'. At Steiner they would compile 'lists' of favourites. The girls would list the boys in terms of who they liked and fancied and the boys would do likewise. Jennifer frequently found her way to the top of the boys' lists. Thor remembers, 'Jennifer was very cute, with long, dark brown hair and great eyes. The best part about her, however, was her smile. She could light up a room with her smile. Still does.'

Thor made it to the top of Jennifer's list on one or two occasions but failed to sustain his position of pre-eminence. His status was not improved by squirting mustard all over Jennifer during some high spirits which, in typical adolescent boy fashion, he took too far. Meanwhile, away from school, Jennifer acquired her first boyfriend, a local boy called Nick. Ironically, considering the views she would later express on dating Greek men, Nick was from a Greek family. She had just become a teenager and was enjoying the attentions of the opposite sex. Things did get out of hand on one memorable occasion in Jennifer's bedroom. The youngsters were kissing so enthusiastically that their braces somehow became intertwined and they were locked together. Fortunately their predicament was discovered by Nancy, but she could not prise them apart. Finally, she had to drive the pair, still inseparable, to an emergency dentist who used pliers to disentangle them, much to Jennifer's embarrassment.

The adolescent Jennifer was becoming more interested in the future and began to harbour serious ambitions to become an actress. She went along with Thor, who did some modelling as a boy, and his younger brother to a photo session with a professional photographer and had pictures taken for the first time. Thor's family had show-business connections and helped her find her first agent although this failed to propel Jennifer to stardom. She also tried to take matters into her own hands when she visited her father on set. He walked into the actors' room to discover his daughter deep in conversation on the telephone with *his* agent fixing herself up with an audition. John Aniston never encouraged his daughter to follow him into a profession which he thought chewed you up and spat you out, although later he did look back with some good humour on her efforts to break into acting.

Bonding between students in such a close-knit environment was inevitable and has led to the Steiner School being almost as secretive as the Masons. That sense of togetherness was fostered still further by the annual visits to the working farm in northern New York where students would spend a week learning about every aspect of farming including how to look after the animals. This was a vacation in all but name and a welcome break from pacy Manhattan. The visits always seemed to coincide with the coldest days of winter but for Jennifer and her friends it was exciting taking the two-hour train journey north and watching the urban sprawl of New York give way to snowy countryside. The trips were like summer school except it was freezing. All the students would stay in bunk beds in the large white farmhouse, while outside in the farmyard chickens and cows roamed around – not an everyday view on West 92nd Street. Lessons were not forsaken, with one of the outbuildings transformed into a woodworking studio. In one memorable lesson Jennifer and her friends were dragged out of bed in the wee small hours to walk down a country road in pitch darkness, wrapped in several layers, to where some telescopes had been set up for them to study the stars.

Competition is not encouraged at the Steiner School. Parents in particular are advised not to let their children play soccer or other competitive sports. Jennifer was not very sporty so that was a bit of a blessing, but she did throw herself into the volleyball team and became an enthusiastic member. The sporting pursuit she most excelled in was skiing which she learned when her father bought a second home in upstate New York where the slopes were snow-covered in winter.

The Steiner rules were there for the young Miss Aniston to break, none more so than the disapproval of television. This temporarily proved a threat to her ambitions of becoming Mrs

Scott Baio – a prospect her father told her he did not relish. The darkly handsome Italian-American actor was a teenie favourite in the classic *Happy Days* when he played Chachi, the young cousin of the Fonz, and Jennifer had a huge crush on him. She would devise all manner of ways of catching the programme, particularly when, in 1982, he moved on to the relatively short-lived spin-off, *Joanie Loves Chachi*: 'I'd sneak it all the time, of course,' she recalled.

She moved on from the desire to be the next Mrs Baio to wanting to be the first Mrs Le Bon. Jennifer had a short-lived incarnation as a 'Durannie', a band of pre-teen and teen girls who would eat, sleep and generally breathe all things Duran Duran. Jennifer's principle interest was the pouting lead singer, Simon Le Bon. She thought he had a sexy voice and described him as 'cute'. Jennifer has always described boys or men that she has fancied as either 'cute' (Simon Le Bon) or 'hot' (Brad Pitt). As well as being for a while in the eighties the biggest band in the UK, Duran Duran were one of the few British groups to travel successfully across the Atlantic. 'The Reflex' was number one in the US as well as on home territory.

Jennifer made sure she collected every Duran Duran album, including the European imports. She would sneak round to a friend's house to watch her idols on MTV and practically wore out her copies of the videos. So she was thrilled to discover that Simon and the boys were going to be at a store in Times Square one Saturday to sign copies of their latest album. Jennifer was up with the larks expecting to be one of the first in the queue. Unfortunately, several hundred fans had the same idea and the line already stretched round the block when she arrived. Patiently she waited, getting nearer and nearer, clutching a red rose for

Simon. Eventually there were only four girls in front of her on the street and she felt that she could almost touch the boys. At that precise moment they locked the doors. The signing was over, leaving Jennifer and the remaining fans distraught. The rose was angrily consigned to a bin on the way to the subway.

FIVE

Fame

Fame was a film that inspired. A youthful energy coursed through the veins of Alan Parker's classic 1980 movie. Perhaps even more importantly, the light of optimism pervaded the corridors of the High School for the Performing Arts where it was set and where the hopes and dreams of the young characters played out. For Jennifer, bogged down in the disciplines of the Steiner School, it represented the possibility of exuberant escape. Jennifer was eleven when the film was released, the same year as her parents were divorced. Like a million other youngsters she was thrilled when the students of the 'Fame school' burst into a spontaneous all-singing, all-dancing jam during lunch. Nothing like that ever happened in regular school.

Fame followed the adventures of a bunch of teenagers auditioning and then studying at the school. In approach it was old-fashioned, following in the footsteps of the putting-on-a-show movies like *Babes in Arms* that Mickey Rooney and Judy Garland had patented to keep spirits up in wartime. In the Sixties, early Cliff Richard films, like *The Young Ones*, trod a similarly exuberant path. *Fame* did, however, try and convey an edge through its suggestion of teenage sexploitation, racial prejudice, drugs and violence. But, all in all, it was pretty tame. The film received an R rating in the USA. In this context, R stood for restricted and basically meant that you had to be accompanied by an adult if you were under seventeen. Jennifer was too young to see the film when it was released, but in 1982 the TV series spin-off from the film brought the lives and loves of the students of the Performing Arts School right into the living room. Jennifer was hooked.

The Fame school, known with affection as PA (Performing Arts) since it was founded in 1947, differed from the Steiner School in one very obvious way. It was a public school which meant that theoretically any boy or girl in New York could apply. You did not have to have parents who could afford $15,000 a year. It was 1984 and while her mother was not exactly tearing her hair out, fifteen-year-old Jennifer was going through a rebellious-teenager phase. She wore lots of heavy black eye make-up and shaved her hair on one side in a semi-Mohican style. She had no idea to begin with that the Fame school was just a short bus ride away in Manhattan, but when she discovered that it was a genuine New York high school where she could take classes in proper acting, not just a drama club, she set about convincing her mother that it would do her the world of good to go there. Despite being a great supporter of the Waldorf method of education, Nancy could see that her daughter was restless at the Steiner School.

Looking back after she had 'made it' Jennifer acknowledged, 'My mom wanted me to do whatever I wanted to do and she was going to stand by me the whole way through. My dad didn't want me to go near acting. He wanted me to have a stable job –

be a lawyer or a doctor: something other than an actress who would struggle and be broke and be a waitress for the rest of her life.'

The audition process for PA was hard, nerve-racking and bore no resemblance whatsoever to the shambolic turns of *The X Factor* wannabes. Prospective students were told to prepare two contrasting one-minute monologues. They were advised to avoid verse, classical works and original material; nothing from novels, short stories or screenplays; nothing with funny accents or weird physical characteristics. This was a drama audition, plain and simple. One of the teachers, Anthony Abeson, who sat on the panel of judges, explains, 'This was a rigorous and remarkable audition process and, as a result, our student body was very, very gifted and very, very special.'

In her year, Jennifer was one of more than 3,000 New York boys and girls competing for just seventy places. After much changing of mind, Jennifer, displaying unwitting prescience, finally decided to perform a piece from the Neil Simon play *I Ought To Be In Pictures* which had been adapted for a movie the year before starring Walter Matthau. The play had been on Broadway for a year at the start of the eighties but was more widely known as a result of the speedy translation to Hollywood. Jennifer, somewhat ironically, read a speech by a smartass teenager from Brooklyn called Libby who decides to go to LA to visit her estranged screenwriter father played by the lugubrious Matthau. It could almost have been written about Jennifer because, ostensibly, Libby wants her father to help her break into the movies. Jennifer may not have been especially aware of it at the time but the Neil Simon approach that blends seriousness and gags is perfect for her comedic style.

For her second choice Jennifer chose a scene from an older play, *The Sign In Sidney Brustein's Window* by the playwright Lorraine Hansbury, who had died from cancer at the age of thirty-five in 1965 while the original production was on Broadway. Hansbury had been the first black woman playwright to have her work produced on Broadway, and had been an ardent political activist campaigning passionately for the rights of both the black population and lesbian groups. *The Sign In Sidney Brustein's Window* challenged the assumption that black playwrights could only write about things relating to their own culture. It was quite a daring piece for Jennifer to interpret at such an important rehearsal.

The whole audition process lasted some four hours, including much nervous waiting around, before a final interview by the judges' panel which was chaired not by a fearsome Simon Cowell lookalike but by Jacob Eskow, the long-standing and much-respected head of drama at the school. The competition for places was intense and Jennifer patiently had to wait the whole summer to hear if she had been successful.

Meanwhile, she needed to catch up academically whether she was going back to Steiner or starting afresh at PA. Jennifer was now certain that she was going to be an actress and any other schoolwork was an unwelcome distraction. Fortunately the solution was just around the corner. She lived within stone-throwing distance of the prestigious Trinity High School, which actually owned her apartment block, and which threw its doors open for 'summer school'. It was perfect for Jennifer – she would be up to speed in the classroom for the September term, she could socialize with all her friends and she could walk to school, thus avoiding the daily grind of New York traffic. The summer-school system is much more popular in the US than in the UK, giving students the chance to explore new subjects not covered by the main curriculum, as well as improving weak academic areas. They were a more serious alternative to summer camps and had the virtue of giving teenagers something to do during the long summer holidays.

One afternoon Jennifer was chatting outside her building with a good friend called Carrie Drosnes when a boy who was taking the same class, Tyler Sterck, strolled by with a very good-looking, tanned buddy. Tyler introduced him as Michael Baroni, who lived locally. The four of them started talking until, after a while, Tyler suggested that they all go back to his home to sunbathe. Jennifer and Carrie needed no second invitation as Tyler lived on the Upper East Side, in a huge Park Avenue house with a massive wraparound terrace. Michael was immediately impressed with the way fifteen-year-old Jennifer filled her bikini. 'She definitely was one of those girls who had matured more quickly for her age,' he recalls. 'I was pretty smitten.'

That first afternoon, Michael, a well-built sixteen-year-old, decided not to take things any further, a decision influenced by the fact that Carrie was an old girlfriend and he was not too sure if she was over him. The following Friday, however, that cautious approach was completely abandoned. The four teenagers were among a group of friends, whiling away a lazy afternoon, when Tyler suggested throwing a party. The girls were keen and left to go home and put on their party frocks while Tyler and Michael invited a bunch of people over to Park Avenue. Luckily, Tyler's mother was out.

That evening Michael could not take his eyes of Jennifer: 'She had on this really hot red dress and, to be honest, looked like a Hollywood star even then. She definitely didn't look like a typical sort of grungy teenager.' Halfway through the evening he spotted her going in to the kitchen to get a drink. He followed her in, shut the door behind him, grabbed Jennifer by the shoulders, spun her round and kissed her passionately on the lips. Cary Grant and Grace Kelly would have been proud of that scene. Michael observes, 'Luckily I didn't get slapped and thrown out the door!' Far from it, because Jennifer was sufficiently impressed by her bold suitor to go down to a phone booth and tell her mother that she was going to be home later than she thought.

When it was eventually time for the couple to come up for air and for Jennifer to go home, she reached into her purse and produced a bright red lipstick which she used carefully to write on a small piece of paper 'Jen 212 580 34 . . .'. Michael recalls, 'I thought it was great because there were pens available in the kitchen but she just pulled out her lipstick. It was very sexy.' That evening was the start of a pretty idyllic Manhattan summer for Jennifer.

Michael Baroni may have been taken initially with Jennifer's striking 'upper-body development', but it soon dawned on him that she had the most amazing eyes: 'Her eyes were very grey and I thought that it was the neatest thing having grey eyes with her darkish skin. They were really beautiful. She also had a fun smile – a really pretty, girlish, fun smile.'

Jennifer's refreshingly realistic view of her teenage shape was that she was big-hipped and, as a result, favoured big sweaters and skirts. 'I never wore jeans,' she confessed. She was, however, much more conscious of her hair. At this time she was lightening her hair and Michael thought she was styling her blonde hair in a Marilyn Monroe fashion: 'It was kind of movie star and she really liked it that way. Jennifer was definitely more into style and wanting to look good. With her hair, her jewellery, her shoes and the clothes she wore, she definitely stood out from the crowd.'

Jennifer's mother may have painted a picture of Jennifer as a vulnerable girl from whom the 'confidence had faded' and Jennifer, herself, later admitted that post-divorce, 'I had started to doubt myself'. That is not, however, how others saw this gregarious, sociable and popular girl. The young men of the neighbourhood all wanted to get closer to her. 'She had a lot of interest from a lot of boys,' recalls Michael.

A short time after he began dating Jennifer, Michael was clearing out a drawer in his bedroom when he came across a picture taken by his grandfather of him playing on the beach at the Hamptons with a little girl. He could not recall her at first, but she was wearing a pink swimsuit and looked familiar. The next evening around at Jennifer's apartment, he produced the picture and asked his new girlfriend, 'Is that you? Are you the girl in the pink swimsuit?' Jennifer reached over, peered at the snap and declared casually, 'Yeah that's me. Oh my gosh! I love that pink swimsuit.' Michael admits it was a really corny moment but also a great memory to have. He suddenly realized that it was Jennifer who had kissed him on the beach all those years ago.

At the time Michael was surprised that Jennifer was not more enthusiastic about what could have been a *When Harry Met Sally* moment, but he soon realized that it brought back painful memories of her father: 'We talked some about her father but he was always a sensitive subject. But her mother Nancy didn't even want to talk to me about it when I brought it up and, when I showed Jennifer the picture, all she wanted to do was put it away and not think about it. There was obvious pain.' Once again, something as trivial as a photograph had found Jennifer Aniston's Achilles heel.

The photograph episode was the only time Jennifer deviated from being fun and focused around Michael. Both teenagers were coming out of quite serious relationships for their age and Michael was very different from Jennifer's first boyfriend, Nick, an altogether artier youngster. Michael was just what Jennifer needed – good-looking and good company. They were too young to go out much to clubs and restaurants so most of the time they would just hang out at each others' apartments and watch movies on the couch. Jennifer's favourite was *Sixteen Candles* (1984) starring Molly Ringwald, the queen of eighties' high-school films. Molly's character has a crush on the best-looking student at her high school, played by Michael Schoeffling. Molly was not the only one. In real life, Jennifer thought Schoeffling, a former male model and wrestler, was gorgeous. 'She was crazy about him,' recalls Michael. 'I remember her going, "Oh my God, that guy is so cute," so I had to playfully tap her on the shoulder and say, "Hey, you, don't say anything about other guys!" It was always good fun with Jennifer.'

Inexplicably, Schoeffling dropped out of Hollywood after appearing in his best-known film, *Mermaids* (1990), as the love interest for Winona Ryder. He was only thirty. One of the last films he starred in was *Longterm Companion* (1990), which was directed by Norman Rene who would later direct Jennifer on Broadway – further proof of just what a small village Hollywood is. Schoeffling's 'retirement' has prompted great interest in recent times as to what happened to him. He was revealed as a happy family man with a wife and two children running a furniture business in a quiet town in Pennsylvania. Perhaps he did not have the focus his young fan in Manhattan possessed.

Michael Baroni thought Jennifer, at fifteen, was 'physically mature and emotionally mature'. Chivalrously, he has never admitted whether his fifteen-year-old girlfriend was also sexually mature. Her previous relationship with Nick had lasted two years and he was her first 'love'. That romance had foundered, Jennifer told Michael, because Nick was getting too serious and she was only fifteen. Michael recalls, 'We may have only been fifteen- and sixteen-year-olds but we probably looked like a twenty- and eighteen-year-old and we acted more like it as well. We never really discussed dating but we just hit it off and liked each other.'

When they were away from the couch, the two of them used to run errands for their mothers, just stroll around the moving theatre of the streets on the Upper West Side, sometimes take a walk in Central Park or go to their favourite burger restaurant on 72nd Street. Sometimes they would listen to music. Jennifer had by this time ditched Duran Duran in favour of Aerosmith and preferred lead singer Steven Tyler to the rather more bouffant charms of Simon Le Bon. For some light relief she would turn to the Eagles. 'Her taste was pretty mainstream,' recalls Michael. Jennifer loved fine art but the nearest she got to the Met with Michael was lazing around on the steps outside. She did tell him that she had once had a painting exhibited there when she was a child.

Ironically Michael probably learnt more about the real Jennifer when he went to the Hamptons for a few weeks for his usual family vacation. 'We spent something like three hours a day on the phone and we probably got much closer during that time than we did when we were together because we'd just talk about each other's emotions and feelings and where we were in life and what we hoped to get out of it.'

By the end of the summer, Michael and Jennifer were no longer dating. Just as she was resigned to returning to Steiner for the tenth grade, she received the fantastic news that she had been accepted by Performing Arts. She was about to move on to an exciting time in her life and summer with Michael was over. They were very relaxed about it and both wanted to play the field. He recalls, 'When it came to guys, she would pursue a guy if she liked him. I don't think anyone could have convinced her otherwise. At fifteen, Jennifer wanted to get out there in the world and have relationships with a variety of different people.

'We were both young and we kind of expressed at the time that we were both getting a little uncomfortable with how much we felt for one another and we both agreed that we were young, and starting to feel serious about someone wasn't a good idea, probably. We had both had serious relationships and weren't ready for another. I never had a single argument with Jennifer, not a bad word, not anything negative.'

Jennifer at fifteen provides a fascinating glimpse of the real Jennifer Aniston. At this stage of her life she neither smoked nor drank alcohol. She was sociable and popular with the ability to light up a room in a way that always grabbed the attention of any man in it – especially when she focused her beautiful eyes on them. But most of all, she was beginning to believe in her future as an actress.

Michael was impressed. 'It jumped out at me pretty early on

that Jennifer was a pretty strong girl with acting. She was so focused on what she wanted for a career. You looked at her and you thought that if anyone can figure out a way to actually navigate her way to the top then she was probably that kind of girl because she seemed kind of pulled together for a teenager.'

SIX

Laughing With Chekhov

Jennifer came alive at the Fame school. Immediately, it was like a great weight had been lifted from her shoulders. She began to thrive in her new academic surroundings. The idea that this was in any way a regular high school is ludicrous. Jennifer literally spent half her day taking drama and the highly intensive education would give students a huge head start in their chosen careers. Imagine you were a fourteen-year-old boy who wanted to be a professional footballer – you practise dribbling from nine until ten, then a spot of heading until eleven, take some free kicks until twelve and then learn how to dive in the penalty area until lunch at one. After lunch you would have regular school. That may seem fanciful but that was literally how Jennifer's school day was divided up except she was learning all the different aspects of acting with four consecutive periods, known at the school as the 'Drama Block'.

Jennifer developed a definite purpose in her life, a certainty that she had a destiny to be an actress. Technically the Performing Arts School was a vocational high school preparing pupils for a chosen career as if they were going to be carpenters or motor mechanics. The decision had been made and she did not have to spend hours every day agonizing about her future. Instead she could enjoy each day learning the dynamics of her future trade. Everything was geared to Broadway and not towards Hollywood, although a majority would be drawn by the magnet of California. The key blueprint or 'text book' for drama at PA was the Stanislavski method. In the 1930s, Konstantin Stanislavski pioneered the process which became known as 'method acting'. Jennifer's studies were not all about acting techniques but about voice and diction, physical skills, theatre history and how to knock 'em dead at auditions. There was a great deal more to it than just rolling up and launching into, 'To be or not to be . . .'

And, crucially, every other student wanted to be at the school as much as Jennifer did. Students, generally, did not act up or cause trouble because every day they were having fun. Anthony Abeson, or Mr A as the kids called him, observes, 'This was a bunch of kids who knew in their early teens that they wanted, needed to act. There was no need for a lot of formality, or for a tremendous amount of discipline because they all wanted to be there and we wanted them to be there.'

Jennifer's class contained many very talented teenagers. One of the best-known names now is Eagle-Eye Cherry, the Swedish-born singer and half-brother of Neneh Cherry. Eagle-Eye has had several hits in the UK and the US, the best known of which is 'Save Tonight'. Eagle-Eye has always drifted towards the avant-garde or experimental. His yearbook message when he left PA was, 'Life is a run-on sentence'. Another student was the New York stand-up comedienne Emily Epstein. The great majority, however, were budding actors and actresses: Dennis Pressey, Joshua Nelson, Curtis McClarin, Doreen Spicer, Lillian Heifetz and Dana Behr are just some of Jennifer's classmates who would try their luck in Hollywood. They had limited success, certainly in comparison to Jennifer.

One classmate in particular drew Jennifer's eye – Peter Waldman, a boy from Brooklyn with a hint of a Leif Garrett haircut about him. Peter was well liked and sociable and he and Jennifer started going out.

Peter was just one factor that made Jennifer love her life at PA. She would go home and regale Nancy with stories which, while not exactly revealing impromptu shows in the cafeteria or dancing around the yellow cabs outside, did demonstrate a group of young teenagers at ease with projecting themselves in public. Even when she was out she was tremendously pleased to be at PA. Michael Baroni, who was by now dating an older girl at PA, was impressed: 'It was a big deal, especially at that time in New York with the *Fame* movie. It was a well-known school but it had a fun attitude.'

The uniqueness of PA was that it brought together a broad cross-section of society. One actor observes, 'Some were street kids. They were really scary. Others were well bred and cultured. But the beauty of it was that they were all ferocious about acting.'

One of the advantages for Jennifer of living on the Upper West Side and going to the Fame school was that there was always a gang of half a dozen or more like-minded boys and girls to hang out with and she loved it. At home, there were just her and Nancy struggling along. The amateur psychologist might point to a need to belong to a group in order to feel like she was part of a large family. That may or may not be true but she has arguably been happiest throughout her life when she has been a member of a large circle of friends in which she could relax and let her real personality shine through. That would certainly be the case when she moved to Los Angeles.

Michael recalls how they would celebrate one another's birthdays, with up to fifteen or more people: 'It was always an occasion and pretty frequently there were large get-togethers for a fun and fairly innocent crowd. We just loved to come together in large groups. It was all very congenial. That was what Jennifer liked. She was just this type of person who loved hanging out with a lot of people and she loved being earthy. People gravitated towards her.

'Jennifer was never in isolation when I knew her . . . She was very much the leader of her own pack and very much the centre of attention. She had a sense of fun that was infectious for people to be around. She would watch people do silly things and just burst out laughing. Or she would always be laughing at her own stories. You definitely knew when she was in the room!'

The need for an extended family was also reflected by her mother. Michael and her friends loved Nancy: 'She was just a really warm, caring woman who cared so much about Jennifer. That was so obvious and she loved throwing parties at Jennifer's house for all her friends.'

Belonging to a large group of friends enabled Jennifer to be funny and extrovert, a side to her character mainly hidden from her public in later years. It was also during this period that she met Andrea Bendewald and forged the principal friendship of her life, one that has lasted more than twenty years and shows no sign of diminishing.

Andrea met Jennifer, who was a year older than her, at the

Performing Arts School: 'She just kind of bounced up to me and went, "Hi," and I went, "Hi," and that's really where it started.' Andrea and Jennifer found that they could laugh at the same things and their gossips in the school canteen were the highlight of their days. Andrea recalled in a television interview that Jennifer wore a lot of make-up and had very darkly made-up eyes: 'She was alternative,' she said. 'She was beautiful.' Andrea, blonde and slender, may have been the opposite of Jennifer in looks and demeanour but the paths of their lives have been strikingly similar. Crucially, both girls came from homes where their parents were divorced. They also had elder brothers who would both find their futures in Hollywood. Mason Bendewald, who also went to PA, is a small-budget film-maker.

They became best pals, bonding in a way that was never competitive. Michael Baroni observes, 'Andrea, at the time, was kind of known as being the ultimate in pure and conservative. The big joke back then was that every guy wanted to be "the one" but she made it clear even at that age that she wasn't going to have any boyfriends at the time.

'She was definitely more toned down than Jennifer who would come across as being much flashier. I never saw any friction which I think is unusual for high-school girls. They never argued about the boys they liked. In fact they never argued about anything. They just always fitted together perfectly.

'My impression is that it was actually an astounding relationship and some of us were kind of amazed that two girls could be that close. I think Andrea is a very nice girl. She never wanted to put Jennifer down in any way and has always been incredibly supportive of her.

'Andrea used to hang out with us a lot and one of my favourite memories is of walking down the street with Jennifer on one arm and Andrea on the other. I was king of the world.'

When Michael threw a party for his seventeenth birthday party, Jennifer arrived with Andrea and was mortified when she realized that she had forgotten to bring a card. She ran into the bathroom with Andrea and made one using red lipstick and toilet paper. 'There you go birthday boy,' she said to Michael handing him his 'card' which said, 'Happy Birthday Michael' surrounded with lots of little hearts. It was a triumph of penmanship to make the Rudolf Steiner School proud.

In 1984, the year Jennifer started at PA, the Fame school amalgamated with the High School of Music and Art. The hallowed corridors of the small, atmospheric building on West 46th Street were abandoned when everyone had to move to a large, new building that would house the establishment to be officially known as the Fiorello H. LaGuardia High School of Music & Art and Performing Arts – a title which did not exactly trip off the tongue. LaGuardia, who also lends his name to one of New York's two international airports, was the city's first Italian–American Mayor and one of the most famous US politicians of the 20th century. Chubby, five-foot tall in his socks and wearing round, black-framed glasses, he had great charisma and during his twelve years as Mayor (1934–46) led the city out of the Great Depression, waged wars on gangsters and was an early and outspoken critic of Hitler. He was also an accomplished musician and conductor and always thought he would be best remembered for creating the high school for music and arts which would eventually merge with PA.

The two schools had become one as far back as 1961 but it

took more than twenty years to finish the new facility, complete with a (then) state-of-the-art concert hall and theatre. The new school, with darkened windows on the outside, looked more like a building that might house the FBI or CIA. Not everyone was pleased with what City Hall called a consolidation especially as, in effect, it consigned the old PA to the scrapheap and with it all the tradition, quirks and immediacy of the old building. The big advantage for Jennifer, however, was that the new building was on Amsterdam between 64th and 65th Streets in the area known as the Lincoln Centre, just a very short hop from her home.

Those who still hankered for the old traditions of PA campaigned for the Performing Arts section to keep its special identity including separate caps and gowns for graduation. For them, even though the building had changed, the school would always be PA and not, as Anthony Abeson puts it, 'that terrible mouthful'. The old building, in the meantime, has become the Jacqueline Kennedy Onassis High School for International Careers which is almost as much of a mouthful.

Something happened to Jennifer at Performing Arts, and while it may not have changed her life, it did cause her to reappraise her attitude to acting, as well as open her eyes as to where her own talents might lie. She had to prepare a scene for performance in the studio in front of her classmates and teachers, including Mr A. He fully supported her choice, a difficult scene from *The Three Sisters* by Chekhov. Anthony recalls, 'Jennifer wanted to be a serious actress and this was a very serious scene but people laughed and she was really bothered by that. Here she was trying to achieve some credibility I guess as a serious actress and people were laughing at it. Afterward, when we went through it, I sat her down and told her, "This is a wonderful gift you have." I really tried to make it clear to her that this was not something to be upset about, that it was really kind of marvellous that she had that ability but that she didn't want to rely upon it to the exclusion of the development of her talent as a whole.'

Anthony's words had a great effect on the teenage Jennifer, who until that time had not seen any legitimacy in her talent to amuse. She even nominated his encouragement as life-changing in the bestselling book *The Right Words At The Right Time* compiled by Marlo Thomas. She acknowledged that she did have a tendency to be superficially funny in a scene rather than go deeper into it. She realized that it was a coping mechanism she had employed to deal with the heartbreak of her parents' divorce and, as she put it, 'the hundred other problems that kids have to face every day as they struggle with their personal insecurities'.

Jennifer had always wanted to be the kind of actress that made her cry when she went to the theatre with her mother or father. She had been truly inspired by a production of *Children Of A Lesser God* in the early eighties. The play, a moving romance about a teacher falling in love with a deaf student he is teaching to speak, was a multiple Tony award winner. Jennifer acknowledges that this play, more than any other, persuaded her to be an actress and pursue a place at Performing Arts. She told *Rolling Stone*, 'I was sitting in the second or third row, and I was just so blown away, and I walked out saying, "That's what I want to do."' A subsequent film of the play was released in 1986 to critical acclaim. The deaf actress Marlee Matlin won an Oscar for her performance.

Now, after the Chekhov incident, Jennifer would always see things differently, accepting her natural tendency to make people laugh and, as Anthony had encouraged her to do, making it part of what she wanted to achieve as an actress: 'Instead of rejecting the funny side of myself, I embraced it and channelled it into something I wanted to do and that makes me unbelievably happy.' Her conversation with Anthony had been a eureka moment. For his part, Anthony always took Jennifer's abilities very seriously and was constantly pressing her to stretch herself and not operate in a comedic comfort zone.

One of the points that Anthony is keen to stress is that he believed Jennifer always had the capacity to be a very fine actress and that an aptitude for comedy in no way diminishes an actor. 'I am always saying in my classes that comedy springs from the truth and here is Jennifer doing Chekhov and she wasn't lying, she wasn't being fake, she wasn't trying to be funny – she was being truthful and naturally funny.' The lay interpretation of his expert view is that Jennifer has an unusual gift easily ignored in slick, disposable television.

Even at an early and inexperienced stage in her career, Jennifer had a vital acting quality which drama coaches call 'inhale'. Many bad actors are on exhale, the over-actors and succulent hams who roll their eyes and grimace as if every part demanded them to be like Jack Nicholson in *The Shining* (1980). Jennifer is not on exhale. 'A lot of actors are out of sync with the universe,' explains Anthony. 'The breath is coming in and out, the tides are coming in and out but some performers are just going out; when you are only going out – on exhale – you're *forced* to be acting. It's only when you're taking in that you can abandon "acting" and simply be *reacting* which is what we want. Jennifer naturally took in. She was always very generous towards other actors, revealing a beneficial lack of ego.' This ability is at the heart of Jennifer's flair for ensemble acting.

As a novice actress, Jennifer was prepared to take risks, hence the decision to try the Chekhov scene. Performing Arts was all about developing talent, not about using it. Anthony observes, 'Don't teach them what they already know.' One of the worst things for acting connoisseurs is what at PA was known as the Romeo syndrome or, more precisely, the idea among bad actors that 'Romeo is a guy just like me'. They do not act the role, they just act themselves. Having butchered Romeo, they move on to Hamlet with a 'Hey, this Hamlet's just like me'. Jennifer was several classes above this.

One aspect of humorous acting that Jennifer alludes to in Marlo Thomas's book is that her favourite actresses growing up were ones that made her laugh like Diane Keaton and Goldie Hawn. Her all-time favourite, however, was the less successful Valerie Bertinelli, teenage star of the long-running US sitcom *One Day At A Time.* She was a real role model, even hero, for the impressionable young Jennifer. Bertinelli won the role in *One Day At A Time* when she was fifteen. Jennifer was able to identify with Bertinelli on two levels: as Bertinelli played one of two teenage daughters of a recently-divorced woman, she was the teenage actress she wanted to be, and she was playing a role that reflected Jennifer's own position. The main male character in the show was not the out-of-the-picture husband but the building superintendent where they lived. Although a sitcom, it was one of the first shows to deal with divorce and the effect it had on children, so it was not hard to understand why Jennifer loved it. The sentiment of 'one day at a time' in dealing with life post divorce could almost have been the mantra for Nancy and Jennifer picking up the pieces on West 92nd Street.

One other Bertinelli 'credential' had an effect on Jennifer.

In 1981, when she was twenty-one, Bertinelli married the heavy-metal guitarist Eddie Van Halen, a rock god – at least in Jennifer's eyes – and from that moment on she was a secret rock chick. If Valerie could capture Eddie then perhaps actress-to-be Jennifer Aniston could dream of snaring her hero, Steven Tyler, the very charismatic, large-lipped lead singer of Aerosmith.

Fame school was a golden time for Jennifer. When she graduated in the summer of 1987 her closing message in her yearbook was, 'It's been a real experience! My friends and PA will live in my Heart forever. I'll miss you DREA xo.' It's a simple but very genuine message. DREA is, of course, Andrea Bendewald, who remains a much-loved person in Jennifer's life. Andrea's own message a year later was more ethereal: 'While I was here I built a rainbow. Now I must find another sky. Let's not forget the times and dreams.' The contrasting thoughts neatly encompass their differing personalities.

Peter Waldman, who Jennifer did not mention in her message, wrote, 'I trust you but send cash.'

SEVEN

For Dear Life

Even though he knew that Jennifer took acting seriously, Anthony Abeson was distinctly impressed when she enrolled at some drama classes he had started downtown on Lafayette Street in a building called the Musical Works Theatre. Some sixty drama students had left LaGuardia Arts at the same time but Jennifer was the only one focused on further improvement right away, joining the three-hour classes on Tuesday and Thursday evenings. Anthony observes, 'It was another sign of her seriousness. A lot of kids graduate from Performing Arts and think, "Oh, I've got a driver's licence to act," but Jennifer thought, "You know what, I want to get more training."'

By this time Anthony too had left Performing Arts to become a much in-demand independent teacher working with, in the main, older students: 'It was very plucky of Jennifer I think to continue her studies downtown in some bizarre building with strangers. She'd been in a very safe, controlled environment but, as well as revealing a serious purpose, it displayed a sign of appetite. That's something you can't teach but which you've got to have to really succeed and realize potential.'

One of the important ingredients in Jennifer's subsequent success was her ability to work with other actors. Anthony noted a refreshing lack of ego about her, an understanding that to make something work it should not always be about her. During one of her classes, another student called Tom Cavanaugh needed to rehearse a monologue he had prepared. It was a very moving scene in which he played a father saying goodbye to his daughter who was dying in hospital. Anthony asked Jennifer if she would mind performing with Tom.

Jennifer was happy to oblige. She lay on the floor and looked suitably close to death's door while Tom lovingly cradled her head and delivered his poignant speech. 'Jennifer was very generous and giving in the class,' recalls Anthony. 'Even with no lines, she would, as we say, "feed" him. She totally understood that being up there was not about her but to help Tom. He began to connect to the idea that Jennifer was his child and that she was dying. Unfortunately he was so absorbed that when I gave him a direction he said, "What?" shrugged with his shoulders *and* hands and dropped poor Jennifer's head on the floor. Bang!

'Many, many actresses would have been annoyed and would have shouted, "Why the hell did you drop me?" or "Aargh!" Jennifer just laughed. Throughout the time I worked with her she was in no way a diva. She put on absolutely no airs.' Tom Cavanaugh recalls, 'She was very gracious about it. She was such a nice, honest girl.' Tom, who had not been to PA, was also impressed with how dedicated Jennifer was, an outlook she shared with others he met from the Fame school.

After the classes the students would pile into the Astor Diner, which was practically next door in Astor Place. Andrea Bendewald would come down with some other friends from PA to join them. Her brother Mason, now a director in Los Angeles, also took the class. Tom adds, 'There were great party times but they were also intent on doing work. I remember there was never any problem with the bill which is unusual with actors. Everyone just paid their share and nobody ever ended up paying fifty dollars for a hamburger.' In some ways it was like an early Woody Allen or Barry Levinson film – conversation with humour and a serious purpose.

Jennifer's acting classes took up two nights of a busy week. She also started evening classes in psychology and learnt the finer points of Freud. 'I like to talk to people,' she explained. 'I wanted to be a shrink if I couldn't be an actor.' The philosophy of human behaviour took a back seat, however, when Jennifer was cast in a play and she never went back to it, although her interviews over the years have always revealed a person immersed in self-analysis.

Jennifer Aniston 'arrived' as a professional actress when the following listing appeared in *New York Magazine* in the issue of 28 March 1988:

> **Dancing on Checkers' Grave** – Jennifer Aniston and Michelle Banks star in Eric Lane's play about two high-school girls in a pet cemetery in Long Island, directed by Marc Helman.

Jennifer had just turned nineteen and had already found herself in the pages of one of the best-known magazines in the US – and the word 'star' was next to her name. The reality, unsurprisingly, was much less glamorous. It was not so much off-Broadway as off the map. The audience paid $8 each to see performances at the Upstairs Theatre at St Mark's Church-in-the-Bowery.

St Mark's, however, does have local prestige. Outside, sparrows and pigeons mingle with passers-by and local residents taking advantage of a seat in the courtyard. This is a place to come for a little tranquillity as the cars cascade down Second Avenue. Inevitably, there are people sleeping in every available doorway, overseen by the mandatory American flag, while inside, the church is bright, airy and secure. It encourages 'community' events in theatre and dance – an ideal venue for the première of what was, even in the modern times of 1989, quite a progressively themed play subtly exploring teenage sexuality, in particular the possibility of a lesbian relationship between two high-school girls. The play required Jennifer to tenderly kiss her young black co-star on stage, every night for four weeks. Jennifer's inter-racial lesbian embrace pre-dated a similar kiss on the long-running soap *EastEnders* by some seventeen years.

Ironically, the media went into a frenzy in early 2007 when rumours surfaced that Jennifer and Courteney Cox would enjoy a 'passionate lip-lock' during an episode of *Dirt*. Jennifer was guest-starring in Courteney's new series, playing a lesbian magazine editor. It turned out to be nothing more than a goodbye kiss and thoroughly tame when compared to the real thing witnessed by a few devotees of challenging, gay drama nearly twenty years before.

Eric Lane has always been a thought-provoking playwright. His best-known work is probably *Cater-Waiter*, an award-winning gay comedy, although the connection with Jennifer Aniston's career will assuredly reach a wider audience. Despite being a short one-act play, *Dancing On Checkers' Grave* is probably one of the most acclaimed pieces of work that Jennifer has on her CV. She plays a seventeen-year-old high-school student called Lisa who is described in the stage directions as 'white, very pretty and takes great care in her appearance. While not intellectual, she is very quick. Tries to hide her insecurities by making sure her physical appearance is perfect.'

The 'Checkers' in the title is the famous cocker spaniel that belonged to Richard Nixon and the device which, it could be argued, saved his career. In 1952, when he was a mere candidate for vice-president, Nixon was accused by his enemies of setting up a secret slush fund. In a television appearance which would have made Tony Blair proud, he said the only gift he had ever received from his political allies was Checkers. He went on to say that his children loved the dog and he would never give it back even it if was a crime. America wept and the rest, as they say, is history. Nixon became Vice-President under President Eisenhower and fifteen years later was elected to the White House.

When Checkers died in 1964, he was buried in a pet cemetery in Long Island, the setting for Eric Lane's play. The drama begins with Lisa's classmate Dina, a seventeen-year-old black girl, searching for Checkers' grave. When she finds it, she calls her friend over to join her. They talk about a composition they have to write but the underlying theme is one of sexual uncertainty between the two, culminating in a kiss which ends when Lisa hears a sound and pushes Dina away, suggesting some guilt or concern that they would be seen. Perhaps Lane was trying to convey the difficulty of recognizing true sexuality when young. It was certainly a challenging role for Jennifer.

She approached the kiss with confidence: 'It was no problem

at all. I was probably thinking, "Wow, this is really cool, kissing a girl".'

Tom Cavanaugh, who went along to support Jennifer, recalls, 'I came out thinking that was pretty brave. It was a great piece of work. It was quite short and I thought very cutting edge.'

The actual kiss was the natural conclusion of the two girls dancing (as in the play's title) while singing the Cindi Lauper hit 'True Colours' together. Lane describes the scene in the stage directions as 'Awkward. Tender.' Tom Cavanaugh thought it 'erotic'. 'True Colours' may not be the most subtle lyric for conveying sexuality – containing the trite sentiment not to be afraid to show your true colours – but it realistically represented the importance of song lyrics to the minds of young people who readily identify with them.

While the use of 'True Colours' is a little obvious, the role of Nixon in the play is more complex. Dancing on the grave of the dog that saved his career suggests a celebration of the passing of Nixon, who was, at least in private, resolutely anti-gay. In 2002, secret tapes were released of Nixon's private conversations in 1971 revealing the depth of his homophobia. He declared that Northern California had become so 'faggy' that he didn't want to shake hands with anyone from there. He also declared, somewhat pertinently considering Jennifer's ancestry: 'You know what happened to the Greeks. Homosexuality destroyed them. Sure, Aristotle was a homo. So was Socrates. We all know that.'

Four years after Jennifer starred in the première of *Dancing On Checkers' Grave*, the play was co-winner as best play in Love Creek Productions' Annual Gay & Lesbian Festival at the Nat Horne Theatre in New York. By then, Jennifer was 2,500 miles away, trying to make it in Los Angeles.

As a young actress Jennifer often described herself as a professional waitress doing some part-time acting. Finding a job serving tables was always considerably easier than securing a role. Fortunately there were countless restaurants within walking distance of her home and the 'auditions' for taking orders were less stressful than competing with other young actresses for Broadway, or, more probably off-Broadway, roles.

Jennifer found a job waitressing at Jackson Hole, a well-known burger joint in Manhattan, just a few blocks from her building. The convenience was just about the only recommendation. It was busy and lively with tables so close together that customers and waitresses were forever squeezing in and out as if performing some elaborate dance. The burgers were huge. You could almost imagine Al Pacino, in his masterful role in the film *Frankie And Johnny* (1991), working here as a short-order cook.

Jennifer is engagingly amusing about her time here, recalling that she was too honest for her own good, quietly tipping off customers if they inadvertently ordered something awful. Although she appears so poised and elegant as a Hollywood star, she is charmingly self-deprecating about her waitressing skills, which suffered from her clumsiness. On one shift she managed to drop an Alpine Burger and a Chilli Burger right into the laps of two tourists: 'They were yelling at the top of their voices, "You stupid woman. You stupid, stupid . . ."'

Notwithstanding this, and despite her good-humoured modesty, Jennifer observed while she was starring in *Friends*, 'I still consider myself a great waitress.'

Between shifts the daily grind of auditions would continue and the only half-decent acting job she secured was in a commercial for Bob's Big Boy burgers. She joked, 'It was one of those where you choose either to have one thing, Bob's Big Boy burger, or the other less appealing burger. I was the other.' Jennifer would often change out of her waitress uniform into her acting clothes in the passenger seat of the car as her mother Nancy dutifully braved the Manhattan traffic to ferry her daughter about. Ironically she had to travel no distance for the next important milestone in her acting career.

Just across Lafayette Street where Jennifer took her drama classes with Anthony Abeson was the renowned Public Theatre, then still part of the legendary Joseph Papp's domain. Papp was one of the great men of New York theatre who would have been a knight of the realm or even a peer if he had been British. His name was inextricably linked in the US with making Shakespeare available to the ordinary man and woman in the street when he founded the New York Shakespeare Festival in 1954. Three years later he won permission to stage Shakespeare at the Delacourt Theatre in Central Park.

This had been a theatrical breakthrough for Papp, but he had not satisfied his ambitions for American theatre and planned to bring important new playwrights to the stage. This led to the establishment of the Public Theatre in 1962, which found a permanent home at the famous Astor Library building on Lafayette Street. Even an audition at the Public Theatre was an exciting prospect and Jennifer was overjoyed to win a part in the Papp production of a new play *For Dear Life* by the OBIE award-winning playwright Susan Miller. Jennifer was still a teenager and here she was about to embark, she thought, on a great stage career at what would be the nearest thing in New York to the National Theatre. From St Mark's Church to the Public Theatre was a huge leap, not least in the ticket price of $25. In context it was assuredly a bigger deal than being cast in the pilot of an untested television show called *Friends*. When the billboards for the play came out Jennifer again witnessed the advantage of having a surname beginning with the first letter of the alphabet: despite being by far the least experienced cast member, her name was at the top while the best-known actor, Tony Shalhoub's, was at the bottom.

Playwright Susan Miller perfectly fitted the profile of the home-grown dramatist that Joseph Papp liked to patronize. She had spent four years working on the play which she had begun in a New York State writers' colony. At that stage, she told the *New York Times*, all she had was the title and a desire to write about people with a zest for language. *For Dear Life* is a very wordy play, describing the lives and conversations of a couple – disc jockey Jake and film critic Catherine – across two decades. Their teenage son Sam wistfully confides that his parents were always trying to tell him something and that they would be waiting for him at breakfast just for the chance to say it.

Jennifer's role was as Sam's girlfriend and, in the context of what was to follow, she was fortunate. She was wide-eyed and innocent in terms of theatrical experience but still exuded confidence. Another young New York actress, Bellina Logan, who was less fortunate to be cast in the role of the daughter of the house, Maggie, recalls, 'I had worked a few years in the theatre and I just remember her asking me so many questions about it.

'It was a big deal to be in a big play. She was really wholly optimistic and excited and a lot of her personality that you see now was very much the way she was then. She was always very wide-eyed.'

Jennifer and Bellina were not the principal actors. The main leads were played by Tony Shalhoub, later to find wider fame in the TV comedy *Monk*, Broadway stalwart Laila Robins and another actress, Christine Estabrook, who also found television notoriety when she played Mrs Huber in *Desperate Housewives* and was bumped off in the first series.

Everyone was optimistic at the beginning. The production had such substance with the inestimable Joe Papp at the top, and the acclaimed Norman Rene as director. By the time of the previews, however, the mood had changed. Norman Rene was doing his best: 'He was great with us,' recalls Bellina. 'It wasn't an easy play because at some point it became clear that this really was a play that shouldn't be up yet. I mean when you have Joseph Papp coming backstage after the first preview going, "It's getting there," you know you have problems. For this play the previews were hell. It did bring us all closer together though.'

The one exception to this general sense of foreboding was Jennifer. Her scene was the best thing in the play, much to the other cast members' chagrin. The play was in three acts but she was only on stage during the second. She had her second stage kiss; this time was with Stephen Mailer, son of the great American author Norman Mailer, who was playing Sam. His mother walks in on them making out on the couch.

Bellina Logan recalls, 'It was a great scene, well written and well acted. Even at the read-through – which is a bit nerve-wracking because in a way you are re-auditioning for not only the people that have hired you but also for your castmates – the scene just read beautifully. I think Jennifer's scene was a joy for Norman Rene. He would always be good with her because her scene was so perfect. The play itself needed to be worked on because it was so uneven. When he had to move on to another scene, maybe he wasn't so enthusiastic.

'Jennifer got to start the second act with a great sense of energy and I know it was the scene that people looked forward to seeing because it was a pure scene – it had a beginning, a middle and an end all in one scene and it was great. We were all a little jealous of the fact that she could come in like a breath of fresh air, especially for the audience who were probably by that point really not sure if they should have stayed through the interval!'

For Jennifer, one aspect of *For Dear Life* was difficult – what to do with her time when she was not on stage. In *Dancing On Checkers' Grave* she was a constant but that was not the case in this much bigger production. She enjoyed smoking and gossiping with Christine in the dressing room they shared, and at other times she would pop into the next-door dressing room which Bellina shared with Laila Robins. Bellina was mainly on stage in the first act so the two girls would have plenty of time to talk in the third. 'We were both really happy to have this job and we would talk about that,' Bellina says. 'But also Jennifer was always inquiring. She wanted to know about acting in Shakespeare and Shaw. Most of the things I had done at college were classical, Juliet for instance, and she would ask me about it. The funny thing was that she sort of looked up to me. "Wait a minute," I used to think, "I'm not much older than you." '

Other than lighting a cigarette and talking about dead-end jobs, Jennifer found the process a little boring as it was a three-hour play. She would ask Bellina, 'How do you do this every night?' or 'Don't you ever lose interest?' which perhaps suggested that she was having doubts about her inner desire to press on as a theatre actress, an idea reinforced by Laila Robins who distinctly recalls Jennifer saying, 'I'm not sure I want to be an actress.'

Ironically, Bellina well remembers the occasion after one of their chats when Jennifer left to go on stage and she thought to herself, 'What a sweet girl, I hope things work out for her!'

For Dear Life opened on 13 December 1988, a big night for Jennifer, who was especially thrilled because her father John had come to see his daughter on stage. 'It was a big deal for her that her father was coming to see the play,' recalls Bellina. 'She was really proud to be doing it and we all felt bad because she was so happy while we, on the other hand, were a bit mortified to be in the play. I felt bad that we were always raining on her parade.'

Jennifer soon settled in to the routine of appearing nightly, blissfully unaware of what was lurking in the wings. She had absolutely no idea that she was acting in what she would later describe as 'the worst play of your life'. For once she had some decent money in her pocket – a take-home wage of some $300 comparing very favourably with her waitressing tips – and she was enjoying the routine, even managing to fit in waiting tables on Mondays, her day off.

The high spot of the play's run was one night when she delivered her funniest line and saw that she was staring straight into the 'huge, gaping cavern that is the mouth of Al Pacino'. Jennifer was stunned, especially as she was aware that Pacino was probably the most famous former student of the Performing Arts School. She suddenly realized that he was sitting next to another of her great heroes, Diane Keaton: 'I couldn't believe it. I made Al Pacino laugh. It was one of the greatest moments – that can carry you for a year or two.' And it would have to carry her because nearly one month after opening, the trap door was opened on the production and everything fell through.

Perhaps the greatest excitement for any actor after, of course, the curtain going up for the first time is opening the newspaper to read the reviews. The word 'excitement' does scant justice to the feeling of nervous anticipation and dread associated with the opinion of Frank Rich of the *New York Times*, the man who can make or break any production. The billing had described the play as a comedy 'about surviving the eighties with dignity and a comic spirit'. When Jennifer opened the paper on 11 January 1989 it became quite clear from the first sentence that Frank Rich had found little to laugh at. He hated it and wrote with a pen dipped in acid that the 'relentlessly right-thinking' characters 'are the kind of people who can't contemplate the change of seasons without anticipating nuclear winter. They can't pour a glass of milk without crying over the snapshot of the missing child on the carton. They can't go to the bathroom without worrying about the depletion of the ozone layer. They're not exactly a fun crowd, and they wear out their welcome pretty quickly . . .'

It was a withering demolition job. And what made it worse was that he exposed an uncertainty the cast themselves felt. Laila Robins observes, 'When a new play doesn't do well you ask yourself is it the writer, the director or the cast? I certainly don't remember any party!'

Probably the only blessing in Frank Rich's review was that he did not single out any actor for opprobrium. Instead, he contented himself with the observation that 'some good actors (and not-so-good ones) look consistently silly'. He did not specify whether he thought Jennifer came under the 'good' or 'not-so-good' heading.

Other reviews had been unfavourable but it was the Frank Rich opinion that counted and, inevitably, it was not long before Joseph Papp appeared. Bellina Logan recalls, 'It was as if God had come in because he ran the thing. It was like the Queen at a première going down the line. He would go backstage and we would all come out of our dressing rooms and he would go down the line saying something to each actor.' On this occasion, his message was simple: 'We are closing early,' he said sombrely. The performance on 22 January would be the last. The play was a flop.

Bellina, although quite relieved that her personal agony was over, recalls, 'I genuinely don't think Tony or Laila thought it would close early. Jennifer was really bummed. You just can't help but take it so personally. We were all pretty down. We just never thought we were going to die like that. There was a genuine depression in the hallways and, when we knew we were going, a sad, low, grey energy set in for the rest of it.'

For Dear Life ran for just forty-six performances. Fortunately, no careers were sacrificed on its failure. Tony Shalhoub won three Emmy awards for *Monk* and early in 2007 was back off-Broadway once again appearing in a new play, while Christine Estabrook was back on Broadway in the autumn of 2006 in the critically acclaimed *Spring Awakening*. Award-winning actress Laila Robins has been a Broadway star for twenty years, most recently in a revival of Shaw's *Heartbreak House*. The playwright Susan Miller has won numerous awards for her best-known plays, *My Left Breast* and *A Map Of Doubt And Rescue* as well as acting as a writer and producer on the TV series *The L Word*. Her play *It's Our Town Too* featured in the anthology *The Actors' Book Of Gay and Lesbian Plays* (1995) edited, coincidentally, by Eric Lane, the author of *Dancing On Checkers' Grave*.

A year after the early closure of *For Dear Life*, Norman Rene directed the film *Longterm Companion*, a title taken from the only way a gay man could be described in the obituary columns – 'survived by his long-term companion'. It chronicled the lives of a group of gay men who, at the start of the 1980s, had never heard of AIDS but who a decade later had been devastated by the disease. The movie was acclaimed as a poignant, unsentimental and intelligent drama about bereavement in the gay community. It was released three years before the Oscar-winning film *Philadelphia* (1993) hit the headlines. Norman Rene died of complications from AIDS in 1996.

Rene enjoyed a reputation as a sensitive director. Significantly, from the point of view of Jennifer's own career, the *New York Times* acknowledged 'his skill at eliciting finely detailed, naturalistic performances from actors and his mastery of an intimate ensemble style'. Acting in a group has always been a particular strength of Jennifer's to which her most famous role in *Friends* is obvious testimony.

That would be her happy future but, for the moment, Jennifer was completely crushed and it would be nearly twenty years before she set foot on a New York stage again. Clearly, if *For Dear Life* had been a huge success, her entire career might have been different.

So where did this leave Jennifer? Back to waitressing of course and the dreary drudge of auditions, with the knowledge that even if she won a part the show could close early. She was becoming more restless – a feeling that became even more pronounced when she celebrated her twentieth birthday still serving burgers, with no boyfriend, feeling fat and unloved, and still living with Mom.

As a change she moved downtown to share a small apartment in the West Village with another young actress called Nancy Balbirer whom she met when they auditioned to be extras on *Saturday Night Live*. (Although the venerable comedy show failed to recognize Jennifer's comedic talents, within ten years she was welcomed back with open arms to be its celebrity host.) It would be nice to think of this as a dry run for *Friends* but the reality was of two struggling young women trying to get a start.

Years later, in 2006, Balbirer appeared at Joe's Pub in New York delivering a monologue in which she talked about a friend called 'Jane' who had lived with her for a couple of months while working at a burger joint. She amused the audience with tales of 'Jane' giving herself bikini waxes lying upside down on the couch. According to the sketch, Jane advised her to try and be 'more fuckable' at auditions and to buy chicken cutlets to stuff her bra. 'Jane' iced her nipples before her own auditions and moaned about her big butt and her nose which, she said, came from her 'Greek half'. 'Jane' moved to Los Angeles, got liposuction, a nose job, a hairline adjustment and lost a lot of weight after going on NutriSlim.

All good knockabout fun, but it did not take journalists more than a nano-second to work out that Jane was a thinly disguised Jennifer, although, in fairness to Balbirer, she never referred to Jennifer by name and has never suggested that this was anything more than a performance. Other than that, she has steadfastly refused to talk about it. The undisputed facts are that she and Jennifer did share an apartment, Jennifer is half Greek, did work in a burger joint, has moaned about her big butt, has admitted some cosmetic surgery, did lose a lot of weight and did move to Los Angeles. (She has never admitted to upside-down bikini waxes.) Jennifer's spokesman called Nancy Balbirer's monologue 'mean-spirited'.

The issue of weight is a recurring one in Jennifer's life. In her memoir, her mother Nancy describes how, shortly after her appearance in *For Dear Life*, Jennifer went on her first diet. It sounded ghastly, involving pouring water on some noxious dry food and eating the result. It worked, however, and she was definitely slimmer by the time she made a life-changing decision. 'I'm thinking of moving to LA,' she confided to Anthony Abeson's wife Sherry. 'Do you think I should?' Sherry thought it would be a good decision.

A number of factors prompted Jennifer to consider a move to the West Coast: she was thoroughly disillusioned with Broadway; there were more opportunities for television parts in LA; her father and brother both lived there and she would have a place to stay; and almost all her classmates from PA were contemplating the same move. Andrea who had graduated the previous year also planned to leave New York to go to college. Jennifer was treading water in New York, but just because the streets of Broadway were not paved with gold did not mean the same was true of Hollywood. Jennifer was clear on one thing: 'I wanted to be self-sufficient.'

The hardest part was telling her mother she would be moving not just down to the West Village this time, but all the way to California. For so many years it had just been the two of them and the goodbyes at the airport were tearful.

Part Two

Ladies of the Canyon

Courteney Cox, who became such a close friend, was asked what she thought was the secret of Jennifer's appeal. She replied, 'She's a real girl's girl. Guys love her, but women really love her and are not threatened by her. It's a really good sign when someone has a lot of good girlfriends.'

EIGHT

In The Footsteps Of Jennifer

Casually, I ask the charming owner of the Laurel Canyon Country Store if he ever came across Jennifer Aniston when she lived up this way. 'Sure, she used to work here,' he said smiling and with more than a hint of an Italian accent. 'That's lucky,' I thought, although there were not too many options in the neighbourhood for an out-of-work actress. She could have worked in a laundry round the corner or, possibly, a shoe repairer's and handbag shop, but the grocery/deli seemed the best choice. The store reminded me of an old-fashioned English village shop in that there seemed to be everything you could ever need crammed onto its shelves. You could stock a Himalayan expedition on a single visit here.

'How interesting,' I say. 'What did she do here?' A young man looks up from the till and pipes up, 'She was me. She did a bit of everything.' He explains that he is the jack of all trades in the store, making sandwiches, stacking shelves and taking the money. His boss tells me that even when she no longer worked there Jennifer would still pop in every day for cigarettes because her boyfriend at the time lived just across the way. Amusingly, he is much more interested in telling me about the time the most famous Italian film star of them all came into the store – the incomparable Sophia Loren. I have to agree with him that Miss Loren is *bellissima* and that it would have been one of the highlights of my life if she'd walked into a shop in the West Country village where I used to live. It's one of those names, isn't it? Sophia Loren just sounds like a million dollars' worth of glamour.

Elizabeth Taylor, Ava Gardner and Marilyn Monroe also sound as if they were born to wear diamonds. Doris Day and Meg Ryan, on the other hand, sound like they would be a girl next door who would be involved in a delightful romantic comedy. I'm not too sure about Jennifer Aniston. It's a name that works well in combination: Brad Pitt and Jennifer Aniston, Vince Vaughn and Jennifer Aniston or Tate Donovan and Jennifer Aniston. You can just see the captions on the red-carpet pictures. It seems to me that it's a name that could go either way but one that is perfect for sitcoms or rom-coms. I'm sure she would never have made it as Jennifer Anastasakis though.

I decide to have my lunch sitting on the veranda of the Laurel Canyon Country Store, having been seduced by seeing them make the deli sandwiches while I was chatting inside. I choose a ham with Swiss cheese combo for $8.99. The temptation to wash it down with a carafe of wine for $3.99 (about £2.00!) is a huge one but I resist knowing that the roads up to Jennifer's old house are full of scary corners.

I can picture Jennifer and her old pals up here sitting round the ad hoc tables, smoking in the sun while the traffic pours past. I wonder if she ever thinks about trying to recapture those happy times. The problem is that now the small car park would be crammed full of paparazzi motorbikes and range rovers. It wouldn't be the same with the click of a lens every time you took a sip of your skinny latte.

The place is an absolute sun trap. I learn that Pamela Anderson has also popped in for groceries but I am still more impressed with La Loren. I take a flyer with me for future reference in case on my way back down the hill I need to buy some firewood, herbal tea, baby food, dog food, bird food, toilet paper or motor oil.

The neighbourhood restaurant is called Pace and is to the side of the stores. It has a pleasant, relaxed atmosphere and is very discrete. Jennifer last ate here about four or five years ago but they are hoping she will come back. Apparently she liked the place because they treat the clientèle here like ordinary people and don't allow punters to bother anyone famous who might come in. This is just common sense for any restaurant hoping to attract celebrities.

Jennifer lived on a street called Ridgemont Drive when she first rented her own place in Los Angeles. It seems very high up and getting there is an adventure in itself. No wonder Matthew Perry mocks Jennifer's driving. He calls her 'the worst driver in the history of drivers'. She must have thrown her SUV around these bends like a rally driver. The houses are just dotted here and there, all different sizes, shapes and colours. Jennifer's house was at the end of the street, but she left here a short time after she started in *Friends* and was earning enough to buy a home of her own.

The afternoon peace is punctured by the sound of barking dogs. When they pipe down it's very quiet again and the views of the hills are invigorating. This may be a cosy, neighbourly place but they still don't want any trespassers. A huge black remote-controlled gate bars the way to where Jennifer used to live. In Los Angeles, even Bohemia needs security.

Jennifer has always insisted that she wanted to make her own money and never wanted to be dependent on a man. Her ambitions when she made it were young and simple – her own home and a Mercedes. She wasted no time in buying a house on Blue Jay Way which is on the way back to Santa Monica where I'm staying. The climate here is terrific. It's autumn and I'm wearing T-shirt and shorts. I remember using a tourist map when I first came to LA that was a guide to movie stars' homes. I have no idea whether Blue Jay Way is on there but it should have been. Tobey Maguire and Keanu Reeves both live at the bottom of the hill while Halle Berry has a rather plain $3-million house on the way up to Jennifer's. If Jennifer's was on the market now it might fetch as much as $5 million. Inevitably there's a security camera trained on the street but it's the views in the other direction that Jennifer loved – you can see the ocean and the whole of Los Angeles from up here. If the Empire State Building was in the view as well, then it would be perfect. This is the place which became a 'love nest' for Jennifer and Brad Pitt before they were married and where they were happiest after. She moved back when they broke up.

Jennifer loved the garden. She loved sitting out on the patio watching the sun go down, gazing at the rabbits on her lawn and waiting for the hummingbirds to come by. It was here that she was photographed sunbathing topless which prompted her to take legal action against the photographer. (It was an invasion of privacy because the photographer shot *into* her property.)

Funny, when I read about Jennifer's 'little' house, I imagine a chocolate-box house – a rural retreat away from the big city. That's not how it is. These are movie-star homes in suburbia, complete with pool and privacy. Hers may not be the size of the over-the-top mansion she lived in when she was Mrs Brad Pitt but you are never going to get someone leaning over the garden gate to admire your roses here. Funnily enough, Jennifer did have roses and was very proud of them.

I decide to track down the restaurant/bar where Jennifer used to go to unwind after filming *Friends*. It's called Merricks and it's on Santa Monica Boulevard, opposite Hamburger Mary's. I drive up and down but can't see it. I park, check the address with an operator and it's not listed. I give directions to a lovely couple from Ohio who are celebrating their silver wedding anniversary and have lost their hotel. Luckily, it's only across the street because the husband is struggling a bit. They made the same mistake as me – imagining they could walk anywhere in LA, but anywhere is miles. It's not like New York. Just yesterday I decided to walk twenty blocks to the ocean in Santa Monica. It took me over an hour. By the time I arrived, my feet hurt and I couldn't be bothered to walk along the front, so I went to a bar for a reviving beer instead and got a cab back to where I was staying.

Where is Merricks? No wonder she liked this place – it's impossible to find. I ask directions and it turns out to be ten yards from where I am standing, just off the main street which is why I could not see it. And it's not called Merricks at all. It's *Marix* and it is heaving. There's a sister place called Basix which has a frontage on Santa Monica. Marix is a Tex Mex place full of chilli and enchiladas but, most of all, overflowing with margaritas. I've met up with some friends so we order a pitcher. I'm tempted by the Kick-Ass Margarita, a house special, but decide

I would like to be alive in the morning. Jennifer would come in with a bunch of girl friends, often including Courteney Cox, and they would establish themselves at a table, order margaritas and open a pack of her favourite Merit cigarettes. Jennifer always enjoyed 'girls' nights', laughing and joking without the distraction of the men in their lives.

It's time to move on. There's a strip joint on Sunset I am keen to try because, rumour has it, Courtney Love once worked there. When we arrive, some girls wearing not much are doing a routine to 'Car Wash', the old Rose Royce disco classic. They are spraying mirrors at the back of the stage and cleaning them with a cloth. The funny thing is that I can tell by the smell that they are using real window cleaner – clearly the Stanislavski method of stripping.

NINE

The Hill

John Aniston was well established as one of the leading actors in daytime soaps when his daughter flew out in the late summer of 1989 to start a new life in Los Angeles. John and his now wife Sherry had left New York for good in the mid eighties when *Search For Tomorrow* had ended and he had secured a new role in the premier show of its type, *Days Of Our Lives*. The show was filmed at the NBC studios in Burbank, just down the road from the set where his daughter would finally find fame in *Friends*. That was more than five years in the future. For the moment, Jennifer, aged twenty, was just one of the countless hopefuls looking for a break in Hollywood.

At least to begin with she was living with her father so she was not struggling on alone without the prospect of seeing a friendly face at the end of the day. Sherry and John had a young baby, Alexander, to contend with and Jennifer was not the centre of the household's attention. She has never spoken about Sherry and there is nothing to indicate that the two did not rub along together. She had been able to visit the West Coast during summer vacations and resolve some of the issues with her father that inevitably as a child she had kept bottled up.

She explained to *TV Guide* the emotional relief she had felt: 'The greatest gift he gave to me was to say, "I'm sorry I wasn't there". He wasn't . . . He wasn't a bad guy but he was typical of his generation. Now he's a great dad.'

John was now, officially, an award-winning actor. He was named Outstanding Actor in a Daytime Serial in 1986 and, much more fun, at the same ceremony he was the 'Outstanding Villain'. A daytime serial is what an award ceremony calls a soap. If we had an outstanding villain award in the UK it would probably have been won countless times by Dirty Den on EastEnders, at least until Richard Hillman came along in Coronation Street. But in the US, the nefarious Viktor Kiriakis had no peers. (Viktor, unsurprisingly, was Greek, a womanizer and a drug baron.)

Days Of Our Lives had begun twenty years earlier, then a half-hour soap set in the fictional town of Salem. One of the programme's little gimmicks has been never to reveal in which state Salem is but it bears no resemblance to Salem, Massachusetts, the very real site of the witchcraft trials which Arthur Miller describes in his play *The Crucible*. Each episode of *Days* traditionally begins with the same, famously kitsch voiceover from the late actor McDonald Carey, who played the character Dr Tom Horton for nearly thirty years: 'Like sands through the hourglass . . . so are the days of our lives.'

The show is an open invitation to parody but does boast a fiercely loyal audience and in 2005 notched up its 10,000th episode. In the UK, where it has never been shown, it ironically became famous to a wide audience when the character Joey from

Friends won a part as Dr Drake Ramore in *Days*. Jennifer found this very funny.

Jennifer's elder brother Johnny was on hand to help if he could. The year before when she had been visiting him, he had secured Jennifer a day as an extra on the film *Mac and Me* (1988) – best described as a dismal *ET* tribute – which was his own first job on a movie, as a production assistant. Johnny had a degree in film but was finding breaking into mainstream movies exceptionally difficult. Jennifer has never had a bad word to say about him while acknowledging that he was not as badly affected as she was by John and Nancy's break-up. She observed, 'He felt badly that I was left with the situation while he had the freedom to live his adult life.'

Jennifer set about establishing her own, new adult life which was, at first, remarkably similar to the one she had left behind in New York – auditions and dead-end jobs. She noted that after a while she began to think that going to auditions was actually her job. The principal point of moving to Hollywood when she did was so that she would be in time for pilot season. This is traditionally an annual rite of spring when new shows are put together for one sample episode in the hope of attracting the attention of the big networks for their autumn schedules. Pilots can be an expensive gamble for independent producers because, if they are not picked up by a network, they are practically worthless and the money is wasted. They are put together with patience and care, written to perhaps capture the television trend of the moment or to emulate the success stories from the previous year. A pilot might also be a spin-off from another popular show or film. *Frasier*, for instance, was a spin-off from *Cheers* and a fantastic success. Jennifer would discover that does not happen every time. Her regular routine for the next five years would be auditioning for a pilot, making the pilot, then waiting and hoping that the show would be picked up for a season and lead to fame and fortune. That was the theory.

Scripts for pilots are mostly pitched in the autumn and actors cast in the first couple of months of the New Year. After casting is complete, the pilot is usually shot in April after camera crews have finished shooting the previous season of established shows. The month of June is when fingernails are bitten while networks decide what they will pick up after doing extensive screenings to gauge audience reaction. This process is called 'going to the networks'.

An actor who appears in the pilot has no guarantee that he or she will be cast again if the series gets commissioned. They may have to re-audition with three or four other candidates for the same role. At this point everyone auditioning will have signed a contract which might tie them up for three or five years if the series becomes a success. The reason for this is to ensure they do not have any leverage for a better deal if they are picked. D. David Morin, who played opposite Jennifer in a pre-*Friends* sitcom, explains, 'It's really kind of a nerve-racking time when you're in the lobby going to network. You're looking around at the others and thinking, "OK, somebody here may blow up and become famous and make lots of money and like be on easy street, and the rest of the buggers, they're not going to get anything!" It's a bit like *The Weakest Link* – "You, Jennifer, go home with nothing".'

The pilot is a showcase for the series. If the network likes it then a number of episodes will be commissioned with the pilot broadcast as episode one. Usually the initial run will be six or thirteen episodes which gives the television companies the chance to see how the series is received. Jennifer was soon to learn that celebrating the commission after just the pilot is premature. The networks, as she discovered, are liable to cancel a show at any time.

Surprisingly, however, Jennifer's first LA role was in a movie. Shortly after she arrived she landed a part in a minor made-for-television film, *Camp Cucamonga*, starring John Ratzenberger, who had become a headliner from playing Cliff Clavin the pedantic postie in *Cheers*. Ratzenberger's voyage to stardom could have been a useful model for his young co-star. He originally auditioned for the role of Norm in *Cheers* but was not what the producers were looking for. They were so impressed by his rant when he realized he was not going to get the part, however, that they wrote another one especially for him. Even so, he was only hired for seven episodes initially and was little more than a minor character at the bar when the show began in 1982. His sparring with George Wendt, who had won the part of Norm, provided so many comic highlights that he eventually went on to appear in 263 episodes.

Sitcom stars would often fit in movie roles during the off-season but *Camp Cucamonga* was a little different because *everybody* in it was literally slumming it from a sitcom. The alternative title, *How I Spent My Summer*, gives the game away – it was a pot-pourri of set pieces about a bunch of teenagers at a summer camp. Billed as 'The zaniest, most hilarious summer vacation ever' – which it wasn't – the film was inoffensive froth. The central plot revolved around the camp's owner mistakenly believing that a local handyman was a camp inspector – a familiar device of mistaken identity which was used far more hilariously in the classic *Fawlty Towers* episode 'The Hotel Inspectors'.

Ratzenberger played the camp's owner and Jennifer his daughter, the unappealingly named Ava Schector. We see Jennifer for the first time in a movie, driving a yellow schoolbus full of annoying, squabbling teenagers. Her first line was, 'You've got to be kidding.' It really was a minor role and Jennifer was surrounded by a group of young actors and actresses who appeared to be going places much more quickly than she was. Names like Chad Allen (Zach Nichols in *My Two Dads*), Candace Cameron (DJ Tanner in *Full House*), Danica McKellar (Winnie Cooper in *The Wonder Years*), and Josh Saviano (Paul Pfeiffer in *The Wonder Years*) were serious teen stars the studio was anxious to build up. Jennifer was just starting out although she was older than these bigger-name co-stars. Despite appearing to cast every young soap actor in Hollywood, not everyone made it to *Camp Cucamonga*. A young actor called Matthew Perry auditioned for a part but was rejected.

Jennifer's role did, however, have some substance. Ava was a serious, responsible girl – the camp counsellor, aiming to support her dumb dad – whose world was temporarily turned upside down when she fell for the camp's Lothario, complete with mullet, in a rather clichéd plot line. The film, however, is good, pointless fun. Like Jennifer's old teen favourite, *Sixteen Candles*, *Camp Cucamonga* is best if you saw it in high school and can now look back on it with fond nostalgia, ignoring the ropey bits like the 'Cucamonga Rap' – 'Come to Camp Cucamonga, Oh yeah'. The movie, in which Jennifer looked both sexy and appealing, is by no means the worst thing on her CV and was far from being a career killer.

One of the best things about *Camp Cucamonga* is that it was filmed at the Paramount Ranch in Agoura, not that far from Sherman Oaks. The ranch, between Malibu and the Valley, is best known for providing the setting for some of the most famous westerns of all time including *The Plainsman* (1936) in which Gary Cooper played Wild Bill Hickock and *Gunfight at the OK Corral* (1957) in which Burt Lancaster portrayed Wyatt Earp while Kirk Douglas was Doc Holliday. Some of the biggest Hollywood stars of all have made the short trek up to the hills to find the Paramount Ranch masquerading as Tombstone or Dodge City. More recently it provided the location for *Dr Quinn Medicine Woman*. Jennifer was beginning to feel right at home in Los Angeles.

In typical Hollywood fashion, by the time the film was released on DVD in 2001, Jennifer had miraculously risen to the top of the cast list and the front cover featured her centre-stage between Ratzenberger and her screen mother, Dorothy Lyman. The young cast of *Camp Cucamonga* now has the makings of a wonderful 'Whatever Happened To . . .?' or 'After They Were Famous' television programme. Chad Allen still pops up in various television shows but is perhaps best known for being outed as gay by the tabloid press in the mid-nineties and, subsequently, becoming an eloquent advocate of gay rights – a commendable thing in a still homophobic Hollywood. Candace Cameron was a child star at five who later found Jesus and highlights her website with the words: 'Growing with God'. Danica McKellar is back acting after majoring in mathematics at the University of California in Los Angeles. Josh Saviano majored in political science at Yale and is now a lawyer in New York. Jennifer Aniston is a multi-millionairess superstar – who could have guessed how it would turn out?

Almost immediately Jennifer was cast in the pilot of a new sitcom called *Molloy*, after just three months of worrying if she had made the right decision in relocating to California. Molloy sounds like the name of a private detective but was, in fact, a teenage girl, Molloy Martin (played by the show's star, Mayim Bialik), who shows up unexpectedly to live with her father and his new family. Jennifer played her elder step-sister and there was also a younger step-brother. The whole thing was an everyday 'family in a living room' comedy and did not capture the imagination, although a first run of thirteen episodes was commissioned.

Mayim Bialik had garnered praise at the age of twelve in the classic weepy *Beaches* (1988), in which she played Bette Midler's character, 'CC', as a young girl. She was named Best Young Actress at the Young Artist Awards and was clearly a star in the making. The two actresses hit it off even though Bialik was six years younger than Jennifer, who by this time must have been starting to feel like an old maid in Hollywood.

Molloy's mother was played by Pamela Brull who had been in *Days Of Our Lives* with John Aniston until her character, Ellen Hawk, was murdered.

On 25 July 1990 American television viewers saw Jennifer Aniston in a sitcom for the first time. Everything was going so well that Jennifer was already thinking about finding her own place to live. Her father and stepmother had a young baby and, while Jennifer was welcome to stay, she wanted her independence. She was soon to taste the disappointments her father had warned her about, however, when *Molloy* was cancelled before the end of the first series; only seven episodes were made. These decisions are usually just based on ratings, although, intriguingly Mayim Bialik found herself in a much better show, *Blossom*, which ran for 114 episodes. Once again it was about a teenage girl – this time called Blossom – growing up in a difficult household, in this case with a divorced father and two brothers.

Jennifer's career is forever revealing just how small a world it is in Hollywood and, in particular, American television. Her orbit is extraordinarily constricted, highlighting connection after connection. One of the actors who appeared in a few episodes of *Blossom*, while struggling for his own big break, was David Schwimmer who would be cast so successfully opposite Jennifer in *Friends*.

After *Molloy*, Jennifer had high hopes for *Ferris Bueller*, the television spin-off from the gloriously funny and hugely successful high-school movie, *Ferris Bueller's Day Off* (1986), directed by John Hughes. (He had also been responsible for Jennifer's former favourite *Sixteen Candles* and a host of other teen favourites.) Three weeks after *Ferris Bueller* premièred Jennifer appeared in her one and only television interview alongside her father. He was a big name in television and she was starting out. She looked lovely and natural and laughed a lot, while her father John was relaxed and indulgent. The impression they gave was that all fences had been mended and they were comfortable together, a regular dad and his daughter. John recalled the time when she was fourteen and had used his agent to try and secure an acting job. He also repeated his view, 'You can't look at this business and think, "This is what I want my child to do."' Jennifer, who was also filmed unconvincingly fixing a meal in her father's kitchen, recalled that her father had told her, 'If you want to make money, be a doctor.' The interview did reveal Jennifer's mindset at the time. She just wanted to try and see what happened. 'I can try and learn from my failures,' she said.

A few weeks later she would be trying to learn from the failure of *Ferris Bueller*. The show was, perhaps, most notable for providing Jennifer with the first opportunity to date someone on set, in this case the star, Charlie Schlatter, who was twenty-four. Schlatter was one of the young actors in Hollywood who were on the fringe of the Brat Pack. He had made his first impression playing Michael, the younger brother of Michael J. Fox's character Jamie, in *Bright Lights, Big City* (1988) although he is better known to UK audiences for his role as drifter Brownie Hansen, having his wicked way with Kylie Minogue in *The Delinquents* (1989). At 5 feet 6 inches tall, Schlatter is one of the few actors who could act in the same frame as either Fox or Kylie without having to stand in a trench. When he flew into Queensland, Schlatter had been unprepared for the Kylie tornado, the constant barrage of questioning and attention aimed at the film. None of it was about him – it was all about Kylie – and he soon became accustomed to the number-one question: will Kylie be naked in the picture? He took it all in good humour.

A little bit of banter was the closest Schlatter got to anything with Kylie but he did go out a few times with Jennifer. Like Jennifer, he grew up on the East Coast and he was born in Fair Lawn, New Jersey, just twenty miles from New York. They were not a serious couple but throughout her career Jennifer has never been shy of gathering a little extra publicity through rumours of dating, although the slightly weird aspect in the case of Charlie Schlatter was that he played her brother.

When *Ferris Bueller* was cancelled after thirteen episodes, Schlatter was literally out of the picture. Jennifer had her own bohemian social life away from the Hollywood glitz and she loved it. Schlatter is now married with three children, loves to play golf and is on British television seemingly every day in *Diagnosis Murder* in which he played Dr Jesse Travis. He filled the place vacated by Jennifer's former heart-throb Scott Baio next to star Dick Van Dyke.

The major problem for *Ferris Bueller* and ultimately the reason it sank was that the original movie was such a classic that it was impossible to follow. The audience liked the film much more than the TV series and ratings slumped. Comparisons are always odious but inevitable. Schlatter was not Matthew Broderick and Jennifer Aniston was not Jennifer Grey who played the part of Jeannie in the movie.

In the second half of 1990 it seemed that Jennifer was absolutely everywhere. The way that scheduling worked out meant that *Molloy* and *Camp Cucamonga* were shown in July and *Ferris Bueller* in August. This surfeit of Aniston gave the impression that she was always working at this time but this was something of an illusion. A pattern, however, had emerged in which Jennifer was cast as the daughter or sister of the lead. She was a reliable young actress, someone with not quite enough star quality or gorgeous looks to be a big name.

Despite the disappointments, Jennifer was revelling in her new life, and she soon became philosophical about her setbacks. She later explained in a television interview, 'It's a weird thing but you get over it in about a week.' When Michael Baroni called from New York to find out how things were going, he light-heartedly asked her what she thought of LA men. 'Oh Brad Pitt, he's hot!' she said. Four more years would pass before she actually met Brad Pitt.

At this time Jennifer formed a much longer-lasting alliance with *Cheers*. She met a young production assistant on the show called Kristin Hahn, who would become one of her closest friends. Kristin, originally from the Watermelon Mountains of New Mexico, introduced Jennifer to the wonderful world of Laurel Canyon which, to some extent, has been her spiritual home ever since.

Laurel Canyon Boulevard, a main street off Sunset Boulevard, lies between West Hollywood and the Valley, where Jennifer was born. It snakes its way up for seven miles into the hills, peaking at Mulholland Drive (made even more famous in 2001 in the David Lynch thriller of the same name). To the side of the boulevard is a warren of winding streets, mostly finishing as dead ends.

The Laurel Canyon neighbourhood has always been a popular hideaway for Hollywood stars, from the silent era right up to the present day. In the 1920s the legendary femme fatale Mary Astor had a house built on Appian Way where she would conduct her numerous trysts with the most powerful men in Hollywood. In the 1970s the Rolling Stones lived in the house for a while and part of their notorious documentary film *Cocksucker Blues* (1972) was filmed there. Today it is the home of the shock rocker Marilyn Manson who has a studio in the pool house.

In the late 1960s, this rustic area of Los Angeles became the epicentre of a musical revolution. Literally every musician who ever passed through LA would pitch up at the home of one of the many music legends who lived there, including Frank Zappa, Mama Cass, David Crosby and John Mayall. Laurel Canyon became a byword for creativity for the greatest singer-songwriters of a generation.

One place in particular, a cottage on the magnificently named Lookout Mountain Avenue, became the focal point for this new, fertile bohemia. The sublimely talented singer and artist Joni Mitchell lived there playing host to the darlings of seventies acoustic rock, Crosby, Stills and Nash. The last named, Graham Nash, was from Manchester, a member of the Hollies and the last person one might have expected to fall in love with a drug based Bohemian culture in the hills above Los Angeles. He loved it, moved in with Joni and wrote the classic 'Our House' in the back yard. A lucky twist of cultural fate brought some of the most talented figures in popular culture together in this small community at the same time. Talent in some ways attracts talent. In the UK, a decade earlier, the Beatles were from Liverpool and suddenly every second band was from the Mersey. Similarly in Manchester in the 80s the Hacienda nightclub energised a generation of innovative and influential music from New Order and The Happy Mondays. The ensemble that gathered in Laurel Canyon would fill a hall of fame.

Perhaps ensemble is the most crucial word where Jennifer is concerned. She was still living with her father when she was invited to a party in Laurel Canyon and met for the first time a dozen or so people all crammed into a tiny apartment who embraced her and offered friendship and a sense of belonging and of family. Jennifer, as we've seen, likes to be in a group of similarly minded people which is one of the principal reasons she did so well at Performing Arts and enjoyed the company of her friends on the Upper West Side when she was a teenager. In particular she hit it off with Kristin who lived in an apartment which she described as being the 'size of a bathroom'. Kristin fondly recalled the first time they met was when she was in the kitchen at a party taking something out of the oven and Jennifer came 'hopping' down the stairs: 'She had a sweet glow about her and we became instantly crazy about each other.'

With Andrea Bendewald studying drama at Wright State University in Dayton, Ohio, Jennifer needed a best friend in LA to talk to about love, life and shopping. Most days when she was not working – which *was* most days – she would drift over to Kristin's and just hang out, moaning about the jobs she was not getting. When Andrea eventually came to LA she too loved the neighbourhood, fitted right in and became best friends with Kristin as well. The friends were very different young women, although all three at one time or another have been actresses. Kristin, outspoken and aware, was the most innovative of the three with ambitions to write and direct. Jennifer once described Andrea as the mother of the group, a reflection of her calming influence on everyone.

Jennifer decided she wanted to live in Laurel Canyon; it was perfect for struggling actors because of the low rents. She found a place at the end of a street called Ridgemont Drive. Strangely, even in those days before she became famous, there was still a large security gate leading to the enclave of houses among which was her new home. Jennifer, Kristin and their friends called the area where they lived 'The Hill' and would talk about converting its laid-back craziness into a sitcom.

Los Angeles can be a very lonely place where to be poor is to be ugly, but that was not the case on The Hill where the spirit of easygoing camaraderie meant there would always be a barbecue on a Sunday to catch up on everyone's week. Then there would be the girls' nights out where all the female residents of The Hill would gather for an evening when the golden rule was not being allowed to talk to men. Kristin told *Elle* magazine, 'It was all about women worshipping each other, drinking and having a blast,' while Jennifer has expressed the view: 'Women are awesome, especially together as a group, so kind and warm and wonderful.'

The pagan quality of life on The Hill – an observation sometimes made about the Steiner method of education – was best illustrated by special female gatherings in the woods around Laurel Canyon. Jennifer and her friends would take candles and personal mementos and sit in a circle, hold hands and just talk, just bond. Jennifer explained that they began the 'circle' as an antidote to the cattiness that can engulf women socially. During the first candlelit circle one of her friends was so moved by the occasion she burst into tears. Perhaps Rudolf Steiner would have approved of discovering the 'spirit within' in this collective fashion. It certainly had a profound effect on Jennifer who described it as a 'huge sort of enlightening kind of experience'. Jennifer has not revealed whether the simpatico vibe was enhanced by passing round a joint or two, although she has admitted to smoking dope.

Another aspect of life on The Hill was that the gang would take off for the weekend en masse, mostly at the instigation of one member, Michael Sanville, a budding photographer. One such adventure was to Santa Barbara, the popular resort town some eighty miles north. Santa Barbara has always been a fashionable haven for Hollywood celebrities, from Chaplin to Spielberg, and Jennifer and Brad Pitt would later own a beautiful home there. On this jaunt, however, eight friends from The Hill would share a room. Kristin recalled, 'Michael would always come up with ideas for crazy shoots, mostly based upon some ploy to get us naked.' A New Yorker like Jennifer and Andrea, Michael was self-taught and took himself more seriously than that. On his website he describes his photography, a little ethereally: 'Shape, light, form, frame, texture, emotion, guidance, passion, compassion, beauty and instinct . . . all of these words describe my process.' The weird and wonderful world of Laurel Canyon was made for him.

The comforting thing about The Hill people is that they are still friends and look out for one another – when Kristin wrote a book entitled *In Search of Grace: A Journey Across America's Landscape of Faith*, published in 2002, her author photograph was taken by Michael Sanville.

Ironically, *Friends* would paint a picture of a group living in lovely apartments, having (mostly) jobs, drinking cappuccino. It was an airbrushed version of The Hill. Meanwhile, one night pre-*Friends*, Kristin introduced Jennifer to a young actor she had invited back for drinks. It was Matthew Perry in the days when he was very slim. Kristin's dog bit him on the backside much to everyone's amusement. Even more amusingly, with hindsight, the dog's name was Brad. Matthew and Jennifer always had a rapport; they were both very funny off screen as well as on. They both also knew what it was like to wonder where the next role was coming from.

From time to time rumours have surfaced of a romantic attachment between Jennifer and Matthew, or Matty as she endearingly calls him as if he's some sort of shaggy dog. She has, however, always insisted that their friendship is strictly of the brother–sister variety. Jennifer has wisely pointed out the difficulties of dating a platonic friend. She did not mention 'Matty' by name but said she had several attractive male friends who she had considered as boyfriends but had decided against it. She observed, 'It's just too difficult. Someone's your friend and suddenly they're your boyfriend and you're naked in front of them!'

TEN

Leprechaun

Days on The Hill drifted by. Jennifer found work at the Laurel Canyon Boulevard, the only grocery for miles around and the centre for all the local gossip

Jennifer spent her days lazing about, talking to Kristin, smoking, watching her father on daytime television and fixing her favourite snack – mayonnaise on white bread. Around this time in 1990 and 1991 the question of her weight arose, not for the first or last time. Ever since her childhood Jennifer had learnt to joke about her chunky frame. She really had no choice especially since her father used to helpfully observe that you could balance a tea tray on Jennifer's backside.

For her part Jennifer has always been upfront about the influence of her Greek heritage on her body shape. In a refreshingly honest appraisal of her 5-foot 4-inch frame she has said: 'I am a Greek woman and that figure is big tits and a big ass.'

Jennifer's problem – one that many of her old admirers never thought she had – was her natural Mediterranean shape. The story of weight loss seems to change each time in the telling but the usual version begins with Jennifer getting a call-back for a second audition and being told to wear a leotard. She tells her agent, 'Well, that should blow it for me', whereupon the agent replies, 'I've been meaning to talk to you about that . . .'

Jennifer went on a diet and reportedly lost thirty pounds. This is the often quoted figure although it does seem an awful lot for someone who certainly did not appear overweight on television with her father in 1990. The figure of thirty pounds may have had something to do with a spot Jennifer did at this time on *The Howard Stern Show* proclaiming the virtues of the Nutri-System weight-loss regime. For many years the role of NutriSlim girl was on her CV.

Her nutritionist at the time, Carrie Wiatt, has denied it was that much. John Aniston confided that Jennifer would be upset if she had gained one-sixteenth of an inch round her waist. He did not fully appreciate the agony of weight assessment that all young women in Hollywood have to go through. Jennifer would later 'curse the day' when she became so body conscious. 'I was just as happy before I was thinner,' she confessed. There is immense pressure to conform to an ideal that is little more than casting-director whimsy. Jennifer hated it but knew she could not beat the perception of a perfect figure and would have to join the parade. She has also always been scathing about the myth that losing weight could spell success, as if one was a consequence of the other: 'Get thin to be successful would never be something that I would personally promote. I think it sends out the wrong message. It's not my message.'

The work situation had not been good. As well as having her job in the local store, Jennifer was also a receptionist, worked in a skin-care centre and sold ice creams. She even tried her hand at selling timeshares in the Pocono Mountains, the popular ski resort region of Pennsylvania. She had to cold-call people and did not have an aptitude for the particular form of insidious chat: 'I didn't like disturbing people,' she confessed. 'I didn't sell one.' When she did squeeze in an audition her agent seemed to be forever telling her that the part had gone to Kristy Swanson, a blonde Californian babe who had been in *Ferris Bueller's Day Off* and was the original Buffy in the film *Buffy the Vampire Slayer* (1992). At the time Kristy was the hare and Jennifer was the tortoise.

The one bright spot on the horizon was a new relationship with a ruggedly handsome young actor and Hill resident, Daniel McDonald. Daniel was six-foot tall, easy-going and an accomplished, if struggling actor. He was born in Scranton, Philadelphia, but grew up in Romulus, a town in upstate New York, where his father was a high-school principal. Unlike Jennifer, he was from a large family, the youngest of seven children. For most of her childhood Jennifer had struggled along with just her mother so she was fascinated to hear Daniel's sibling tales.

He too had acting credentials in the family but instead of following in his father's footsteps, it was his elder brother Christopher who was making a name for himself. By the time Daniel pitched up in Los Angeles, Christopher had already been there for ten years making a succession of films. On television Christopher had been a guest star in one of the funniest episodes of *Cheers* in which he played a pitcher going through a slump who borrows Sam's lucky bottle top. Despite some promising roles, however, Christopher never quite made it to the very top of the bill. When Jennifer first came across the McDonald brothers, Christopher had just finished a role in the classic road movie

Thelma and Louise (1991) in which he played Darryl, the couch potato husband of Thelma (Susan Sarandon). The film would prove to be the big breakthrough for an actor a couple of places below Christopher in the cast list: *Thelma and Louise* turned Brad Pitt into a star.

Both brothers took their acting very seriously and Daniel followed Christopher to London to study at the Royal Academy of Dramatic Art (RADA). He was a devotee and member of the Actors Studio which, under the leadership of the renowned Lee Strasburg had become so influential in post-war acting. Strasburg and a host of famous 'students' brought worldwide recognition to the organization. Marlon Brando, Paul Newman and James Dean were just three of the huge film stars of the fifties who legitimized Strasburg's methods. The Actors Studio was not a student group in any shape or form but a workshop for professional actors seeking to improve their performances away from a commercial context. Jennifer has never belonged but her acting bears some strong influences. Some of the more recently acclaimed actors emerging from the Actors Studio include Al Pacino and Ellen Barkin, who were high-school students at PA, just like Jennifer. Later in her career, her acting in *The Good Girl* would reflect the influence of Stanislavski and Strasburg.

While still in New York Daniel took classes at the American Mime Company before studying with the respected acting coach Stanford Meisner, another teacher strongly influenced by Stanislavski. He developed what became known as the Meisner Technique and, as a result, was considerably overqualified for his first Hollywood break in 1984 when he was cast in *Where The Boys Are '84*, alongside his brother. He observed, 'They paid me peanuts but I had a great time. I didn't know it would be the worst film of the decade. The movie's terrible.' He was not lying. The film was a very forgettable comedy about four co-eds on vacation in Fort Lauderdale, Florida. It was Daniel's *Camp Cucamonga*, although not as good. Just like Jennifer, he moved from movie to television securing parts here and there in *Cagney and Lacey* and *Murder She Wrote*. They paid the bills but, nine years older than Jennifer, he had turned thirty by the time they met on The Hill. His serious approach to his profession, though, was a beneficial influence on his new girlfriend, reinforcing her desire to always do her best work.

First of all, however, Daniel had to pass the rigorous 'audition' of Jennifer's girl gang before he could be deemed 'worthy' and approved as proper boyfriend material. The girls were far worse than any intimidating dad as they took pride in subjecting male interlopers to intense scrutiny. When he passed, Daniel became Jennifer's 'first, real mature relationship'. Charmingly, three months after they started dating, Daniel got down on one knee in front of Jennifer and asked, 'Will you be my girlfriend?' She loved the romance of that gesture and although they both had their own places, in reality they became a couple living together.

People who met Daniel were impressed by his sincerity, often a rare commodity in Hollywood. Actor D. David Morin, who met Daniel when he worked with Jennifer, recalls, 'He was a good bloke. Like Jennifer, he was someone who had no airs. He was kind of a sensitive artist, serious and a little bit more intelligent than the norm. He wasn't the court jester or anything. He was introspective, very smart and very sweet – a nice guy.'

Jennifer, it seemed, had struck lucky with her first serious boyfriend in California.

'Jen and Dan' as they were known on The Hill, never acted together but one curious television series almost brought them together. They were cast in the distinctly offbeat but fondly remembered sitcom *Herman's Head*. Daniel was in an episode called 'Sweet Obsessions' in March 1992 while Jennifer appeared in two – 'Twisted Sister' in May of that year and 'Jay is for Jealousy' in November the following year. Yet again Jennifer played the sister of the main character, Herman Brookes, causing him a great deal of anxiety when she slept with his best friend. Herman was an aspiring writer working as a fact checker in New York. His innermost thoughts, in 'Herman's head', were played out by a Greek chorus of four characters Animal (representing libido), Angel (compassion), Genius (intellect) and Wimp (fear of getting into trouble). In effect it was two sitcoms in one, the second involving the people living in 'Herman's head'. The show ran for several seasons and more than seventy episodes but was ultimately a bit too strange for primetime. For Jennifer and Daniel, happily ensconced in Laurel Canyon, it was just a pay cheque.

Later in 1992 Jennifer appeared in a sketch show called *The Edge*, which had nothing to do with the U2 guitarist or the excellent 1997 Anthony Hopkins thriller of the same name. This type of show is invariably destined to appear dated within a few years but it had high energy and moved perkily along in the manner of some British shows. It was hardly *The Fast Show* but was imaginative and fresh for an American audience. Jennifer showed a versatile touch as part of a group of burgeoning talent that included Wayne Knight who would become a regular on *Seinfeld* – one of the few comedies to beat *Friends* in the ratings in the nineties. *The Edge* sought to emulate the success of *Saturday Night Live*, an American institution but one probably well past its sell-by date.

Jennifer's first two abortive ventures into the world of television comedy, *Molloy* and *Ferris Bueller*, did have the advantage of paying the rent and the bills for the year, although they meant that she missed out on pilot season the following year. Nothing came her way so, with the situation a bit desperate, she auditioned for the main female role in a low-budget horror film. *Leprechaun* was a lifesaver, although today Jennifer playfully denies ever having been in the movie. The director, Mark Jones, was immediately struck by her charisma and recalls thinking to himself, 'I hope she can act'. Jennifer sailed through the audition and Jones told the studio that he had found his leading actress. The studio was happy provided that Jennifer bleached her hair blonde. When the director phoned her to tell her the news, the line went quiet before Jennifer said, 'Oh Mark, I really don't think I can do that.' Jones hit upon the solution. With just three weeks to filming, he simply told Jennifer to turn up how she liked, adopting the strategy that they had a tight schedule to fill and nobody was going to worry about the colour of Jennifer's hair. She arrived with her usual auburn tint and nothing more was said.

Filming began in October 1991 in Simi Valley, the location for the popular seventies television show *Little House on the Prairie*, some forty miles north of downtown Los Angeles, past San Fernando Valley. The movie was distinctly low budget coming in at no more than one million dollars for a four-week shoot.

Jennifer may half-heartedly try to distance herself from the movie now but one of her co stars, Ken Olandt, who had the muscular, cut-off T-shirt role, distinctly recalls her being 'excited' about being in the film. Jennifer was the second on the cast list, although not above the title. Once again the star of the piece was younger than Jennifer. Warwick Davis was already a movie veteran at twenty-one, playing the title role in the Ron Howard-directed fantasy adventure, *Willow* (1988), which boasted a $35-million budget. He had received his acting break when George Lucas cast him in *Star Wars: Return Of The Jedi* (1984) as Wicket the Ewok. At the time he was two feet eleven inches tall. He was three foot six when he was cast as the malicious leprechaun.

The plot of *Leprechaun* appeared like something conjured by a bad acid trip. This particular leprechaun is no jolly green dwarf but a malevolent creature terrorizing a town in North Dakota in the search for his stolen gold. Jennifer plays Tory Reding, whose father buys the house where the leprechaun has been trapped for ten years in a crate sealed with a four-leaf clover, the one object which holds power over the evil puck. Needless to say, he escapes, and murderous mayhem ensues.

Jennifer's role called for her to be the 'beautiful' daughter, once again countering the idea that Jennifer was regarded in any way other than as an extremely attractive woman by all who came across her. Perhaps the way she looked in the film has more to do with her future denial of her role than the quality of the movie itself. She is more Jennifer Lopez than Jennifer Aniston –

slim but with a decidedly curvaceous rear. She also spends the majority of the film running around in a tight pair of multi-coloured shorts showing off a pair of powerful pins. A weight-conscious actress would have to spend the whole film covering her eyes. Mark Jones acknowledges, 'Jennifer never forgave me for putting her in those shorts.' Ken Olandt, however, was not the first or last of her co-stars to notice her 'pretty blue' eyes and 'great' smile.

Her character is that of a spoilt little rich girl living off Daddy's money who the audience grows to like as the story unfolds, a little like the prototype for Rachel Green in *Friends*. The role was relatively undemanding and, to be honest, not that interesting, but she impressed everyone with her professionalism. Ken Olandt recalls, 'Some actresses are nothing but drama. They are such high maintenance but Jennifer was very cool, a real trooper. There really wasn't much dialogue because the director preferred quick cuts but Jennifer was always prepared.' Jennifer's best piece of dialogue was the unforgettable line, 'Nathan, that's no f***ing bear'.

Jennifer also impressed with a quality that always shone through her work – she had confidence. Her belief in her own ability – at least on the outside – is noticed time and again by her colleagues. 'She had great poise,' observes Olandt. 'She was also really funny off-camera. I would say her humour was quite sophisticated, witty if you like, and she had great fun with the crew members.'

Ken and Jennifer became great buddies, although not romantically involved, for the duration of the filming. Jennifer would unhappily learn in the future just how easy it was for the peculiar environment of location work to change two actors from being comrades in arms to lovers in arms. For this film Ken was able to keep her grounded: 'It's location not a vacation,' was his maxim. At the time Jennifer was driving a beat-up old SUV and after late-night filming sessions she and Ken would talk constantly on the telephone while they drove home – to keep each other awake more than anything else. Mostly it would be gossiping about the movie and the director Mark Jones, who had also written the script.

Jones had cut his Hollywood teeth writing scripts for *The A Team* but *Leprechaun* was his directorial debut and he had definite views on how he wanted to put the movie together, in particular using strong primary colours and, seemingly, never shooting anybody square on. He was fighting a running battle with the producers who, Ken recalls, thought the film was becoming too light and wanted a darker touch.

Ken also remembers the director taking a shine to Jennifer, in a light-hearted way: 'I think Mark Jones was quite attracted to her which is always difficult for an actress. He was also a little jealous and we would laugh about what direction I would get from him versus her. Hers were long and involved with detail while mine were short, two-word directions like "More surprise," or "Less surprise," whatever emotion was required. It was funny because it's so common on sets for this to happen. But Mark kept us laughing because he wouldn't hide it and is a very funny guy and a talented writer.'

Jennifer enjoyed being able to stay at home in Laurel Canyon while shooting the movie but the bad thing about it was the cold. The location could have been described as 'The Little House Without Central Heating On The Prairie' and Ken and Jennifer would sit around in the vans drinking hot coffee, trying to keep warm. In the business this is known as 'downtime'. Much of that time they were waiting around for Warwick Davis to finish his elaborate make-up which took more than three hours to apply and caused him much discomfort.

Filming was not without drama. In one scene Ken's character Nathan, his leg pinned by a bear trap, has to wield a flashlight to keep the murderous leprechaun at bay. He accidentally whacked him on the hand, breaking it. This being Hollywood though, it was the poor stunt double who suffered the injury while Warwick Davis was having a cup of tea in his trailer. Jennifer also suffered an on-set injury when she had to poke the leprechaun in the eye with a truncheon as it attacked her in a police car. She scratched her hand on a jagged door lock and still has the 'war wound', a scar on the back of her left hand between her thumb and forefinger.

Jennifer also hurt her ankle running over the rugged ground. On one occasion she was rubbing her ankle before shooting a scene in which she had to flee the leprechaun. Mark Jones told her, 'We can get the stunt double to do it, Jennifer. Of course her legs aren't as nice as yours.' Jennifer immediately sprung up, declaring, 'Oh, I can run. I'll be all right.'

While Jennifer was shooting *Leprechaun*, Nancy Aniston decided to leave New York to be nearer her children in Los Angeles. She now realized that Jennifer was doing well in her new life and would not be returning to New York so she moved into a one-bedroom condominium in Toluca Lake, twenty minutes from Jennifer, and started a photographic studio. She visited Jennifer on set but was disappointed at how little she saw of her daughter. Jennifer later observed that her mother found it difficult accepting that her daughter had the support and comfort of her new social circle on The Hill. She told *Elle* magazine, 'She didn't understand how special and protective these people were. If only she knew, I think she would have felt less threatened by them.'

At the end of the month's filming there was a wrap party at Chasen's on Beverly Boulevard in West Hollywood. Dinner at Chasen's, one of the most famous restaurants in Los Angeles, was still quite a thrill for any actor. The golden age of Hollywood was the golden age of Chasen's where the greatest movie stars rubbed shoulders. Now they might go to Spago but in the 1940s Clark Gable, Gary Cooper, Cary Grant et al would all go to Chasen's. Humphrey Bogart, one drunken night, made off with the restaurant safe but had to abandon it in the street when it proved too heavy for him and fellow *Casablanca* star Peter Lorre to carry home. James Stewart held his bachelor party there in 1949, while a couple of years later Ronald Reagan proposed to Nancy Davis in the red-upholstered booth number two. Forty years later he would treat Mrs Thatcher to dinner there. Jennifer was fortunate to go to Chasen's when she did as the legendary Hollywood landmark closed in 1995 to make way for a new shopping mall.

Some post-production hiccups resulted in a twelve-month delay before the film was released on 1 January 1993, the first new movie of that year. In the meantime Jennifer appeared in one episode of the cult sci-fi drama series *Quantum Leap*. The hero, Dr Sam Beckett, played by Scott Bakula, is a scientist who is transported backwards and forwards in time into the bodies and lives of various people. He then has to solve their most pressing problems, thereby changing the course of history. It was a bit like *The Bill* or *Midsomer Murders* in that many familiar actors like Teri Hatcher, Susan Anton and Roddy McDowell drifted through. Brooke Shields was the guest star the week before Jennifer. In Jennifer's episode, 'Nowhere To Run', Dr Sam leaps into the body of a paraplegic Vietnam veteran who has to sort out the suicidal tendencies of his paralysed roommate.

The publicity for Jennifer on the release of *Leprechaun* neatly encapsulates her standing at this point: 'Los Angeles-born actress Jennifer Aniston trained with Anthony Abeson at Theatre Works and the High School of Performing Arts in New York City. Following work with the New York Shakespeare Festival's production of *For Dear Life* and Second Story Theatre's *Dancing on Checkers' Grave*, nineteen-year-old Ms Aniston returned to Los Angeles to accept a role on the Twentieth Century Fox television series *Molloy*. Ms Aniston's other television series credits include regular roles on *Ferris Bueller* and *Sunday Funnies* both for NBC. Additional credits include the NBC television movie *Camp Cucamonga*.'

Publicity always serves its purpose, usually more to obscure than to illuminate. In this case it did reveal Jennifer's desire to push her credentials as a serious actress. The blurb, obviously, makes no mention of the reality – *For Dear Life* was a flop and closed early, *Dancing on Checkers' Grave* was a one-act play in a local church, *Molloy* and *Ferris Bueller* had flopped and both been cancelled. *Sunday Funnies* never saw the light of day. The great irony is that *Leprechaun* was actually a success, revealing a profit of more than ten times the original budget, which is always the sort of figures that Hollywood likes to hear, whatever the scale. Jennifer, however, was unimpressed and sneaked out of a screening before the end, claiming she was horrified but not in a good way.

Amusingly, as far as tormenting Jennifer is concerned, *Leprechaun* just will not go away, spawning as many sequels as *Rocky: Leprechaun 2* (1994), *Leprechaun 3* (1995), *Leprechaun 4: In Space* (1997), *Leprechaun In The Hood* (2000) – co-starring Coolio and Ice-T – and lastly, so far, *Leprechaun Back 2 Tha Hood* (2003).

Warwick Davis has been hugely successful, winning parts in some of the most successful films of recent times including playing Filius Flitwick in the *Harry Potter* series. Ken Olandt moved into producing until he decided he wanted more security for his family and set up as a mortgage broker in Northern California. He strongly believes Jennifer is being mean about *Leprechaun* by not acknowledging it: 'There is nothing negative to say about the film. There's no bad acting. There's no gratuitous nudity. It's just a light-hearted, scary movie. If Disney was to make a horror movie then this would be it.'

When the film was released the opening credit ran 'Warwick Davis in *Leprechaun*'. When the film was released on DVD, post-*Friends*, the front cover read, 'Jennifer Aniston in *Leprechaun*'. For her part, Jennifer will never want to hear herself deliver the line, 'That thing is a Leprechaun and we've got to figure out how to stop it.'

ELEVEN

Muddling Through

While Jennifer was spending the latter part of 1993 hoping nobody would recognize her as the girl in *Leprechaun*, a new idea for a sitcom was being put together by a fledgling production team as part of a development deal with Warner Brothers. Bright/Kauffman/Crane productions was born of the success of a comedy called *Dream On* which was very influential in the early nineties but only enjoyed minor exposure in the UK. *Dream On* came about because the film director John Landis wanted to devise a programme which would utilize Universal's old library stock, particularly their anthologies featuring the great entertainers of the past. He then asked the writing partnership of David Crane and Marta Kauffman to come up with something. The result, *Dream On*, was about a divorced book editor trying to meet and relate to women. It was quite risqué at the time with lots of naked flesh and sexual references. The numerous black and white archive clips were fun and fresh at first, although a one-trick pony which ultimately would limit the show's shelf life.

Crane and Kauffman had met and started writing together while at Brandeis University near Boston, noteworthy as the only non-sectarian university in the US sponsored by the Jewish community. They became friends and collaborators in college musicals, co-directing a production of *Godspell*. After college they moved to New York where they teamed up with a young composer called Michael Skloff (who Marta would marry) to write several musicals. The collaboration started well when they supplied material for *A . . . My Name Is Alice* which won an Outer Circle Critics Award as Best Revue of 1984 and ran off-Broadway for a year. The nature of the revue gave Crane and Kauffman the chance to write sketch material which would later work so well in the television comedy format. They enjoyed more success by writing the lyrics for *Personals*, an off-Broadway show, based around people who place personal ads, which ran for 265 performances in the mid-eighties. The multi-talented Skloff was conductor, composer, musical director and pianist. He was also responsible for the vocal arrangements and played a synthesizer. The show's star was Jason Alexander who would find greater fame playing George Costanza in *Seinfeld*. He was another actor who would transfer successfully from Broadway to small-screen situation comedy.

Dream On was a success. Both Kauffman and Crane were nominated for Emmy Awards for Outstanding Individual Achievement in Writing. Michael Skloff was nominated for the theme tune. Coincidentally one of the episodes of *Dream On* was called 'Oral Sex, Lies and Videotape' and featured Jason Alexander, their former off-Broadway associate. He too was nominated for an Emmy, for Outstanding Guest Actor. The executive producer of *Dream On* was Kevin Bright who had also begun his career in New York, producing variety shows featuring, among others, Dolly Parton and Johnny Cash. When he moved to the

West Coast he produced comedy specials including one for Robin Williams and an award-winning spoof documentary drama *The History of White People in America*, in which Steve Martin played himself. By the time he became associated with *Dream On*, he had already won an Emmy as supervising producer on *In Living Colour*, a sketch show which featured Jim Carrey, Chris Rock and Jamie Foxx before they became film stars. Despite the presence of Carrey, the show was primarily written and created by black comedian Keenan Ivory Wayans and was considered a pioneer in African-American orientated entertainment. Another future star to garner attention on the show was a young member of the regular hip-hop dance troupe, Jennifer Lopez.

Kevin Bright was extremely adept at handling a large cast which would prove invaluable when he went into partnership with David Crane and Marta Kauffman who were now based in Los Angeles. The new 'dream team' was more a 'dream on team' when their first show together for CBS, *Family Album*, was a flop and cancelled after just a few episodes. That particular sitcom was another of the 'family in a living room' school which Jennifer had come to know so well and which, at the time, was not going down well with the American audience. Other shows they were involved in after *Dream On* also failed, but all shared one important characteristic – they were someone else's original concept. In one of their early shows called *Couples* which never went past pilot, one of the actors who auditioned for the lead – and was very nearly chosen – was David Schwimmer. In the end he lost out to his high-school pal Jonathan Silverman, but missing out on *Couples* was David Schwimmer's big break.

In November 1993, Marta and David met with Kevin to tell him about their latest idea, inspired by their own twentysomething lifestyles – a comedy about a group of 'singles' in New York, all in their twenties with all of life's choices in front of them. Like many of the best ideas, it was a very simple one. The crucial aspect, however, was that all three of them had lived it. They had all started their careers in New York and been in a group of friends. They were also facing an uncertain professional future, a prospect that often encourages nostalgia for the 'good old days'.

Describing the creative process to writer David Wild for his book *Friends . . .'Til The End*, Marta Kauffman explained how the breakthrough came when she and her husband Michael were driving down Beverly Boulevard in West Hollywood and they saw a sign on a storefront which read 'Insomnia Café'. She realized that the words encapsulated the new show-to-be. It was 'over-caffeinated'.

The following month, in December, they had a seven-page treatment ready to pitch to NBC which explained that the comedy was about 'sex, love, relationships, careers, and a time in your life when everything's possible. And it's about friendship because when you're single and in the city, your friends are your family.' The original idea included a romance which would develop throughout the series: Monica and Joey would fall in love. They did not pitch any sort of love affair between the characters of Ross and Rachel, the part that would eventually be played by Jennifer. Marta and David envisaged Monica and Joey becoming the 'love interest' on the show because, at this early stage, they were the two most sexual characters they had sketched out. NBC liked the idea enough to commission a pilot. Marta and David were pretty over-caffeinated themselves at this point because they went away and wrote the pilot episode in just three days. 'It wrote itself,' said Marta. At this point it was called *Friends Like Us* or, possibly, *Across the Hall.*

The ace in the hole for what would become *Friends* at this early, planning stage was the director James Burrows. Having the multiple Emmy award-winning director on board was a jackpot appointment for any sitcom, the TV equivalent of finding out that Scorsese was going to direct your film script. His credentials were impeccable. Since he won his first directing Emmy for *Taxi* in 1980, he had been at the forefront of comedy in US television, responsible for, among others, the ubiquitous *Cheers* and *Frasier*. Perhaps even more importantly for the brainchild of David Crane and Marta Kauffman, Jimmy, as everyone called him, had directed the first-ever episodes of *Cheers* (1982) and *Frasier* (1993). He was a master of setting the scene and grabbing the attention of an audience so that they will make a mental note to tune in the following week. Time and time again critics deride first episodes as being slow or spending so much time introducing the characters that there's no plot. Both of these very successful shows embraced brevity and pace. They moved along so that the whole episode was over before you blinked. It is one of the reasons why they and *Friends* can stand so many repeats – you can easily miss a gag, a nuance or just a funny look first time around. The deadpan humour of all his shows is relentless.

By the time *Cheers* finished its eleven-year run in May 1993, Burrows, whose company produced the show, was already a multi-millionaire. He did not need the money but just loved directing situation comedy. He was also a very shrewd judge of what might make a hit. With him at the helm, at least at the beginning, there was confidence at the top.

While Marta and David were polishing the first script, the

start of another year brought another new pilot for Jennifer. One of the few advantages of Jennifer's turnover was that she was improving as a sitcom actress. Obviously she was hoping one of her shows would trigger the breakthrough but the reality was that she and Daniel were coasting along. He hankered after more legitimate acting experience, perhaps trying his luck back in New York. Jennifer, meanwhile, still saw her future in Los Angeles. Perhaps the aptly named *Muddling Through* would finally crack it for her.

One problem for Jennifer was that the sitcom life was so easy. D. David Morin, who played her father in *Muddling Through*, observes, 'I think most people would agree that next to voice-over this is one of the easiest gigs in town. The hours are really simple. When you are doing episodic work you always have long hours but for sitcom stuff you roll in at ten, you leave at three or four. You have one long night which is the fifth night when you're taping but yeah, it's cool.

'The sitcom lifestyle is a wonderful, wonderful gig because you can have a life, raise a family, live in town and have a short drive to work. It's a dream.'

Jennifer was certainly not stretched by *Muddling Through*. This time she was not the sister of the star, but the daughter. Stand-up comedienne Stephanie Hodge was the lead in the show, playing Connie Drego who returns home to the family roadhouse after spending two years in jail for shooting her cheating husband (Morin) in the behind. Jennifer played Drego's sensible eldest daughter who had managed to keep the motel open while her mother had been absent. She spent much of her time being a waitress – the classic Jennifer Aniston role. To complicate matters Jennifer's character Madeline had married the dim state trooper who had arrested her mother. For a little contrast, the writers had thrown in another more wayward, pubescent daughter while Connie's husband also still lived in one of the rooms. The basic storyline added a little edge to a very traditional sitcom plot of 'family in a living room' conflict.

Stephanie Hodge had been noticed in the Saturday night comedy *Nurses*, while D. David Morin had been a familiar television face for ten years in all manner of series from *Knots Landing* to *Northern Exposure*, *Dallas* and, almost compulsorily, *Cheers*. Lurking below Jennifer in the pecking order was an actor called Scott Waara, who played her husband. He was a Tony award winner thus providing a salutary example for both Jennifer and Daniel that serious exposure on Broadway was no guaranteed passport to success on the West Coast.

When he was cast as Jennifer Aniston's father for the pilot of *Muddling Through* David Morin was thirty-eight. Jennifer was twenty-four. The two were near enough in age to become close pals. Jennifer was now such an old hand at 'pilot season' that she was able to relax and be herself from the outset: 'Right from the beginning I felt she was just a genuine, hard-working actress.'

David was instantly impressed with Jennifer's aptitude for comedy, something which her drama coach Anthony Abeson had so readily identified nearly ten years before. The 'twentysomething' Jennifer, however, knew exactly what she was doing. 'Her timing was innate,' explains David. 'My friends call it throwing strikes. It's the ball you would always want to throw in baseball. If you're really on your game you're throwing strikes, always putting the ball right on the corner of the plate, on the spot, because you're really that good. Jennifer always threw strikes – every rehearsal and every performance. Funnily, she knew exactly how to play a line so she really never got enough notice for what she was doing.'

Jennifer had become very accomplished at performing in front of a 'live studio audience' – an acting skill in itself. Her schooling and earlier training, especially performing off-Broadway, was useful preparation. David observes, 'She could just give a look. She knew just how to milk it in the right way – not too much, not too little.' David's appraisal reflects a development in Jennifer's ability to 'inhale' as an actress, another characteristic from her days with Anthony Abeson.

Making the most of a funny line is almost an art form in itself. David explains, 'If you have a good line, you've got to stop and wait till things settle or else you're walking on the laugh. Personally, I had to get used to that. Sometimes you will get some coaching. After rehearsal the director will have seen where there's a laugh and will tell you when to hold. Jennifer knew it instinctively.'

In these pre-fame, days Jennifer would begin her working day with a trip to the gym on Melrose. Jennifer was now playing the Hollywood game of exercise, diet and weight-watching. Just rolling up and delivering a few lines was not going to win many auditions in the long run. She and David used to meet up there for a session running on the treadmill, side by side, watched over by their personal trainers. This was the time when Jennifer was intent on improving her body tone which, combined with her dramatic weight loss, changed her shape from Greek chunky to Californian slender. She was definitely working much harder at the way she looked in 1994.

Muddling Through was probably fundamentally flawed as a serious contender for a long-running show; the problem was that the two main characters were distinctly unlikeable. David Morin observes, 'You couldn't cheer for any of them. The Stephanie Hodge character shot me in the ass and went to prison and now she's come back and is still mad at the world. She was a sarcastic dog in most of it which was funny for a while but then not so much. You couldn't cheer for me because I'm this playboy rogue who's totally irresponsible.

'Jennifer had a thankless role. She was the straight girl while everyone else was sort of eccentric and had one-liners. They had the joke in the last line, not Jennifer. She was almost a foil, the caring, protective innocent, trying to be a good daughter that nobody really saw or appreciated. She was like the Cinderella character in the show. Jennifer was clearly very funny but I don't think her part was written funny. She didn't have the zingers.'

Two important decisions affected Jennifer's life in 1994. The first and, at the time, more important of the two, was that Daniel decided to try his luck in New York. To begin with, he attempted to be in two places at once and would fly back and come to the studios to support Jennifer. David, who knew Daniel and had worked with his brother Christopher recalls, 'At the time she was doing *Muddling Through*, Dan was definitely her boyfriend and he was in New York and in town on occasion. I don't remember him as this appendage everywhere she went. It wasn't like that at all.'

In the end, keeping a relationship going while they spent the majority of their time on different coasts proved too difficult, and Jennifer and Daniel decided to split. Jennifer was discovering for the first time that the unavoidable absences in the world of show business did not make the heart grow fonder. They drifted apart when their day-to-day lives grew less entwined. It was entirely amicable and Jennifer would always be nice about Daniel in interviews. 'He's fabulous,' she once admitted. He needed to devote himself to what was in effect a new career. Jennifer has never considered it but perhaps this particular break-up gave her own situation a fresh energy. She was a single woman again and, within a short space of time, her whole life would start to change.

As things turned out, it would take Daniel much longer to make a breakthrough in New York but, ultimately, he did achieve great success. He made his Broadway debut in the spring of 1997, revealing a light baritone voice in a new musical, which was quite a surprise. The musical was called *Steel Pier* and came from the songwriting team of Kander and Ebb who were responsible for both *Cabaret* and *Chicago*. He played a stunt pilot who meets and falls in love with a woman at a dance marathon in Atlantic City. It proved a critical triumph, nominated for no fewer than eleven Tony Awards including one for Daniel as Best Actor in a Musical. He failed to win that one but did win the Drama Desk Award and the Theatre World Award. Surprisingly the show only ran for two months, closing earlier than expected, but Daniel's new career was assured. During rehearsals for the show he met an actress called Mujah Muraini-Melehi and would beat Jennifer to the altar, marrying in 1999.

The newly single Jennifer was, in early 1994, not the chic A-list Hollywood star she would one day become. At this time she was a brunette with a quite ordinary hairstyle and general demeanour. David Morin observes, 'I think maybe she was more of a girl next door when we did *Muddling Through* but she was still very attractive with the most beautiful eyes. She has this ability to make everyone feel at home. She was genuinely interested in everybody and that made them feel special. It was just effortless with Jennifer.'

Her sex appeal, however, is always something that has been underestimated. She has a habit of putting herself down, hence the 'ugly duckling' remarks, but the majority of men she meets have never thought that for a second. From her early teenage years as a curvy sexpot to the more toned Jennifer of *Muddling Through*, she has had the precious gift of making any man feel like he is the only man in the world, an attribute especially useful when becoming popular with cast and crew. And everyone notices her eyes.

Jennifer's personality and professionalism had made her very casting-friendly. Getting work in Los Angeles is not easy at any level and Jennifer's career in television to date was by no means a failure. She had been in two films (twice playing daughters), three sitcoms (two sisters, one daughter) in which she was a regular cast member, a sketch show and at least four other guest spots. Her career was far more successful than her father's had been when he started out and she was also getting more work than Daniel during that same period. The only thing lacking was a hit. She was like a record that gets considerable air play but never makes the charts.

Did *Muddling Through* have that extra touch of magic to be picked up for the autumn schedules? Having recorded the pilot earlier in the year, Jennifer and the cast then endured the usual anxious wait to see if it would be noticed. Jennifer had made some cash appearing in an episode of *Burke's Law*, the old sixties whodunnit series which someone thought ripe for revival. Burke,

Charlie Schlatter was the first actor romantically linked with Jennifer. She gets close to him in a publicity shot for the ill-fated comedy show *Ferris Bueller* (*above*), with co-stars Ami Dolenz and Brandon Douglas, and at an NBC party in 1990 (*below*).

Jennifer's yearbook picture from the 'Fame School' in New York was taken a few weeks before her eighteenth birthday in 1987.

Jennifer would never have been in *Friends* if *Muddling Through* had been a hit. In this scene she is in the kitchen flanked by co-stars Stephanie Hodge and Hal Landon Junior, while her screen father D. David Morin is on the far right.

Sporting a million-dollar smile for the 1997 New York première of *Picture Perfect*, supported by her father, John Aniston, and her half brother, Johnny Melick.

The fine cheek bones of Nancy Aniston, Jennifer's mother. This photo was taken in 1999 during her long estrangement from Jennifer, which led to her missing her daughter's wedding.

Many thought Jennifer would marry actor Tate Donovan. He had a goofy smile she found irresistible . . . for a while.

From the very beginning the cast of *Friends* had a close rapport that made the show believable. From left to right: Matthew Perry, Lisa Kudrow, Matt LeBlanc, Courteney Cox, Jennifer and David Schwimmer.

Phoebe, Rachel and Monica – The Ones with the Kissable Lips.

At least Jennifer's real-life work as a waitress came in handy when Rachel got a job at Central Perk.

Two key ingredients that made *Friends* a blockbuster: the on-screen chemistry with David Schwimmer, who she finally kissed in Season Two (*inset*), and 'the Rachel', the notorious haircut that launched a thousand snips. Jennifer hated it.

Look at me: Jennifer poses à la Streisand to show off her engagement ring with Brad Pitt at a Sting concert in New York, November 1999.

The look of love: Jennifer and Brad on their wedding day, 29 July 2000.

Don't look now: trucks thunder by on the freeway through Malibu, yards from where the showbusiness wedding of the year is being held.

Mr and Mrs Pitt's $14 million dream house in Beverly Hills.

Jennifer looks happy at the première of *The Good Girl* in 2002, even though some hobo appears to have taken the place of Brad.

Jennifer was supported by Kevin Bacon (*above left*) and Jay Mohr when she took centre stage in a film for the first time in *Picture Perfect* (1997).

It's only a film: Jennifer and co-star Paul Rudd create a happy scene on the set of *The Object of my Affection* with Lauren Pratt (1998).

As downbeat Justine, Jennifer fell for a younger man, the brooding Holden, played by Jake Gyllenhaal, in *The Good Girl*, her finest film role to date (2002).

played by Gene Barry, was a smooth millionaire police chief in LA who had to solve a different unsolvable crime each week. At the end of every episode all the suspects would gather in a room and he would rule them out one by one until unmasking the actual murderer. The series had been very popular in its heyday but was a bit creaky thirty years later. Burke himself was now a 'retired' police chief (Gene Barry was seventy-five) and the whole premise failed to catch fire although it was commissioned for two series. Each episode had the same generic title – 'Who Killed the Starlet?' or 'Who Killed the Fashion King?'. In Jennifer's episode the question was 'Who Killed the Beauty Queen?'. It was the same device they had used in the original series and one that would prove even more effective when *Friends* came along with its trademark 'The One With . . .' Funnily enough Jennifer was not cast as the beauty queen – at that stage of her career she did not have pin-up status.

The future for *Muddling Through* was undecided. They did, however, get an initial order for ten episodes which began broadcasting in July 1994. Jennifer had signed her 'pilot' contract with CBS as well as one with the producer Barton Dean. The ratings were reasonable so there were grounds for optimism that they would get another order, this time for the more prestigious autumn time slots.

While she was waiting to see if there would be good news about *Muddling Through*, Jennifer, as usual, looked for other work. She was about to get very lucky. The often repeated words of wisdom are that you only need one slice of luck to make it. In music, Robbie Williams, for instance, was a boy-band has-been, sinking in a sea of booze and drugs before the classic song

'Angels' turned it all around for him. In television, Ricky Gervais was a failed pop star, manager and bit-part actor before *The Office* propelled him to international stardom at the age of forty.

Jennifer made her second big decision of 1994. She agreed to audition for a new sitcom with a title that kept changing.

TWELVE

Casting

Jennifer Aniston was not the first to be cast in *Insomnia Café*, nor was she the first choice to play Rachel Green. The first definite was David Schwimmer. Writers David Crane and Marta Kauffman had been impressed by him during the casting of *Couples* and had him in mind for Ross Geller, the geeky palaeontologist, from the start. Schwimmer, it seemed, had been around the fringes of stardom for a long time but he was only twenty-seven. He also had no track record in comedy. 'When I told my friends I was going to be on a sitcom, they said, "Why would they want to put you in a sitcom? You're not funny."'

Schwimmer, tall, dark and so-so looking, was born in the Queens borough of New York, but his successful lawyer parents relocated to Los Angeles where his mother Elaine handled high-profile divorce cases for stars including Roseanne Barr and Elizabeth Taylor. David went to the famous Beverly Hills High School whose alumni include Angelina Jolie, although she is ten years younger than David. In this ultra-glamorous environment he saw himself as a fat boy who wore the most unattractive braces in the world. He thought he looked something like a horse in a harness which was social suicide at an institution where so much emphasis among his peers was placed on appearance. He also tells the story of his acute embarrassment when he grew a moustache at the age of thirteen. He admitted, 'I was the geek in high school,' which resulted in him having no social life. His standing was not helped by sporting a dreadful eighties mullet, another victim of the Leif Garrett look or, for British audiences, the haircut modelled by Jason Donovan in *Neighbours*.

David fell in love with the theatre during a summer school in acting at Northwestern University in Evanston near Chicago. He recalled that he loved making his parents laugh, one of the greatest joys in the world. He went back to Northwestern as a drama student and began to appreciate how much more there was to acting. He took it very seriously and was a young actor born for the 'method' approach of Stanislavski. He once heard of a vacancy for a waiter in a roller-skating restaurant. He proceeded to wear roller skates every minute of the day, including in all his classes at college until after two weeks he could skate backwards, forwards and round in little circles. He got the job.

After graduating, he joined four friends to write and conceive a performance play, *Alice In Wonderland*, based on the children's classic. The off-campus production was bankrolled by Schwimmer using his bar mitzvah money which he had sensibly kept in a bank earning interest. The production was such a hit they took it to the Edinburgh Festival in 1988 and, while in Scotland, decided they should start their own theatrical company. The Lookingglass Theatre Company of Chicago was formed and the inaugural production, *Through The Looking Glass*, took to the stage in 1989.

The company is still going strong today thanks largely to his support and involvement. He explained his commitment: 'I feel I am most challenged and fulfilled when I'm working with the company. It is my home, my family, my brothers and sisters.' In 2000 Schwimmer gave the company a quarter of a million dollars to help fund a new home in the Water Tower and Pumping Station development in Chicago.

The theatre has always been Schwimmer's first love so it was quite a surprise when he pitched up in Los Angeles trying to break into television. David had to suffer just as many rejections as Jennifer. Curiously, in some ways, they missed out on roles for the same fundamental reason. Jennifer was too Greek in shape and stature. Schwimmer was too Jewish or, as he more tactfully put it, 'too ethnic'. He appeared in a few episodes of *The Wonder Years* and *L.A. Law* but made more of an impression as '4B' in the acclaimed ensemble police series *NYPD Blue*. He appeared in the pilot and then the next three episodes as Josh '4B' Goldstein, so named because he lived in apartment 4B. *NYPD Blue* is one of those landmark series that seems to have been on many years ago but, in fact, only began in 1993. In an action-packed few weeks Schwimmer's character shoots a mugger before getting shot himself on a station platform.

Schwimmer was disappointed not to win the lead role in *Couples* for Bright/Kauffman/Crane. One role he did get, but wishes he had missed, was in a sitcom called *Monty*. The show starred Henry Winkler in his sitcom comeback role, ten years after he last played one of the great comedy characters, the Fonz in *Happy Days*. In *Monty*, Winkler played the title character, an ultra-conservative talk-show host, while David Schwimmer played his son. Rather like *Muddling Through* it seemed one of those comedies where the audience found it difficult to cheer for the characters. When the show was cancelled in February 1994 Schwimmer decided he had suffered enough in sitcom land and went back to the theatre in Chicago. He promised himself that he would never, ever do television again and immersed himself in the Lookingglass production of *The Master and Margarita*, an adaptation of one of the great Russian novels of the twentieth century by Mikhail Bulgakov.

From 1930s Moscow to Central Perk was quite a jump but David was tempted back by the prospect of an 'ensemble' comedy. He had hated the way *Monty* was built around one star and nobody else mattered. He loved the script that was sent to him in Chicago but was still undecided until he was called by the actor and director Robbie Benson who sang the praises of the production team. Like his friend Burrows, Benson was one of the most respected figures in television comedy and had already directed David in *Monty*. His opinion counted for the young actor. He persuaded Schwimmer to fly to LA for a meeting where he met everyone, including Jim Burrows, and decided he had nothing to lose. Benson knew just about everybody. As well as his work on *Monty*, he had directed the flop *Family Album*, and Jennifer in *Muddling Through*. He kept popping up so it was unsurprising that he would later direct some of the funniest episodes of *Friends*. While Schwimmer was dithering, the producers did audition Eric McCormack, later to star in the hit comedy *Will and Grace*, but they had always written Ross with David in mind.

David Schwimmer is a serious-minded individual with ideals and intelligence. He once turned down $50,000 to make a comedy pilot because he did not like the script. At the time he was working as a waiter. He grew up with a love of the law and appreciates the significance of his country's history, in particular the stories of World War Two, declaring that he is 'humbled' by the efforts of that generation. His empathy is sincere. His dislike of the 'one-star' system would prove to be very profitable for Jennifer and her co-stars. He would become the driving force behind them standing together as a group in all negotiations – all for one, one for all.

David Schwimmer is of great significance in Jennifer Aniston's story. He was never her boyfriend or even her best friend among the cast of *Friends*. They, however, had a spark on screen that gave their romance as Ross and Rachel the 'believable' factor. Without that storyline, *Friends* may never have reached the heights of popularity it attained. Jennifer observed, 'He looks a lot like my high-school sweetheart. So yeah, I'd be attracted to him. I love that sweet puppy-dog-eyed kind of thing.' Schwimmer it seems was a winning combination of Peter Waldman and Norman, her beloved dog.

Lisa Kudrow was thirty-one and the oldest of the group. She was too old to play Phoebe but was tall, blonde, glamorous and very funny. When the twentysomething comedy finished in 2004, Lisa was forty-one. Lisa was a very different personality from Jennifer. Growing up in the San Fernando Valley, California, she had no connection with acting whatsoever. She was neither blonde then nor particularly attractive, reportedly undergoing a nose job when she was thirteen. Like Jennifer, previous generations of her family were from Europe but not from the sun-kissed Mediterranean islands of Greece. They were from Poland and many relatives had died in the Nazi concentration camps. Her father, Lee, was an eminent physician, renowned for his research into headaches. Lisa was a brainy – and sporty – child who graduated from Vassar College in Poughkeepsie, New York, with a degree in psychobiology. When she left university in 1985 she fully intended to pursue a career in research, specializing in headaches. Her two brothers were both neurologists and she began working with her father. She was a long way in mind and spirit from the Performing Arts School.

Back in Los Angeles, however, her brother was friendly with the comedian Jon Lovitz who noticed Lisa had a natural aptitude for being funny. Lovitz is perhaps best known in the UK for duetting with Robbie Williams on the track 'Well Did You Evah' on the number-one album *Swing When You're Winning*. In the US, however, he was synonymous with *Saturday Night Live*. He encouraged Lisa to audition for an improv comedy troupe called The Groundlings. She started to learn her trade under the guidance of the improv coach and TV actress Cynthia Szigeti. It was like going back to college for Lisa and she studied until 1989 when she started looking for television work. Although she was six years older than Jennifer, she started her TV career at the same time. They both unsuccessfully auditioned for *Saturday Night Live* in 1990 but lost out to comedienne Julia Sweeney.

Her first big break became a major disappointment, although with hindsight, proved to be lucky. She was cast as Roz Doyle, the radio producer in *Frasier* – one of the few comedy series of the nineties to seriously rival the popularity of *Friends* – but during the making of the pilot it became clear that Lisa was not working out in the role. Ironically the man who effectively fired Lisa from *Frasier* was Jimmy Burrows. The pilot for any show, however strong the idea, has to be exactly right. Towards the end of the first episode, Roz gives a speech in which she tells Frasier that he has to accept his father. It is a key moment for the entire show. Lisa, according to Burrows, was brilliant but 'off-centre'. She was a little too daffy, perhaps too Phoebe-like, to make the audience believe something so sincere. The role was recast in favour of Texan actress Peri Gilpin who played Roz for 261 episodes in a run almost identical to that of *Friends*. In the world of comedy connections, however, Burrows did not forget Lisa or what she could offer to a new show.

Lisa admitted to being 'devastated' but pulled herself together by exercising and going blonde. In September 1993, Lisa appeared in the hit comedy series *Mad About You* as a waitress. It was clearly compulsory for all young actresses trying to make it in Los Angeles to play a waitress as often as possible. This could have been problematic for the new show because Lisa's character was called Ursula Buffay and would be returning in future episodes. She decided only to audition for shows that would allow her to resume the role of Ursula whenever that script demanded. *Friends* was on the same NBC network, she knew Jimmy Burrows and had good reports of the writers.

From the very first audition, she loved the character Phoebe Buffay and brought layers to the character that even the writers had not envisaged. Christine Cavanaugh, who would become the voice of Babe the pig, was also up for the part but Lisa quickly made it her own. The producers already knew her work on *Mad About You* so Phoebe was the least trouble to cast, and they solved the problem of Lisa appearing in two shows at the same time by making her separate characters twin sisters. Hence, Lisa Kudrow is the intelligent brunette who has made a career out of playing if not dumb then eccentric 'off-centre' blondes. David Schwimmer observed, 'Lisa has a razor-sharp mind.'

Lisa and Jennifer were poles apart as personalities and while they never became as close as the friends of The Hill, they had lunch with Courteney Cox and the boys most days for ten years. They had both undergone therapy and smoked like chimneys. Shrewdly, Lisa once summarized Jennifer's appeal: 'She is emotionally available.'

The role of Chandler, it seemed at first, would be as easy to cast as Phoebe. It was offered to Craig Bierko, an actor with a face full of expression who had worked with Crane and Kauffman on *The Powers That Be*. He turned it down which was not the smartest career move, although he has since been on UK television in 2007 in the acclaimed *Boston Legal*, playing attorney Jeffrey Coho. One of Bierko's friends, however, who was also one of Jennifer's old pals from The Hill, gained insider knowledge of the role by helping Bierko to learn his lines. By the time *he* came to audition, Matthew Perry knew the lines and did not need to refer to the script.

Perry was the youngest of the *Friends* co-stars, six months younger than Jennifer. Contrary to popular assumption, he is no relation to heart-throb actor Luke Perry, the star of *Beverly Hills 90210*. Like Jennifer, his father was a television actor but he was brought up by his mother in Ottawa where she was press secretary to the Canadian premier Pierre Trudeau. Poignantly, both Jennifer and Matthew saw more of their fathers on television than in real life. 'I got to see my dad through the TV,' explained Matthew. 'He would phone and say, "I get shot on *Mannix* on Tuesday night," so I could watch him.'

Matthew's life does follow a similar pattern to Jennifer's in that, after graduating from high school, he drifted back to Los Angeles where his father, John Bennett Perry, was living. He had already achieved one credit, at the age of ten, when he was cast in the adventure show *240-Robert*, in which his father starred. At fifteen, he appeared in an episode of *Charles In Charge*, starring the ubiquitous Jennifer favourite, Scott Baio.

The teenage Perry bore a passing resemblance to the young Leonardo DiCaprio. He was very popular with the opposite sex and in real life his success rate with girls was much more Joey than Chandler. The young Matthew would not have been seen dead with Janice, his recurring nightmare of a girlfriend in *Friends*. Part of his youthful attraction was his athletic prowess as a tennis player. As a schoolboy, he was national standard and harboured serious ambitions of being a professional tennis player but his skill did not develop as a senior and he decided, after graduating, to leave Ottawa to try his luck in Los Angeles instead.

Matthew's first decent part was in the sitcom *Second Chance* when he was seventeen. The second chance was given to a dead man who could go back in time and advise his teenage self (Perry) on the important decisions in life. Perry was very funny in the role. It ran for a couple of seasons and established him as a face on the sitcom circuit. Matthew had some luck early on his career when he was spotted by director William Richert in a restaurant. Richert was impressed with the fact that Matthew was with three girls, all of whom were hanging on his every word. He thought he would be perfect for the part of Fred, friend of the title character in his film *A Night in the Life of Jimmy Reardon* (1988), which starred the ill-fated River Phoenix. In the end, Richert managed to persuade a sceptical Matthew to audition, but not before reassuring him that he would not have to take his clothes off.

More importantly for his future, he impressed David Crane and Marta Kauffman when he guest starred in an episode of

Dream On in October 1992. By the time they were trying to cast *Insomnia Café*, he had a longer list of failed pilots than even Jennifer could boast.

By coincidence, he too was waiting to hear if a series he was contracted to would be picked up when he heard about the new comedy from Craig Bierko. He had already made the pilot for *LAX 2194*. It was a sci-fi comedy about baggage handlers at Los Angeles Airport in the year 2194 and co-starred the Hawaiian beauty Kelly Hu, who was in the same episode of *Burke's Law* as Jennifer. You would be forgiven for thinking there was a repertory company of about twelve actors and actresses who shared out every single role between them. Fortunately for Matthew, *LAX 2194* was not commissioned.

Surprisingly, considering his obvious natural talent, Matthew is the member of the *Friends* cast with the most insecurities about acting. When he lost out to Andrew Shue for the part of Billy in *Melrose Place* he admitted to becoming neurotic: 'As an actor you are always worried whether you are ever going to work again.' In real life Perry is probably the funniest of the *Friends* cast, followed by Jennifer. She loves his wit but observed, 'He's not just a funny guy but he's also very sensitive. He's just a good guy, not a guy's guy.' That appraisal did not stop him buying a Porsche and a football table for his Hollywood Hills home when he had cashed the first season's pay cheque for *Friends*.

He was also the only member of the cast who would regularly come up with killer ideas to help the writers. The others, including Jennifer, would have ideas as well but theirs tended to be deathly. This was no accident because Perry was actually a frustrated writer. In 1993, he and friend Andrew Hill Newman wrote a sitcom called *Maxwell's House* about a group of twentysomething friends. NBC decided they liked the one written by Crane and Kauffman better, so, adopting the old adage of 'If you can't beat them join them,' he auditioned for the new show. He needed to move fast because the producers were also considering a promising young actor called Vince Vaughn. Like a TV Solomon Grundy, Matthew auditioned for the producers on a Wednesday, for the production company on the Thursday, for the network on the Friday and started filming on the Monday. He knew the role of Chandler was a perfect fit for him.

Courteney Cox was the star of *Friends*, or at least, the actress who was expected to be the star. She was called in to audition for the part of Rachel because Kevin, David and Marta thought she would be perfect for the role of the spoilt daddy's girl. Courteney, however, wanted to read for Monica. Jim Burrows recalled, 'I thought she would be great as Rachel but she wanted to play Monica and she was right.' At this pilot stage she could have been forgiven for thinking that Monica was the better role: her storyline was superficially the strongest and Monica appeared to be the central character. Courteney now admits that you cannot really know how a character will develop from a pilot. She explained, 'She seemed kind of strong and I thought she would be fun to play. These are all just chances that you take. In reality I had no idea.'

The producers were concerned that Courteney was not tough enough to play Monica. She told them, 'I lived in New York when I was seventeen. I'm tough enough.' She could not tell then that Monica would transform from the babe who sleeps with Paul on their first date to a neurotic mom figure for the rest of the gang, leaving the sex-symbol role wide open for Jennifer to seize and the best 'zingers' to the other five.

Courteney was easily the best known of the auditioning cast having co-starred in early 1994 with Jim Carrey in the unexpected box-office smash *Ace Ventura: Pet Detective*. Her salary for the movie, which made more than $100 million at the box office, was estimated at $200,000 so she was considerably better off financially than her co-stars. She had a movie-star boyfriend, Michael Keaton, who was twelve years her senior, and she was also the only one who was a southern belle.

She would become Jennifer's closest friend on the show and has remained so even after the show has ended, living in the same exclusive street in Beverly Hills and the same stretch of Malibu beach. Their backgrounds may appear to be poles apart but they shared one important goal from an early age. They both admitted to wanting to make something of themselves and to a desire for the real independence and money needed to achieve that. They had also shared a life-changing experience. Courteney's parents divorced when she was ten and she faced the same emotional difficulties that Jennifer had suffered, although Courteney found herself the youngest of a large family with four brothers and sisters and a further nine step-siblings. She was brought up in Mountain Brook, Alabama, a posh suburb of Birmingham, the state's largest city. Her father owned a construction company.

Rather like Jennifer, Courteney went through a bit of a rebellious stage as a teenager but, after dropping out of college where she was studying architecture and moving to New York, she found her classic looks much in demand for modelling. Two early 'roles' have almost attained iconic status. She was the first person to say the taboo word 'period' on US television in a Tampax commercial. And, more famously, she was the teenager (although she was actually twenty at the time) dragged spontaneously out of the audience at a Bruce Springsteen concert to dance on stage during 'Dancing in the Dark'. It was all staged for a video directed by Brian De Palma and Courteney was paid $350 to be the adoring fan during the two-day shoot. It was a one-off payment and she receives nothing for the thousands of times the video has been shown – a lesson learned and one that would mean her strong support later for David Schwimmer and the *Friends* cast collective.

A course of acting lessons helped rid the southern belle of her Scarlett O'Hara drawl and she joined the pilot season auditions in the mid-eighties. She had early success when she was cast as Michael J. Fox's girlfriend, Lauren, in the final two seasons of his hit comedy *Family Ties*. Fox, an underrated actor, was a master of his craft and taught his inexperienced co-star the importance of timing in comedy. Her career had a lull but she did appear in *Dream On* in 1992, just a couple of months before Matthew Perry, thus getting the chance to impress Bright/Kauffman/Crane before they set about casting *Friends*. They also noticed her in the forgettable sitcom *The Trouble With Larry* in which she starred for all of its six episodes.

The subsequent attention given to Jennifer's looks, hair and movie-star partners tends to obscure the fact that Courteney Cox was one of the most beautiful actresses in Hollywood. Her early drama coach, Alice Spivak, was struck by how pretty Courteney was: 'She was totally uninvolved with her beauty.' She also successfully sent up her modelling past and her size-two figure with the storyline that Monica was enormously fat as a girl. The same year as she was cast in *Friends* she starred in a murder movie called *Sketch Artist II: Hands That See*, a pretty dismal effort in which she played a blind woman who is raped but helps the police catch the killer. The producer Brad Krevoy offered her the part when he saw her coming out of the sea in Malibu: 'You have not seen Courteney Cox in the proper light until you've seen her walking across the sand in a bikini. She makes Bo Derek look like a five.'

Courteney reportedly regretted her decision to swap roles, especially when Monica had no strong storylines. She was much happier when, later in the run, Monica and Chandler formed a relationship. Fortunately for their friendship, there has never been the suggestion of bitchy jealousy between Jennifer and Courteney, although the circumstances of their stardom could easily have led to that. Instead they have supported each other through the bad emotional times when troubles could be sunk as quickly as a couple of margaritas on Sunset. Perhaps it helped that they would both become multi-millionaires through *Friends*, earning a million dollars a week for lounging around on a sofa pretending to drink coffee. Jennifer is godmother to Courteney's daughter Coco and they still see each other most days, or at the very least, talk on the phone. Courteney very simply describes Jennifer as being like a sister to her, and she means it.

When Courteney secured the role of Monica, it left the producers back at square one casting Rachel. Almost without exception, other actors or actresses will be considered for the role you want. It's part of the game. Producers will always give the network a choice of possibles even if they have their heart set on a particular one. David Schwimmer was probably the only secure casting from the start. The popular Jon Cryer turned down the role of Chandler before Matthew Perry was cast. Even Courteney Cox had competition from another actress, Nancy McKeon.

A third actress, Janeane Garofalo, wise-cracking co-star in *The Ben Stiller Show*, was reportedly offered the role but turned it down. A fourth, Leah Rimini, who would later make 200 episodes of *The King of Queens*, tried out for the part. The Monica situation was confusing because at first the producers thought Courteney would be Rachel.

Jennifer's many rivals included the delectable Tea Leoni, now married to David Duchovny. Promising actresses including Elizabeth Berkeley, Denise Richards and Melissa Rivers all read for the part. Both Berkeley and Richards had been in the same episode of *Burke's Law* as Jennifer. Other actresses Nicollette Sheridan, Parker Posey and Jami Gertz were said to have turned down the opportunity to audition. When Jennifer eventually read, she went straight to the top of the list. Two hours later, the producers rang her at home and said the part was hers provided the situation regarding *Muddling Through* was resolved and she could be released from her contract. She recalled, 'I was beyond thrilled.' Filming did overlap for a couple of weeks but in the end it worked out for the best.

The last role to be cast was Joey. Matt LeBlanc was probably the least successful of the six, reputedly having just $11 in the world when he auditioned for the part. At this stage Joey was almost an afterthought for the show's creators. His role in the pilot was relatively unimportant and other roles needed to be sorted out first. As Matthew LeBlanc he had been on the pilot merry-go-round for five years before he read for the part of the loveable and simple Joey. He had quite similar ancestry to Jennifer in that he was half Mediterranean, with an Italian mother, and half potpourri, including Irish and French. Although the character Joey probably seems the most 'New Yorker' of the six friends LeBlanc was born in the town of Newton, Massachusetts, about one hundred miles from Williamstown, the birthplace of the other Matthew on the show, Matthew Perry. His father was a mechanic and his mother an office manager but they divorced when he was seven. The majority of the *Friends* cast were therefore from broken homes.

Le Blanc was more interested in sports as a youngster than anything academic. He entertained thoughts of being a professional motor cyclist before settling on a career as a carpenter. That all changed when he moved to New York and took drama classes. He had only gone along to support a friend but the teacher, Florence Greenberg, immediately saw his potential although she recalled him stating categorically that he was a carpenter and too shy for acting. He did, however, have aspirations beyond the grotty Lower East Side apartment where he lived and where at dinner times a rat would often run across the floor.

His natural, boyish Latin looks led to a post-high school career as a model which included being on the cover of the *Spartacus International Gay Guide*, although it was never suggested that he himself was gay. His ability to sound as if he is from Brooklyn is primarily down to the acting classes he took in New York before he moved to Los Angeles to try his luck in television. His delivery of his most famous line from *Friends*, 'How *you* doin!', is down to plenty of practice in bars using the same line on girls when he was living in New York.

His Hollywood career was not a total failure by any means. In 1989 he was in thirteen episodes of a high-school drama *TV 101* but it lasted less than one season. The only memorable thing about it, for the British football fan at least, was that the main character's name was Kevin Keegan; Matt played Chuck Bender.

Of greater significance for *Friends* was his casting in the popular *Married With Children* as the Italian boyfriend of Kelly Bundy. The character – Vinnie Verducci – was the archetypal dim-witted Italian, a prototype for Joey although this was conveniently forgotten when *Friends* began. Joey was not particularly developed in the pilot but Matt came along with the idea of Vinnie in his head when he auditioned; he actually played Vinnie in two other spin-off failures, *Top of The Heap* and *Vinnie and Bobby*, so knew the character well.

Matt secured the part of Joey Tribbiani by making Marta Kauffman laugh during his audition. He had a nasty cut across his nose and when she asked about it, he replied, 'It's a *long* story, you don't want to hear about it, trust me.' He told David Wild that the reality was that he had tripped in a friend's bathroom and cut his nose on the toilet seat.

Matt was able to define Joey right at the start of the show by suggesting that he could only get along with the three female characters if he treated them like sisters and did not hit on them every three seconds. It made the friendship believable and his character could grow from there. Marta Kauffman observed, 'Joey was a womanizer and not necessarily likeable but Matt brought his tremendous heart to his work.' David Crane added, 'He made Joey sweet.'

At the very first read-through with the six chosen cast members, everyone was aware of something special. Jim Burrows acknowledged, 'It was up to us not to screw it up.' And in real life the six-strong cast bonded right from the very beginning. Crane recalled, 'The chemistry was great. They seemed like people who *were* friends.' Before the start of every recording the six Friends would gather round in a circle like a group of football players and have a 'huddle'. Despite their strong friendship, Matt has confessed to having a small crush on Jennifer at first but he was not alone in that. She has never lost the art of making every man feel like he is special.

THIRTEEN

The Rachel

Jennifer began shooting the pilot for *Six of One* as it was now feebly called in the summer of 1994. She was under contract to Barton Dene and he had first call on her for *Muddling Through* whatever the reaction to this new show. When they did some early publicity shots for the new comedy, Jennifer had to slide out of some shots in case they needed to replace her. Behind the scenes, Marta, David and Kevin were all involved in a battle with the bosses at NBC about the script and, in particular, the central storyline in which Monica has sex on her first date with Paul the wine guy and then discovers he feeds all his dates the same sob story about impotence in order to get them into bed.

The president of NBC Entertainment, Don Ohlmeyer, was not convinced that this would be readily accepted by a primetime audience. It was a stand-off between angry scriptwriters and the moneymen. In these circumstances the moneymen usually have the final say but, as a compromise, it was agreed that the studio audience would fill in a questionnaire after watching the filming. The audience was asked: did they want to keep the story the way it is; prefer it if Monica and Paul did not sleep together; or prefer it if Monica and Paul did not sleep together but made plans to spend the weekend together in the mountains instead? When the forms were collected it was clear that the audience had not minded one bit. It may seem slightly absurd that the studio were worried about such a tame piece of morality but primetime US television was much more conservative than British TV and the reaction of the midwest Republicans was important.

In retrospect, Marta, David and Kevin joke about this episode in the *Friends* story along the lines of: do you think for sleeping with a man on the first date Monica is a) a slut b) a whore c) a tramp or d) a dream date. Millions of dollars in the bank later and it's easy to have some knockabout fun but, at the time, this was a serious concern, and it was not the only one. Executives were also concerned that in the days before Starbucks ruled the world, the audience would not appreciate the Central Perk coffee house setting. Americans were used to ham, eggs 'over-easy' and waffles with maple syrup, not cappuccino, latte and mocha. Perhaps it would be better to use a diner like the one in *Seinfeld*? The next bright idea they had to fight off was a suggestion that the show needed an older character who could give avuncular advice to the young friends. Marta Kauffman recalled that they even toyed with introducing a character called Pat the Cop but, fortunately, everyone thought it was a 'terrible' idea.

Having successfully negotiated the pitfalls of Pat the Cop, Central Perk Diner and Monica the Slapper, another potential stumbling block arose when the pilot itself was far from rapturously received. After a series of screenings a 'programme test report' is compiled giving the show a mark out of one hundred. *Friends*, as it was now thankfully called, scored a disappointing forty-one and was described as weak. The lowly figure did not inevitably mean it would fail, or that it would be rejected by NBC. *Seinfeld*, one of the most successful of all comedies also scored poorly but *ER* was said to have been given a rating, or 'predictor' as it was called, of ninety-one. One intriguing aspect of the report was that it clearly made the assumption that Courteney Cox was the star of *Friends*. It said, 'Courteney Cox was familiar to many viewers. As Monica, she came across as charming, attractive, confident, and motivated – the leader of the group. Among her group of friends she seemed to be the one who was the most stable and together. Men thought she was sexy and women liked her sense of humour.' Jennifer, as Rachel, was barely worthy of comment: 'None of the supporting cast members reached even moderate levels with the target audience.'

The best conclusion about the report is that, with hindsight, it is not worth the paper it's written on. It did, in fairness, reveal the crucial factor that would enable *Friends* to be such a massive hit in the modern age of television: 'Younger adults 18–34 and teens felt most of the characters seemed like nice people and they could be potentially interesting when they had a chance to grow.' Older adults 35 plus found the characters 'smug, superficial and self-absorbed'.

Timing is everything and *Friends* was lucky that the age of Beckham, Robbie, Kylie and *heat* magazine was about to start. There was nothing wrong with 'smug, superficial and self-absorbed' in the new age of celebrity. The nineties would introduce the *I* age of Internet, IPods, ITunes, and I Want that everyone takes for granted now. The young audience would adopt new shows like *Friends* and, later, *The Office* and *Little*

Britain. They would watch all the repeats, buy all the merchandise and ask for the DVD for Christmas. Targeting a young audience was the recipe for success.

Monica's perceived sluttishness is only one of several feisty ingredients in the pilot episode – Rachel ditches her fiancé at the altar and Ross is dumped by his wife who, it turns out, is a lesbian and has absconded with another woman. The basic rule in episodic comedy is to have a main plot line and a sub-plot. The pilot for *Friends* set its own precedent of having three plot strands in every episode. The writers needed to do this to maintain interest in all six main characters, building the point that this was an ensemble and they could not deviate from the collective. One legacy of *Friends* is that three plot strands passes by almost without comment because the audience is used to it. *Ugly Betty* in 2007, for instance, also employs the formula with huge success.

Jennifer, individually, made a flying start in *Six of One/ Friends*. Monica may have been perceived as the lead but Rachel took centre-stage in the pilot episode. In the famous opening sequence where the cast frolic in a fountain, she comes on first looking sexy in a white turtle neck, short black skirt and black tights. The famous dancing around the fountain sequence which began all 236 episodes of *Friends* was filmed at the studios at four in the morning using heated water. The cast looked happy dancing to 'I'll Be There For You' by The Rembrandts but the song had yet to be written and they were in fact grooving to a soul record the producers had brought along. Jennifer's name was first on screen, another triumph for alphabetical order.

After the credits have rolled, she commands attention in the opening scene in the coffee shop mainly because she enters wearing a white wedding dress showing just a discreet amount of cleavage. The writers also plant the idea at the end of the episode that something might happen in the future between Ross and Rachel after he admits to having had a major crush on her in high school. In one scene she has a paper bag over part of her face and gives one of those killer looks with her eyes that David Morin noticed was one of her strengths. In another, she is watching an old television programme which happens to be showing the wedding of *Joanie Loves Chachi*, her favourite sitcom as a teenager.

Fittingly Jennifer ends the episode serving coffee to her friends in the role of her new job as a waitress. Just from the pilot episode it was clear that Jennifer was breathing life into a difficult character. David Crane explained, 'In the wrong hands Rachel is kind of annoying and spoiled and unlikeable. You need an actress who can bring what Jennifer brings to it, for you to really root for this girl.' Jennifer Aniston is a professional actress and was not just playing herself in her performance of Rachel Green. She was always acting.

As summer drew to a close Jennifer still had no idea whether she would be spending the autumn filming *Muddling Through* or *Friends*. The latter seemed like it might be more fun. Andrea Bendewald recalled Jennifer telling her how she had loved making the pilot. She always enjoyed the company of Matthew Perry and also had an instant rapport with Courteney Cox. But it all hinged on whether Barton Dene would release her from her contract. For a short while, Jennifer was shooting *Muddling Through* for CBS and *Friends* for NBC at the same time. She tried to remain calm, explaining, 'I'm just going to make it work, go back and forth at the same time. It's all been worked out.'

Behind the scenes it was not at all worked out, with the producers of *Friends* well aware that if CBS committed to more *Muddling Through* then they would have to recast the role of Rachel and reshoot *everything*.

In the end she was lucky. David Morin recalls, 'We were still hanging on to see if we would get another order but Barton was gracious enough to say to Jennifer to go ahead with *Friends*. He basically let her out of the deal. I think he could probably see the writing on the wall for *Muddling Through* and there was no sense in tying up a young actress who had to go somewhere else. Going from a thankless role on *Muddling Through* to a great role as Rachel, where she absolutely shines, was no contest. When you watch the pilot for *Friends* you can see the difference.'

Barton Dene's decision to let Jennifer go was made easier by Stephanie Hodge being cast in a new show, *Unhappily Ever After*. Dene was also a veteran of the comedy world, having worked as a writer on *Taxi*, one of the shows that forged the reputation of Jimmy Burrows. He would have been well aware of the potential of *Friends*. The show was being talked about even before it started its run. Much of that was down to Jimmy Burrows and the rumour that he was about to present a huge new hit, the next *Cheers*. The network also decided to give the show a big publicity campaign and the cast took it in turns to give interviews when nobody really had a clue who they were. In one of them Jennifer highlighted the show's biggest selling point: 'It's the first show that I am aware of that deals with young people embarking on life.'

The final episode of *Muddling Through* was broadcast on 7 September 1994. It was the last time Jennifer would have to play a waitress until 22 September 1994 when the pilot episode of *Friends*, 'The One Where Monica Gets A Roommate', aired.

Before the pilot was broadcast Jennifer joined her five co-stars on a trip to Las Vegas. Burrows persuaded Warner Brothers to lend him the company plane, demonstrating the confidence in the new show, and he treated them to a meal at Wolfgang Puck's restaurant in the famous MGM Grand Hotel. Nobody bothered them. James Burrows was the most famous person in the group and he looked like a well-groomed Captain Birdseye. The young ensemble was unknown and broke. All, except perhaps Courteney, had to borrow money off the director so they could have some fun gambling afterwards in the hotel casino. Famously, Jimmy gathered his young cast around and warned, 'This is your last shot at anonymity'.

After the pilot episode was broadcast, it was time to wait for the all-important ratings. Rather like an unimpressed critic could close a theatrical show – as with *For Dear Life* – so poor ratings could dash hopes and ambitions on television at a stroke. *Friends* premièred at number fifteen, a fine result and one that would soon render Jimmy Burrows's words about anonymity absolutely true. NBC had given it every chance, putting it on from 8.30 to 9pm, sandwiched between two top-rated shows, *Mad About You* and *Seinfeld*. They hit the ground running. Jennifer and the five others were on a salary of $22,500 an episode for the season, with increments in place if it did well which would take that figure up to $35,000 an episode. Success grew rapidly as did critical acclaim. Epsiode 2, 'The One With The Sonogram At The End', was screened the week after the pilot followed by a burst of a further seven weekly instalments before a mid-season break.

Everybody seemed to be humming the cheesy theme tune, just the way they did with the equally catchy *Neighbours* theme.

The trick for a hit show is to make it something that viewers would stay in for and talk about at work or at school the following morning. This is known as a 'water-cooler hit' and *Friends* achieved that in a matter of weeks with a series of classic episodes. David Crane observed, 'There are many episodes that first season that I absolutely adore to this day,' echoing the views of the majority of *Friends* devotees. By the end of the debut season on 18 May 1995 the show was regularly in the top ten.

Not everything went smoothly. One regular member of the cast fast became Jennifer's weekly nemesis – Marcel, Ross's pet monkey, would chase her around the set, grab her and pull her hair. He would also delight in showing 'it' to her. Jennifer and everyone else were unimpressed, and the writers were soon trying to work out how to rid themselves of this turbulent beast. David Crane recalled they worked on a plot which involved Marcel (who in real life was two equally obnoxious monkeys) 'humping a toaster' and accidentally being electrocuted. Reluctantly they had to abandon that idea in favour of a happy life in San Diego Zoo. Everyone was heartily relieved, especially Jennifer, the object of their affections.

During the first season of *Friends*, Jennifer as Rachel had done her own laundry for the first time, accidentally dying her white clothes pink, cleaned an apartment for the first time, been seen naked in the shower by Chandler, had her heart broken by Paolo, an Italian cad, lost Marcel the monkey, almost got back with Barry, the dentist she ditched at the altar in the pilot, and had sexual dreams about Chandler, Joey and Ross (even though she had no idea of his true feelings for her). The writers scripted a rollercoaster life for the twentysomething. They did not, however, seem to notice the most momentous event in Season One which transformed Jennifer Aniston into the ultimate cover girl of the nineties. She had a new hairstyle.

Jennifer professed to being quite entertained by what she called the whole 'blublah' about her hair but her publicist let slip, 'We are not that excited about it because she's not a hairstyle, she's an actress.' In reality Jennifer hates her iconic haircut with a great passion.

Jennifer's hair is naturally very curly and she was sick of the amount of time she had to spend every day giving it a good iron. One afternoon she was in the salon of Chris McMillan, trying to work something out, when he simply took a razor blade to her curly tresses and scythed his way through. He was not her regular stylist but they had started chatting when she met him on the set of *Friends*.

'He cut it in the most bizarre style,' she told *The Times*. 'There was nothing planned about it.' The idea was to find a style that suited her personality and one that would show off a face that was being overwhelmed by her old 'blunt' haircut. There was method in McMillan's madness – he created a series of angles culminating in one at the front just below the chin. The whole effect was eerily reminiscent of David Cassidy in the seventies.

The actions of a flamboyant hairdresser may have been spontaneous but he hit upon a style that perfectly framed Jennifer's face. Her hair was now highlighted with blonde streaks in the front and looked lighter, shinier and sleeker than that sported by the Pilot Queen of Laurel Canyon. Was this really the same actress who, two years earlier, had screamed at a nasty little leprechaun?

She did not realize it at the time but she left the salon sporting what would become the most famous and imitated hairstyle of the nineties – 'the Rachel'. It was an accident and not exactly one she welcomed: 'It looked terrible on me.' She suddenly discovered that she very much enjoyed wearing hats and tried to encourage the *Friends* writers to start putting the characters in a variety of headgear. Ross may have been madly in love with Rachel but he seemed to have missed her new look.

In basic terms, the Rachel is a shoulder-length layered shag, a sort of sleek and perky bob. As soon as the style surfaced on primetime Thursday nights, picture editors devoured it and women all over the world wanted to copy it. In no time it was the most requested style, copied by millions. More importantly for her future success, she became the face of *Friends*. When Courteney Cox sported a very similar style, nobody went to the hairdresser and requested 'the Monica'. The Rachel made Jennifer look cute and emphasized that she was a good five years younger than her two female co-stars.

Jennifer may have hated 'the Rachel' but she did strike up a lasting relationship with the stylist Chris McMillan who has become one of the most successful hairdressers in Hollywood based on the success of that now infamous cut. He is not the first or the last hairdresser to become a client's friend and confidant. She trusted him with her hair on her wedding day and, when she was tearing her hair out at the prospect of divorce, his was a welcome shoulder on which to cry. She even stayed with him temporarily. Chris is ensconced in the inner circle of Jennifer's friends and, as such, enjoys her loyalty and confidence. She may suffer agonies whenever the Rachel is mentioned but she has never stopped using Chris. He has also been responsible for her hair on more than one movie.

Jennifer may want to forget about 'the Rachel' but the association will never leave her. She loathes having to answers questions about her hair, especially before she grew out the style. 'It feels nice, being reduced to a hairstyle,' she said sarcastically. 'I know everyone loves it but I'm sick of it.' A poll in 2004 declared the style to be the most influential of all time, followed by the Farrah and Princess Diana's much-copied cut. The only consolation and proof that focusing too much on hair can be a little silly was the high placing enjoyed by Homer Simpson's wife's shocking blue beehive. Not too many women enter their salon with the words, 'I'd like a Marge please'.

Jennifer's lack of enthusiasm for 'the Rachel' obviously stems from the feeling that she was being appreciated more for her hairstyle than for her acting skills. 'What am I doing wrong if they're looking at my hair?' she cried in a television interview. That did not prevent her image from endorsing all sorts of products, in particular L'Oréal hair products for which advertisements seemed to be aired every single commercial break. Jennifer began to dominate the pages of the glossy magazines in a way that none of her co-stars ever did. A decade earlier Farrah Fawcett had achieved the same eclipse on her *Charlie's Angels* co-stars and, although Jennifer will never admit it, the reason was the same in both her case and Farrah's – it was the hair that launched a thousand covers. (Coincidentally, Farrah's was the hairstyle she most admired growing up on the Upper West Side.)

From Jennifer's point of view the debut season of *Friends* was a triumph, not just because of her hairstyle, but because her character had moved centre-stage by episode Number 24, 'The One Where Rachel Finds Out'. Her character, of course, finds out that Ross is secretly in love with her. She is the last to know. She goes to meet him at the airport on his return from China, not realizing that he has become involved with another woman. The satisfying thing for Jennifer as an actress was that her storyline was the one that would sustain fans through the summer break. Monica and Paul the wine guy were a distant memory. Rachel and Ross were the focus. Lisa Kudrow observed, 'They [the viewers] ended up getting involved with that couple as if they were people they knew.' Jennifer told writer David Wild, 'Maybe it's unrequited love that touches people? Rooting for two people that you *know* should be together. And Marta and David were smart enough to keep them apart as long as they could.'

Jennifer, however, did not have the best 'zinger' in that final episode of the debut season. That honour belonged to Lisa Kudrow who, as Phoebe, delivers one of the funniest lines ever in a sitcom. Phoebe finds out that Joey is going to make a buck by selling his sperm: 'Wow, you're going to be making money hand over fist,' she tells him.

FOURTEEN

Stage 24

Jennifer and the other five Friends first realized that the show was a huge hit during the summer hiatus when reruns of the debut season began and proved to be hugely popular, taking the show to number one in the ratings and beating both *ER* and *Seinfeld*. Early fans were watching for a second time and now an audience who had picked up on the hype and media coverage were tuning in as well.

The cast were being a little ingenuous, however, because 18 May 1995, the day when the last episode of Season One was broadcast, was also the day when they made the cover of *Rolling Stone* magazine, a sure sign of stardom. They were pictured, hair flowing, in an old-fashioned convertible. It was a retro image mimicking an Edwardian postcard and looked like a movie poster for a screwball comedy. Meanwhile, Jennifer appeared solo on the world-famous *The Tonight Show with Jay Leno*, in June. The 7-foot 1-inch basketball legend Kareem Abdul-Jabbar was also a guest and proceeded to coach Jennifer in some tricks. She was proving to be an old hand at showbiz shmooze, the candy-floss of fame.

Friends was shown for the first time in the UK in April 1995 and became an instant success, regularly topping Channel 4's weekly ratings. The beauty for the showbiz-hungry British media was that there were six glamorous young stars to write about and, just as importantly, they looked great in pictures – especially Jennifer and her hair.

Up until the summer, the cast had been absorbed in working on the show itself. Jennifer explained, 'We were not paying attention to out *there*. We were just focused on in *here*.' Matthew Perry added that they had realized, 'This is a little bit more than a hit show'. The significance of the *Rolling Stone* cover was that it pictured all six and this collective approach would prove to be the secret of the show's long-running success, regardless of any individual attention Jennifer was receiving. Urged on by David Schwimmer, the gang of six decided they would make every decision as a group. Collectively, they could protect their success. As a gesture of solidarity they insisted on Emmy consideration as supporting actors and actresses and not as competing lead performers. In the event Lisa Kudrow and David Schwimmer were nominated but neither won. The show itself was also nominated for Outstanding Comedy Series but missed out, losing to *Frasier*.

Jennifer's bank account certainly noticed the success. By the end of Season One she had earned a not-too-shabby sum in excess of $500,000 – more than enough to buy the car and house she wanted.

The rest of the cast headed straight for the Porsche dealership but Jennifer's dream car – for the moment – was a 1970 280 SL Mercedes. In an interview in *FHM* magazine she explained, 'For an antique, gorgeous car it wasn't that expensive. It's been a fantasy car of mine for a long time.' Sentimentally, she still kept the beat-up old Land Rover which had served her so well as her audition limo before she made it. She still liked to use it to bomb around the bends in the Hollywood Hills.

The house Jennifer found on Blue Jay Way became a hideaway in the hills; a hideaway from the paparazzi, who, in the not too distant future, would wait outside hour after hour when they knew that Brad Pitt was inside, and would then wait outside hour after hour when they knew that he wasn't. It was relatively modest by the standards of the star she was becoming but she was not yet on superstar money. The pool was small and square and inside there were just two bedrooms but the view down to the ocean was breathtaking, while the lemon trees and the palms hid the increasingly private Jennifer away from unwelcome scrutiny.

This was the first home she had ever owned. She wanted it to be special and to savour the joy of finding just the right pieces of furnishing. Fortunately, as the fifties-style house was quite small by Hollywood standards, she was able to gut it and start again, slowly. She had a dining table and chairs specially made, she hired a gardener who cultivated rosebushes on the patio and planted a hedge around the perimeter. She had that delight of spending afternoons hunting around antique shops and coming home with a killer rug. She had developed a love of antiques growing up when her mother developed an interest in them. Jennifer, however, may have seen something as an antique which her mother thought second-hand and thrifty. She also loved having family pictures smartly presented in frames and enjoyed finding just the right spot for them. The family could be reunited on a glass-topped coffee table even if they would never again be in the same room in person.

As money became less of an issue – until, in no time at all, it was no issue – she improved the home so that it became her oasis of calm and one she would never be happy leaving. She filled the rooms with antiques and candles, put in a private gym, an office and a tiled bathroom with a Jacuzzi. Amusingly, she is a tidy person much more in the manner of Monica than Rachel. Everything in her house has to be just right: 'I can't stand it when thing are out of place,' she explained.

Everything was changing in her life very quickly. Her friend Kristin Hahn likened the *Friends* explosion of popularity to something like that of the Beatles. One of the unexpected side effects of her new life and new home was that she saw much less of old friends. Kristin explained that they did not see Jennifer for about a year and a half. She admitted that there was some jealousy from Jennifer's 'old' friends. She told *Elle* magazine, 'Here she was in a show called *Friends* and we were her real ones. There was a period where we were waiting for her to come out to the other side. And she did.'

That same summer of 1995 Jennifer also realized for the first time just how much her day-to-day life was changing. She could not go out to buy groceries without a crowd gathering. She recalled going to a pharmacy and standing in the queue clutching toilet paper and Q-tips while a group of fans asked for her autograph. The effect was as one of stalkers working in a relay. She was even approached in a sauna when she was 'butt naked' and asked by an equally naked and steamy woman, 'Is it you?'

Her hate–hate relationship with the tabloid media and intrusive photographers was gaining strength. She discovered that once an event in your life is latched onto it becomes inexorably linked with you for the rest of your days. Anybody you say good morning to suddenly becomes a hot date and is trotted out on the list of past suitors. In Jennifer's case her date list post-Daniel McDonald included *ER* actor Noah Wyle, who, in February 1995, appeared in a very funny episode – Number 17 – of *Friends* with George Clooney entitled 'The One With Two Parts, Part Two'; they played 'cute' doctors lusted after by Rachel and Monica.

Jennifer was also linked with Jonathan Silverman, an old school friend of David Schwimmer whom he had beaten to the lead role in the short-lived *Couples*. Silverman starred opposite Courteney Cox in the dreadful *Sketch Artist* film and then popped up in an episode – Number 23 – of *Friends* as well. He was in 'The One With The Birth' where, coincidentally, he played a doctor – perhaps Jennifer had a thing for men in white coats. She flirts with him in the show while he looks after the pregnant Carol, lesbian ex-wife of Ross. The actress Jane Sibbert, who played Carol in many episodes of *Friends*, has had a career spookily similar to Jennifer's. She was in *Herman's Head*, *Quantum Leap* and *Burke's Law* before finding a niche in *Friends*.

Wyle's episode was aired in February 1995, while Silverman's was in May, so Jennifer was busy. There was always time, however, for the perennial rumour to spring up suggesting she was dating Matthew Perry. More interestingly she was linked for the first time with two rock stars. The first was Anthony Kiedis, lead singer of the Red Hot Chilli Peppers and the second Adam Duritz of Counting Crows.

Kiedis was also a part-time actor under the pseudonym Cole Dammett, a name which sounded like someone Wyatt Earp would have gunned down in Tombstone. He has always surrounded himself with beautiful women and so there would have been nothing unusual about him dating Jennifer. He did not, however, mention Jennifer in his autobiography, *Scar Tissue*, in 2004 although one actress he definitely did date was the beautiful and ethereal Ione Skye, daughter of the Sixties' musician Donovan. Ione was the star of the first film Jennifer made after joining *Friends* so it is possible that Jennifer might have met him through her co-star, but there is no evidence it was anything more than that.

Adam Duritz, the charismatic lead singer of Counting Crows was, with his trademark dreadlocks, a bit like Mick Hucknall. He kept on dating beautiful women but nobody knew how he did it. He was an unlikely suitor for Jennifer Aniston, or so people thought. But Jennifer was always a bit of a rock chick and, if Steve Tyler was not available, why not date Adam Duritz?

Although not hugely popular in the UK, Counting Crows was a well-known nineties' band in the US. They were formed in San Francisco and were only getting started when Jennifer and Adam went out. They had a big hit in 1994 with the upbeat 'Mr Jones' and, although at an early stage in their career, had gained a devoted following, particularly Duritz who specialized in thought-provoking and emotional lyrics. Some welcomed his sensitive introspection; other thought him a bit miserable. But his star was definitely in the ascendant.

Duritz is quite philosophical about his reputation for dating actresses and to his credit he has always been a gentleman where Jennifer is concerned: 'A lot of these relationships were completely invented by the press. I could date someone for a week and still be reading about it three years later. There are whole albums credited to Jennifer Aniston, who is a very nice girl I dated for about a week. I don't, myself, remember writing a song about her. It's just a great story for the press. Everyone in LA is an actress.'

He is being a little coy about the fascination with his brief relationship with Jennifer, made even more interesting by the fact that he moved on to date Courteney Cox – and he did write a song for her, reportedly the track 'Monkey' on the Crows' 1996 album *Recovering the Satellites*. He also wrote one for the beautiful former *Boston Legal* star Monica Potter, 'Mrs Potter's Lullaby'. 'I didn't write songs about them because they were actresses. I wrote songs about them because they were cool people.' Perhaps the relationship with Jennifer was not important enough to merit a song.

Observers thought it was a testament to the strength of her friendship with Courteney that there was no fall-out over her dating Jennifer's ex.

Courteney went out with Duritz after ending her six-year relationship with Michael Keaton. Jennifer's last important relationship had also been with an actor, Daniel McDonald. Clearly the articulate Duritz was a welcome antidote to actors. He was different. But it would soon be time to go back to dating actors.

Jennifer once said, 'It's fun being in a successful show – you get to meet a lot of interesting people.' But her alleged dalliances were not too well received by *Friends* disciples who considered it almost an act of infidelity for her to be dating anybody other than Ross. Since the very beginning, she has had to contend with the public confusing Jennifer Aniston the person with Rachel Green the character she played on screen.

While Jennifer and Courteney were playing the dating game, Lisa Kudrow was the first of the Friends to settle down. She married Michel Stern, a French advertising executive, on 27 May 1995, just nine days after the end of the first season. Unusually she let it be known that she was a virgin at the time because, she said, her Jewish mother, Nedra, had told her it was a gift for her husband alone. A few stars have played the virginity card over the years but in the case of Lisa, a witty and intelligent woman, it seemed a completely honourable revelation. Only David Schwimmer of the gang of six missed the wedding in Malibu. He was filming his movie starring debut, *The Pallbearer*, in New York.

Dating, getting married and buying a new house were all important tasks for the off season, the six months' breathing space when repeats kept the Friends in the public eye. Jennifer also happily posed for pictures next to her mother Nancy at the wedding of her half-brother Johnny Melick and his girlfriend Shannon. It was a very rare family get-together and one of the few times since Jennifer became famous that mother and daughter have been photographed together.

The time off also gave Jennifer and the cast the opportunity to 'break-out', the entertainment term for television stars trying to make it in movies. The *Friends* collective were all bombarded with possible movie scripts and, understandably, allowing for the years of struggling along as pilot actors, they were keen to make the most of their new-found fame. The rule of thumb was that you could shoot a movie during the summer 'holiday' when you could go on location and then it would be released the following summer when you would have to participate in the all-important promotional work.

Movies were considerably scarier than the relatively easy life of sitcoms. On *Friends*, the stars even had stand-ins to walk around the stage so that the camera marks could be worked out for the actual performance. The 'stars' would sit around and drink coffee while men and women who could have come straight from the Ricky Gervais comedy *Extras* were directed here and there, identified only by a sign hanging round their neck, 'Jennifer', 'Courteney' and so on. In future years Jennifer would be able to shoot more than one film at the same time as making *Friends*.

An accomplished actor can sleepwalk through a writer-led series like *Friends*. (In Jennifer's case that would not be a problem – she has confessed to one or two sleepwalking episodes in her life including setting off the alarm at her house when she stumbled outside in somnambulant mode.) On set, if your line does not get a laugh, then a writer will step in and write you another one that will. Jennifer's re-entry into the world of movies was surprisingly low-key. Her confidence in her ability to act the part of Rachel Green did not stretch to acting in movies. All through her career her co-stars have noted her confidence and professionalism, yet she has always maintained this to be an illusion. She was *acting* the part of an actress who knew what she was doing. Her modesty may be part of an innate protection system but the way she approached her transformation from TV star to movie star endorses her self-appraisal. She eschewed the fanfares that would have accompanied her post-Rachel big-screen debut.

The confidence others saw in her reflected her assurance as part of a group. *Friends* suited her so well because it was an ensemble. Similarly her theatrical roles in New York and early forays into TV and film in Los Angeles were all as a supporting actress. When faced with the reality of how she looked and acted on the big screen, as in the case of *Leprechaun*, she had sneaked out of the cinema. She told *GQ* magazine, 'I used to dread watching myself. I was like, "I should not be on a screen this big."'

Her first film project, *Dreams Of An Insomniac*, therefore was small and discreet. She was not the star but, in some ways a step back, was the best friend of the star, Ione Skye. Ironically, given Jennifer's previous roles, Ione played a waitress, Frankie, who has great difficulty sleeping and is also obsessed by unlikely words of wisdom. She's like a walking dictionary of popular quotes including John Lennon's 'All You Need Is Love' and Kurt Cobain's 'I wish I was like you, easily amused'. A famous quote of Kierkegaard, a favourite of biographers, also features: 'Life can only be understood backwards.' The slightly enigmatic title of the film belies its basic rom-com plot – girl meets boy, trouble in paradise when he turns out to have a live-in girlfriend, happy ending. Jennifer has gone on to appear in practically every variation of this 'date movie' plot in the past twelve years.

Most of the action takes place in a café – not Central Perk but one called Café Blue Eyes due to the owner, Frankie's uncle, being a big Sinatra fan. The gimmick is that the film begins in black and white to reflect Frankie's general misery, but when a handsome young songwriter comes in, switches to glorious colour à la *Wizard of Oz*. The songwriter, played by Mackenzie Astin, has writer's block. He makes a pact with Frankie to cure her insomnia if she will do the same with his inability to write a new song. The only problem is that she is due to leave town in a couple of days to start a new life in Los Angeles where she and best friend Allison (Jennifer) intend to become actresses.

Jennifer's sub-plot as Allison involves Uncle Leo's gay son

Rob who is afraid to come out to his father. Instead he enlists her help to pretend they are boyfriend and girlfriend. Allison, meanwhile, is more concerned about perfecting a wide range of accents for any acting eventuality. She starts off with French and moves on to Southern, taking in Canadian in case she is hired by a Toronto film-maker.

The movie was first shown at the San Francisco Film Festival in April 1996 but a disappointing response meant it took a further two years before it gained a limited release in the US. When it did eventually surface in June 1998 it appeared to be Jennifer's fifth since *Friends* began. The reviews were mixed but not overly harsh and, on balance, Jennifer finished well in credit. The *New York Times* thought it 'much too cute' but the two newspapers in San Francisco, where the movie is set, were much kinder – at least to Jennifer. In *The Discerning Film Lover's Guide*, David Bleiler notes the amount of inane banter about caffeine. In the *Examiner* Barbara Shulgasser described Jennifer's performance as 'terribly funny' while Mick LaSalle in the *Chronicle* wrote, 'It's talky, clumsy and a bit trivial, but the talk is rarely dull and there's an integrity about its clumsiness. Aniston, as the best friend, does nothing but waltz in every few minutes to throw her charm around and look very, very, very pretty. Who's complaining?'

Dreams of an Insomniac is a small movie but, if you like this sort of thing, then it is good, harmless fun. In some ways it is a sitcom stretched to the big screen. Jennifer is not extending herself but is comfortably the best thing in it. The whole enterprise shouts 'safe'. Jennifer does not have to carry the movie, nor is it a giant leap from the ensemble acting in which she flourishes. The movie went straight to video in the UK, which means it popped up on the shelves of Blockbuster leaving people wondering how they could have missed a Jennifer Aniston film at the local multiplex.

If *Dreams Of An Insomnic* had been Jennifer's first release, it would not have killed her career. Instead, filmgoers who were not at the San Francisco Film Festival had to wait to see what 'Rachel' could do on the big screen for the first time in the comedy *She's The One*, which promised much. The movie was the second film venture of the previous year's *wunderkind*, Edward Burns, who had burst onto the Hollywood radar with *The Brothers McMullen*, one of the most acclaimed romantic comedies of the nineties. That film was made on a shoestring and, for once, shoestring is not a misused cliché. Burns's father, a police sergeant, had put up $10,000 to help his son make the film. The total budget came in at about $24,000 and was shot mainly in his parents' Long Island home. In a now legendary move, Burns cornered Robert Redford in a New York lift and pressed a copy into his hand. Redford, impressed by the Burns chutzpah, watched the film, enjoyed it and decided to screen it at his world famous Sundance Film Festival. *The Brothers McMullen* won best film – a course of events a Hollywood scriptwriter would have turned down as too far-fetched. Fox Searchlight took the film on, which was a shrewd move because it took more than ten million dollars in the US alone – nothing less than a phenomenal return on budget.

The Brothers McMullen was a gentle, conversational film about the lives and loves of three Irish–American brothers in New York. The multi-talented Burns, himself an Irish–American, wrote, directed, produced and played the lead role. He decided he could pull off the same trick for *She's The One*, only this time he had a budget of three and a half million dollars. Money, however, did not buy success and the film made less money than its illustrious predecessor and considerably less profit.

She's The One is by no means a bad film but it disappointed the many who thought the previous film was a breath of fresh air in the mid-nineties Hollywood tired of blockbusters. Once again it was about the lives and loves of a pair of brothers played by Burns and Mike McGlone. Many of the cast from his first film were reunited but this time with two key additions. One was Jennifer Aniston, the number-one television pin-up of the age. The other was the delectable Cameron Diaz. How could this film fail?

Jennifer played Renee, the neglected wife of Francis Fitzpatrick, an irritating Wall Street trader. The role was reasonably thankless although she does get to say 'penis' on screen for the first time, something which would have made the Leprechaun turn red with embarrassment. Renee is being ignored by her husband because he is having an affair with Heather, his brother's ex-fiancée and a former hooker played in very street-smart fashion by Diaz. (The role of Heather was a much juicier one than that of Renee.) Burns played the nicer brother Mickey, a cab driver, while his real life girlfriend, Maxine Bahns, played the girl he meets in his taxi who invites him to drive her to New Orleans. At least one critic pointed out that it was a pity that Jennifer did not play this role.

The film, while amiable enough, stretched credibility in that it seemed unbelievable that either the Aniston or the Diaz character would be interested in the ghastly Francis. *Time Out* called it a 'bland, so-so romantic comedy without the charm to see it through', and thought it a disappointment after *The Brothers*

McMullen – a widely held sentiment. *Time Out* also thought the film generally reeked of 'unalloyed chauvinism', an observation which went to the heart of the problem: the characters were not especially likeable, not even Jennifer's mistreated Renee. Brian Webster in the *Apollo Guide* thought Francis a jerk and labelled Jennifer's character 'a sarcastic whiner', but his overall verdict was that *She's The One* was 'by no means an awful movie. While it's awfully talky, it has some witty moments and some sweet ones too.'

The years blend easily into one another when stars regularly churn out movies. Cameron Diaz somehow seems to have been around longer than Jennifer Aniston but when the film was released in the US in August 1996, Jennifer was the bigger star. *Friends* was a television phenomenon, she sported the most famous haircut in the world and she was in a high-profile relationship with Tate Donovan. Cameron Diaz was an ex-model with no TV experience and just two films to her credit. Her debut in *The Mask* (1994) had been eye-catching but the film's enormous success was almost entirely due to the popularity of its star, Jim Carrey. At the time Jennifer would have had far more star muscle, if she had chosen to use it. Instead, Diaz, three years younger and four inches taller, took the attention. Roger Ebert in the *Chicago Sun-Times* said of Diaz, 'She proves again that she is a real actress, in addition to being one of the most beautiful women in the movies.'

For two such disparate actresses as Jennifer Aniston and Cameron Diaz, there are some interesting similarities. They could easily turn up in the same movie again. They each broke into big box office in Jim Carrey movies – both *The Mask* and *Bruce Almighty* (in which Jennifer co-starred) made more than $100 million. They have both made quirky comedies with Ben Stiller in which they played the girl in the title: Cameron made *There's Something About Mary* while Jennifer appeared in *Along Came Polly*. In the films the brilliant Stiller made a fool of himself with both women. They have both starred in a series of rom-coms over the years in which either actress could have played the lead. Neither actress has baulked at looking plain in a movie – Jennifer in *The Good Girl* and Cameron in *Being John Malkovich* (1999).

They also both spent five years with a superstar heart-throb – Brad Pitt and Justin Timberlake respectively – before ending up alone. Intriguingly, their respective CVs look as if Jennifer has followed Cameron's blueprint, although one could never imagine her as one of Charlie's Angels. The comparison is fun but the reality is that Hollywood is a small place with an apparently limited stock of ideas and personnel. Both actresses were just testing the water in *She's The One* and have moved on to much better and more demanding roles since then.

Edward Burns, who is married to the supermodel Christy Turlington, has continued to write and direct films but is better known these days as an actor. He co-starred in the acclaimed *Saving Private Ryan* (1998) and was also reunited with Cameron Diaz in the light comedy *The Holiday* (2006). The ensemble nature of his own films suggests that he could also be reunited with Jennifer at some point in the future.

She's The One did very little for Jennifer's film ambitions. She had gone neither forwards nor backwards. The film was neither so bad that she became tainted nor so good that she was beating Julia Roberts to roles. The film was so safe for Jennifer that it seemed as if she were trying to hide, just popping her head over the parapet for a second before retreating to the safety of the barracks, in this case the new sound stage for *Friends* at the Burbank Studios. The upgrading of the facilities for the second season of *Friends* – including the addition of a pasta bar and a sushi bar – was further proof, if any were needed, of the success of the show and the regard in which it was held at the studio.

FIFTEEN

The Goofball

When *Friends* began, the publicity was able to hint at six young, wet-behind-the-ears actors putting on a show. They were of course seasoned pros but it all added up to a feeling of freshness, an antidote to the cosy over-familiarity of *Frasier* and *Seinfeld*. The problem would come when the media decided that everyone was sick of them and that *Friends*, at not much more than a year old, was past its sell-by date.

Jennifer was blissfully unaware of this prospect when she returned to Burbank to shoot Season Two. The first matter to be resolved was 'The One With Ross's New Girlfriend', the opening episode, in which Rachel's hopes of revealing her true feelings to Ross are scuppered by the discovery that he has a new girlfriend, Julie. To make things worse, he won't stop going on about how great she is. Rachel sleeps with the Italian rat Paolo again in an attempt to cheer herself up.

The developing storyline of Ross and Rachel was a fascinating one because the audience now sympathized with Rachel, who, at the beginning of the first season was the spoilt rich girl dumping her fiancé at the altar. Now *she* is the victim. And, in the classic way that fantasy and reality become blurred, Jennifer Aniston's public persona was touched by that perception. As a result of this merging of Jennifer and Rachel in the minds of her enormous fan base, everyone was rooting just as much for Jennifer to have a happy ending as they were for Rachel.

In the seventh episode of the series – Number 31 – Ross realizes Rachel reciprocates his own feelings for her and they kiss for the first time. The kiss was the biggest television event of the year. Jennifer recalled, 'The studio audience were screaming and cheering and it was all quite emotional. We had no idea how much everyone had invested in these two people.' In the end the expectation and involvement of the studio audience made it impossible for Jennifer and David to perform the actual kiss in 'public'. 'It was too huge a pressure,' she explained. They kissed away from the set and the continuity was organized in the editing suite.

Meanwhile, a short time before the kiss between Rachel and Ross was broadcast at the beginning of November 1995, Jennifer was relaxing with friends in a bar after a day at the studio when she was introduced to an actor called Tate Donovan, six feet tall with a winning smile and a slightly quirky attitude which she found attractive. Tate, who was five years her senior, put his success with women down to acting like a 'goofball'. He explained, 'Oddly enough women like me because of it. I have really lucked out in that way, because this goofball hasn't been cool a day in his life.' He (goofily) asked Jennifer out on a date and she accepted.

The first date could have been a complete disaster but somehow getting through it gave impetus to the relationship. It was a bit like a sitcom and could almost have featured Rachel. Tate planned a low-key evening not realizing that Jennifer was making a big, almost red-carpet effort. He chose a little Japanese café in a strip mall, the sort of place which is ubiquitous in Los Angeles. Jennifer had to grin and bear it. Imagine if the Queen popped in to a curry house in Windsor for dinner. The evening did not improve when Tate ordered them both some noodles, a dish Jennifer cannot bear. They did, however, chat easily which was promising.

Tate was similar to Jennifer's previous long-standing boyfriend Daniel McDonald in that he came from a large East-coast family. He was the youngest of six children in a close-knit Irish Catholic family. His father, J. Timothy Donovan, was a surgeon and Tate enjoyed a middle-class upbringing in the affluent suburb of Tenafly, New Jersey, no more than ten miles away from where Jennifer was brought up, but light years away from the crack addicts on the corner. He attended the Dwight-Englewood High School which also boasts Brooke Shields and Mira Sorvino among its former pupils.

Tate was always keen to break into television and chose to study drama at the University of Southern California in Los Angeles where he forged an enduring friendship with George Clooney and his long-time collaborator Grant Heslov. His natural good looks enabled him to find plenty of early work as a teenage actor, specializing in that Hollywood stand-by, the troubled teen. By far his best early role was in the film *Memphis Belle* (1990) in which he played 1st lieutenant Luke Sinclair, the charismatic yet arrogant co-pilot of the World War Two bomber which gave the film its title.

By the time he started dating Jennifer in October 1995, he had already had one high-profile relationship with a famous actress, Sandra Bullock. They were engaged for a time. Sandra Bullock shares Jennifer's unconventional good looks, is also curvaceous rather than stick-thin and is a gifted comedienne. And she worked as a waitress in New York before trying her luck in Los Angeles. She and Tate fell in love on the set of *Love Potion No. 9* (1992), a silly, small-budget, small box-office comedy. Bullock was probably the best thing about it and her star was definitely in the ascendant. Her career was turned around by the popular thriller *Speed* (1994). Cynics pointed out that she and Donovan split when her career hit the freeway while his was still leaving the driveway, the implication being that the ambitious Donovan could not cope with being eclipsed by his glamorous fiancée.

Tate was once described as the most talented actor that no one recognizes. He could walk down the street totally anonymous, a luxury no longer enjoyed by Jennifer. Jennifer thought him an excellent actor and he would give her invaluable advice, going through lines with her, especially when she was moving into films. Actors most commonly date other actors. The same is true in every area of show business; the opportunity to meet 'ordinary' folk, let alone date them, just does not exist. Jennifer was living in a cocoon now that she was a success. She could date her hairdresser (unlikely) or her yoga instructor (usually female) but she was never going to meet anybody with a 'proper job'. Fellow actors understand the pleasure and pain of acting. If you don't act, you don't know – it really is as simple as that.

Tate had high hopes for a new comedy called *Partners* which premièred ten days before the second season of *Friends* began. Jimmy Burrows was again involved and Donovan's co-star was the popular Jon Cryer who had so nearly been in *Friends*. The dull-sounding premise was that they were both architects but Jennifer was encouraging and readily agreed to be a guest star in a suitable episode after she returned from a skiing holiday she planned in Aspen, Colorado, during her mid-season break. Tate was not invited. Jennifer was not yet sure if he was boyfriend material although she told *Rolling Stone* magazine, 'It's so new and I'm scared and sceptical. I'm dating and I like him very much but when do I start to call him like a boyfriend?' Jennifer's uncertainty is quite surprising considering she was nearly twenty-seven at the time.

Instead of Tate, Jennifer travelled with her now restored tribe of friends from The Hill. She had realized that these were friends for life so she rented a house on the edge of the popular ski resort and invited twelve of the gang to share it with her. She could afford the best hotels but the ramshackle mob, some now with children, rolled up with their sleeping bags and blankets as tribute to the great days of Laurel Canyon. Andrea Bendewald was among them. She observed, 'This is something she was dying to do. She needed a break because she worked so frickin' hard this year.'

The slight dichotomy in Jennifer's view of the media at this point is nicely illustrated by this very private trip with friends. Quite rightly, she baulked at the interest from the cameras as she queued for the ski lift, knowing that a picture of her falling on her bottom in the snow would be seen the world over. On the other hand, a writer from *Rolling Stone* magazine was invited along for a glass of wine and a cosy chat. 'The Rachel' was all over the place. Even an FBI agent would have found it hard to tail Jennifer for the day without losing her in a sea of long, fluffy shag cuts. At least the resulting magazine article brought Jennifer to life. More than that, the edition of 7 March 1996 featured Jennifer on the cover for the first time under the banner of 'The Girl Friend'. She was naked and it caused a great deal of fuss at the time because 'Rachel stripped off', but it was very tame. She was lying on her front on a stripy bed, breasts well hidden by a strategically placed hand, although the curve of a bare bottom was clearly visible. It fulfilled its purpose of getting talked about. She was even stopped in the street by bewildered members of the public who could not understand why Rachel Green would do something like that. In retrospect it is noteworthy, not so much for the fact that Jennifer was naked, but because it superbly showed off the world's most famous haircut. The hated 'Rachel' never looked better. Jennifer must have been so proud, although she does not care for old pictures of herself unless they are family ones.

True to her word Jennifer did appear as a guest in *Partners*. She played an accountant in an episode called 'Follow The Claims', aired in February. It was the seventeenth episode that season. The show was cancelled after twenty-two, leaving Tate out of work while his girlfriend's star continued its inexorable rise. Surprisingly, however, Jennifer was finding it hard to bask in her new-found glory. She was suffering a personal crisis about deserving her success which explains to some extent her pitching her movie career to date at too low a level.

In *Friends*, at the beginning of the year, Rachel Green's screen mother Sandra, played by Marlo Thomas, showed up for the first time in the episode 'The One With The Lesbian Wedding'. She comes to visit and tells Rachel she is thinking of leaving her father. Jennifer became friendly with Marlo and a few years later agreed to contribute to her book entitled *The Right Words At The Right Time*. She provided two illuminating stories. The first concerned the words of Anthony Abeson when she had felt humiliated in class, having been laughed at by her peers during her performance of Chekhov. The second provided an insight into why she was accepting such inconsequential movie roles that did not stretch her as an actress. She revealed that she went through a personal crisis when *Friends* became a success. She wrote, 'I was really at a place where I felt undeserving.' She could not accept her standing as someone thought fabulous and famous by people who did not really know anything about her.

Jennifer's epiphany arrived when a friend sent her an extract from a book by the popular evangelist Marianne Williamson, *A Return To Love: Reflections on the Course in Miracles*. The often-quoted exhortation begins, 'Our deepest fear is not that we are inadequate. Our deepest fear is that we are powerful beyond measure.' The text poses the question that Jennifer has been asking herself, namely, 'Who am I to be brilliant, gorgeous, talented and fabulous?' and answers it with the words, 'Who are you *not* to be?' It is a truly inspiring quotation and one which had a profound effect on Jennifer, struggling to come to terms with such unexpected and extreme fame and prestige. She was a little Greek girl from the twenty-third floor of a block on West 92nd Street who was being treated like a deity by people she did not know and who had Jennifer Aniston confused with a television character called Rachel Green.

The irony of Marianne Williamson's words of wisdom is that they were widely believed to have been quoted by Nelson Mandela at his inauguration speech as President of South Africa in

1994, in particular the sentence, 'As we are liberated from our own fear, our presence automatically liberates others.' Mandela never said it, which is a pity, but Jennifer certainly believed he did. Like many others she was moved by the magnitude of Mandela. In Marlo Thomas's book she declares that reading Mandela's words inspired her to believe that she had a valid place in the world and that making people laugh on a grand scale was part of that.

The words may not have been Mandela's but the message they impart is the same and they gave validation and comfort to Jennifer Aniston. Her work may not change the world, but it was a good thing to make people laugh.

Meanwhile Season Two of *Friends* was not going as swimmingly as everyone had hoped. The media backlash was taking shape. The worst sufferer from negative stories in the early days was probably Courteney Cox, originally the biggest of the six stars. She was rumoured to have an eating disorder and was constantly having to deny that she was anorexic or bulimic. The usual antidote to this unwelcome publicity is to make sure that you always have a large plate of food whenever you are interviewed. Sure enough, when Courteney, a size two, was interviewed by *People* magazine in November 1995, she was diving into a buffet table laden with doughnuts, cookies and crisps. She laughed off the unfunny rumours that she was just skin and bone by declaring, 'There are no skeletons in my closet'.

The main criticism of the *Friends* cast, it seemed, was of overexposure. Author and *Friends* expert David Wild observed, 'In all fairness during Season Two, the show's young stars were indeed moving from high profile toward a sort of multimedia omnipresence.' Kevin Bright confirmed, 'It just felt like maybe these people who were so fresh and new in the first season, all of a sudden you were getting to know them a little too much.'

The cast themselves were aware of it although they could hardly be blamed for their enthusiasm to make the most of an opportunity they had all wanted so much. David Schwimmer said, 'We were everywhere and it was too much and there was a huge backlash.' Jennifer too was aware of overexposure, especially uncertain about their involvement in a campaign for Diet Coke. 'We knew we were doing too much, too soon, but somehow we got talked into it.' Sensibly, they made a conscious decision not to accept the opening of every envelope. James Michael Tyler, who played Rachel's adoring Gunther, commented, 'I think they handled it quite well and they did cut back.' Tyler had been hired in Season One as a glorified extra because he knew how to work a cappuccino machine. In Season Two he was thrilled when Marta Kauffman told him he had his first line of dialogue. It was 'Yes'.

Not everyone was aware of the *Friends* success story. Back in New York, Anthony Abeson, who watched very little television, saw the 'milk moustache' poster featuring Jennifer and Lisa and was thrilled to see that Jennifer was working. The last he had heard she was starring in *Leprechaun*, which did not gladden his drama teacher's heart. He rang her up and said, 'Jennifer, why are you doing the milk ad?' She replied, 'Oh, well, I'm doing this show called *Friends*.' Anthony had never heard of it: '*Friends*? It must be doing very well.' Jennifer replied, 'Yeah, people seem to like it.'

The show itself went from strength to strength during Season Two reaching number three in the ratings. The highlight was securing the time slot after the 30th Super Bowl won by the Dallas Cowboys. The episode, broadcast on 28 January 1996, was memorable for two reasons: it featured Julia Roberts as guest star and the less welcome return of Marcel who, with an irony worthy of The Simpsons, is now a movie star. The joke was made even better because in real life Marcel was the first member of the cast to make a movie, the thriller *Outbreak* (1995). Julia, just about the biggest female star in the world, made a good impression on Jennifer: 'She just knocked it out of the park.'

Roberts played a former girlfriend of Chandler, who he had humiliated at school by lifting up her skirt and giving her the nickname Susie Underpants. She gets her revenge by enticing him to ask her out on a date and getting him to wear her panties and nothing else. Rachel meanwhile gets asked out by Jean-Claude Van Damme playing himself.

The high spot for Rachel in Season Two is that she and Ross sleep together, although for many the actual season highlight came in Number 30 – 'The One With The Baby On The Bus' – in which Phoebe sings her signature song 'Smelly Cat' for the first time.

Privately, Jennifer was facing a personal crisis in her always volatile relationship with her mother. After the happy family day at Johnny's wedding, Jennifer also joined everyone for Christmas, but that togetherness would all change a couple of months later in February 1996 when Nancy was interviewed at the Peninsula Hotel in Beverly Hills for a television programme about the Steiner School. Or so she thought. (Nancy would later write that she was 'duped by the rogue tabloid press'.) During the interview she made some casual remarks about Jennifer's hair and about her success on *Friends*. When the show aired, there was no mention of the Steiner School. Instead it revealed a chatty mother talking about her famous daughter. According to Nancy, Jennifer rang that evening and went ballistic, telling her that she would never forgive her. Nancy claimed that Jennifer's voice was so distorted by rage that she did not recognize it at first. She also claimed that Jennifer abruptly hung up.

If Nancy's version is accurate, then it reveals a side to Jennifer not normally seen; her parents, it would seem, remain very much her Achilles heel. The course of events as described by Nancy raises as many questions as it answers about the relationship of mother and daughter. What sort of relationship did they have at that point if Jennifer did not know in advance that her mother was going to appear on television? It was the first time Nancy had been interviewed. It was clearly a big deal and yet her daughter seemed not to have known anything about it. Afterwards, Jennifer cut off all contact with her mother. Perhaps they had drifted far apart before this.

Occasionally, both Jennifer and her mother have given clues as to why they were already cast adrift before the television programme provided the final gust of wind. Jennifer has hinted that Nancy could be quite controlling, while undermining her confidence. The classic instance is in making Jennifer feel like 'the ugliest ducking on the planet'. Jennifer told *Rolling Stone* that Nancy, as a former model, was very focused on beauty and would advise her to use make-up to enhance her features. Jennifer called it 'funny and pathetic'. As a young teenager Jennifer used to cake her face in make-up and continued to do so after her move to Los Angeles until Daniel McDonald told her that she was beautiful without make-up and did not need so much.

Jennifer was angry and resentful at the way her mother had

allowed her destiny to be controlled by the key man in her life, John Aniston. Perversely, her anger at her father for leaving them was defused when Jennifer became an adult and moved to Los Angeles. She forgave her father but her anger at her mother appears to have been unresolved. Jennifer's leaving home would seem to have been crucial for both women. Nancy discloses in her book that she and Jennifer attended joint counselling sessions, at her daughter's request, at which it seemed the finger of blame was being pointed at her, the mother.

For her part, Nancy Aniston did not like Jennifer's friends and the influence she believed they had over her daughter. In her memoir, Nancy reveals her feelings about Jennifer's 'new friends' or 'hip crowd' as she disparagingly called them. She says they were not her kind of people. She did not like their bad language or whispering and described the behaviour of The Hill people as blatantly ill-mannered, displaying a lack of human consideration. Her mother's antipathy towards her closest friends attaches a greater relevance to Jennifer calling the her 'chosen family'.

The realization that she had nothing in common with Jennifer's friends led Nancy to stop visiting her daughter at her home. Instead she would only see her at the Warner Studios in Burbank, an impersonal environment.

Nancy was probably correct in declaring that she had nothing in common with Jennifer's friends. The strong-minded feminism they espoused was never going to sit cosily next to Nancy's old-fashioned values. Jennifer, in effect, reflected this when she said that she would never want to be governed by a man: 'I will never depend on any man as much as my mom depended on my father.'

In context this fissure between mother and daughter occurred at a time, in early 1996, when Jennifer was intent on grasping the opportunity provided by *Friends* with both hands. She was concerned that negative publicity was undermining her ambitions and the last thing she thought she needed was her mother blabbing away and possibly revealing things Jennifer would have preferred to have kept well hidden.

Then, Jennifer had been quite slow off the block, lacking, at first, the self-esteem to believe she could be a fully-fledged movie star. Her castmates in Central Perk had moved more quickly with varying results and, generally speaking, the actresses from *Friends* have had considerably more success than the actors.

David Schwimmer had raced out of the traps by starring in *The Pallbearer* (1996), but this did very small business, and his second film, *Breast Men* (1997), in which he was also the star, was equally unsuccessful although did boast a release in Sweden under the title *Big Tits*. Matt LeBlanc starred in *Ed* (1996), which was no more successful than *The Pallbearer*. Matthew Perry led the cast of *Fools Rush In* (1997) which did reasonably well, although the plaudits were shared by the stunning Salma Hayek. He went backwards with his next release *Almost Heroes* (1998) which languished in the sub-ten-million-dollar range occupied by Schwimmer and LeBlanc. The problem for Ross, Joey and Chandler is that all the best comedic roles in Hollywood for the last ten years have been hoovered up by either Ben Stiller or Adam Sandler. Matthew Perry could be ideal for Bill Murray-type roles in about twenty years' time.

Lisa Kudrow, meanwhile, did well in *Romy and Michelle's High School Reunion* (1997) before taking on a small indie film, *Clockwatchers* (1998), which was nominated for a prize at the Sundance Film Festival. These efforts, however, pale into insignificance when compared with the good fortune of Courteney

Cox who was cast in the spoof horror film *Scream* (1996) when actress Janeane Garofalo turned down the role of newsgirl Gale Weathers. *Scream* reached the landmark return of more than $100 million in the US alone a month before Jennifer put her own ambitions to the test with *Picture Perfect*. Garofalo (who was also the original choice to play Monica in *Friends*) had turned down the role in *Scream*, preferring to make a movie called *Sweethearts* (1996) which went straight to video. Cox, meanwhile, was reportedly paid $5 million for *Scream 2* (1997) and $7 million for *Scream 3* (2000). Besides not making the best career decisions, Garofalo is interesting because she has a reputation of being a highly skilled comedic 'actress', a judgement Jennifer craves. She keeps on popping up in the story because she was also in *Romy and Michelle's High School Reunion*.

As well as earning her millions of dollars, *Scream* also provided a personal landmark in Courteney's life: she met the actor David Arquette on set. He played Deputy Dewey Riley, one of the very few characters to survive in the spoof horror and he, like Courteney, appeared in all three *Scream* films. The extrovert and slightly off-the-wall Arquette would not have seemed an obvious match for Courteney (for one thing, he was seven years her junior) and when reports that they were dating first surfaced they were not taken too seriously. The media should have taken greater note, however, especially when he made the almost obligatory 'partner' appearance in an episode of *Friends* at the beginning of Season Three. He played Malcolm, who stalked Phoebe – funnier than it sounds – in 'The One With The Jam', Number 51. Courteney acknowledged that they were complete opposites but that when they were together they would 'laugh their asses off', which has been a recipe for longevity where their relationship is concerned. Arquette has also been a solid friend and supporter of Jennifer through the good and the bad times.

Courteney Cox would appear to be a very good judge of her own talents and her commercial appeal. She does not like romantic comedies and has never been a rival to Jennifer, which is one reason why they have an enduring friendship: they do not covet the same roles. Jennifer, on the other hand, agonized about whether *Picture Perfect* was the right role for her 'breakout'. She told *USA Weekend*, 'You want to make the right choice because you want to hang around for a while.' In the end she listened to her father John Aniston who advised her to accept. He receives a mention in the credits: 'John Aniston . . . Thanks'.

On the inside Jennifer may have been nervous at being the marquee player in *Picture Perfect*, but that was not how it appeared on the outside. Bellina Logan, the actress who had appeared with her in *For Dear Life*, was still living in New York and secured a small role in *Picture Perfect*. She recalls sitting in her dressing room wondering if the star of the film would remember her when Jennifer popped her head round the door and declared, 'My God, Bellina!' It was a moment that summed Jennifer up: 'She was so sweet. I didn't want to put myself in the position of not being remembered, but she not only remembered me but she would talk and laugh so much. She's like that, Jennifer. She is completely genuine. She's not like a lot of people that can become famous and have that kind of "What do you want from me?" thing.'

Professionally, on set, there was no doubt that Jennifer was the star, although she did not have an entourage, a crew of yes men and women pandering to her every whim. Pre-Brad Pitt her world was calmer. Bellina observes, 'When she was doing *Picture*

Perfect she could still be Jennifer, an actress who was up and coming. Things are different for her now.' Bellina, however, did recall that she had a 'self-possessed thing that you can only have when you've become successful'. Jennifer certainly did not act as if she was under pressure, although the film's director, Glenn Gordon Caron, was mindful of her situation. 'He was very nice to her because I think it was very stressful for her,' recalls Bellina.

Bellina now lives happily in Los Angeles with her young family, but has bumped into Jennifer occasionally: 'I have to say to this day, whenever I meet her, it's almost like we just did the play. You just don't feel uncomfortable around her. She's truly the real deal in that respect.'

SIXTEEN

Picture Imperfect

Jennifer was pleased that Tate fitted easily into her group of pals. She observed, 'He is unbelievably sensitive and funny and warm.' Six months after they started dating, Tate took Jennifer to visit his family who still lived in Tenafly, New Jersey, in the same house he grew up in. He even showed her his boyhood bedroom. Jennifer, who can be hard-boiled about sentimentality, thought it was 'pretty romantic'. She remains jealous of a Waltonesque environment. She would have loved half a dozen siblings and her father saying, 'Goodnight JenJo,' when the lights of the house were turned out.

Jennifer was keen to repay the compliment and take Tate to Greece to show him some of her family history. That would have to wait for the moment because she was committed to starting *Picture Perfect* in New York and he was also scheduled to be away on location in Washington and Texas. Jennifer was not thrilled by their separations, discovering, not for the last time, that the inevitable absences of acting partners were not conducive to a healthy relationship. At one stage they talked of renting an apartment together in Manhattan but decided against it that summer.

Jennifer was able to take a holiday before reporting back to begin shooting the third season of *Friends*, so she and Tate travelled to Europe where, among other things, they embarked on a two-week bicycle tour of Provence in France, cycling thirty miles a day through the Rhone Valley and taking in romantic tourist spots like Avignon and Aix-en-Provence. They moved on to Greece where they spent nearly a week in Santorini which was unseasonably chilly. She also took him to Crete and showed him the town where her father was born and the places she remembered from her brief childhood sojourn there. Jennifer never confirmed strong rumours that the couple became engaged on that trip and she did not sport a ring on her return. She did wear one a short time afterwards but it was not an engagement ring.

The holiday, where they could escape from the pressures of work and those of Jennifer's celebrity, did wonders for their relationship. On their first anniversary they gave each other gold friendship rings or, to be more accurate, Claddagh rings which are Irish wedding bands. Jennifer described it as a commitment ring and wore hers on her wedding finger. She used to fiddle with it and twist it playfully around her finger. She was clearly very much in love with Tate. She said he was 'a boyfriend who's heaven'. She would even describe him as the 'love of her life' which, at the time, he was. The presence of a ring, any kind of ring, meant that Jennifer would forever be answering the inevitable question of any celebrity interview: 'When are you getting married?' Her replies were generally optimistic and suggested it was something she would like to do.

Season Three of *Friends*, meanwhile, had begun in a swirl of controversy triggered by a row over money. The cast were portrayed as grasping for trying to secure the best deal for themselves. Jennifer was particularly upset by a piece written in the *New York Post* by Liz Smith, a renowned columnist who Jennifer had almost grown up reading. 'We don't want to be disliked,' said Jennifer. 'When she wrote, "Who do these Friends think they are? Remember where you were two years ago," or something like that, I was like, "Oh, my God. Liz Smith hates us!"'

The network, NBC, had announced a $4-million-per-episode syndication in 1996, contingent on the show running for five years. If the cast walked, there was no show so their bargaining position was strong. Led by David Schwimmer, they asked for $100,000 each per episode at the start of Season Three and were offered $75,000. At this point, stories started appearing suggesting the cast would go on strike if the offer was not improved. Those articles could have been put out by cast or company, each trying to secure a better position. In the event Jennifer et al settled on a sliding scale, beginning at $75,000 with increments bringing it up to $125,000 an episode by the year 2000. For good measure their Christmas bonus in December 1996 was $200,000.

Jennifer was also commanding a seven-figure salary in her blossoming film career – she was paid $3 million for *Picture Perfect* – so the financial gap between her and Tate, which had been relatively small when they met, was now of Grand-Canyon size. Tate used to joke about it but he would have had to be one of the most successful actors in Hollywood to match Jennifer. Eighteen months into their relationship, Jennifer was asked if there was any friction between them over the widening divide in their earning power. She was quick to deflect that particular line of inquiry pointing out that Tate had not stopped working since *Partners*, including two movies and the voice of Hercules in the Disney film of that name. By Disney standards, however, *Hercules* (1997) was only a qualified success, although Jennifer found it highly amusing telling everyone that she was dating a god – not exactly true as Hercules was but the son of a god. She also failed to point out that there was a considerable difference between working and *starring*. Tate was working, Jennifer was starring. He was down the cast list for both of his movies, *Murder at 1600* (1997), a thriller starring Wesley Snipes, and a Diane Keaton romantic drama, *The Only Thrill* (1997). Neither film did great business.

Jennifer had embarked on a gruelling schedule, trying to juggle her film career with maintaining a strong presence in *Friends*. She was doing some reshoots on *Picture Perfect* as well as honouring a commitment to a smaller film called *'Til There Was You*. Every three weeks she would have one week off from *Friends*. She would finish at Burbank on a Tuesday night and then work on *'Til There Was You* on Wednesday. On Thursday she would fly to New York and shoot *Picture Perfect* on Friday, Saturday and Sunday. She would then fly back to Los Angeles on the overnight flight known as the red-eye so that she could be on the *Friends* set on Monday. It really was a lifestyle better suited to a single woman. She denied claims that she grew fed up with the demands on her time, however, telling journalist Gill Pringle, 'This is what I've been preparing for all my life.'

The big storyline of Season Three in *Friends* was the Ross-and-Rachel split which took place over two episodes – Numbers

63 and 64 – 'The One Where Ross and Rachel Take A Break' and 'The One With The Morning After'. Ross has a one-night stand with Chloe, an attractive girl from the copy shop, after Rachel has suggested they need a break. Ross's excuse after Rachel finds out is the classic 'We were on a break'. They split up for good in a wet-hankie exchange at the end: 'This can't be it,' cries Ross. 'Then how come it is?' replies Rachel. Once again Rachel was the victim here, treated badly by a fickle man. The ongoing ill feeling between Ross and Rachel dominated the season until in the finale Rachel admits that she still loves him. In Jennifer's expert hands Rachel became the character with whom most women could identify. Monica was whiney and Phoebe was odd but Rachel was very much a real girl juggling the demands of love, work and shopping. Jennifer had imbued Rachel with a vulnerability that would also become an important ingredient in her film acting.

Jennifer's real relationship was, in the meantime, faring much better. Tate may have modestly ascribed his success with women to being a goofball but he was also adept at tugging the heart-strings. On Valentine's Day 1997, Jennifer was filming *Friends* at Burbank. During one scene she had time to walk back to her dressing room to relax for a few moments. Sitting on a chair looking up at her was an adorable little Australian sheepdog puppy with a big red bow tied around his neck. He was a gift from Tate and Jennifer called him Enzo. 'He's a good boy,' she said (meaning Enzo not Tate). She considered the gesture the most romantic thing anyone had ever done for her.

One major problem for Jennifer and the rest of the *Friends* cast was the contemptuous way television stars were viewed when they tried to break into movies. The scepticism was all too apparent when they were collectively nominated for the Razzie Award in March 1997. Jennifer et al were placed under the dubious title of 'Friends Cast Members Turned Movie-Star-Wanna-Be's'. The Razzies, otherwise known as The Golden Raspberry Awards, are part of the annual fun in Hollywood but still not something a serious actor wants to win. At least on this occasion they were pipped by Pamela Anderson in the execrable *Barb Wire* (1996).

'Til There Was You was released in the US at the end of the third season of *Friends*, in May 1997. It was very much in the same vein as *Dreams Of An Insomniac* and *She's The One*. They were modest films and she was not the star nor was she expected to carry them. You could be forgiven for believing that Jennifer's only good reason for appearing in them was that she was allowed to smoke. In *'Til There Was You* Jennifer had a Rachel-like role as Debbie who was, horror, another best friend. She was fourth on the cast list and her character did not even have a surname. The actress who comes out best is Sarah Jessica Parker, who would soon be the star of *Sex And The City*. She played a ghastly former child star who unwittingly brings the two romantic leads, Jeanne Tripplehorn and Dylan McDermott, together. It is a tale of kismet suggesting the rather trite philosophy that there's someone out there for everyone.

The film follows the lives of two people, one writing the Parker character's biography, the other an architect restyling her home, until inevitably they meet just in time for the closing credits. The idea had been seen to much better and more popular effect in *Sleepless In Seattle* (1993). Jennifer's character Debbie is an uninspiring woman who ends up as a matronly doctor carving turkey in her suburban home. Once again, it would have been interesting to see what Jennifer might have made of the Sarah Jessica Parker role, which is by far the funniest. The director, Scott Winant, was television flavour of the month for his Emmy-winning work on the hit comedy *thirtysomething*, which might account for the generous budget of $23 million for a film that returned less than half that investment at the box office.

Leonard Klady in *Variety* gave a review which indicated how the film might perform, calling it a 'tired piece of romantic cornball fare' and a 'badly conceived, poorly executed fairy tale'. He rightly predicted that a fleeting theatrical run was the best it might expect followed by a late-night cable slot. He did, however, single out Jennifer for praise, deeming her performance 'a stunning but abbreviated turn'. The implication, almost certainly correct, was that Jennifer could have been the film's ace in the hole but, for whatever reason, her contribution was not fully realized. Perhaps she was being stretched too thinly across three projects.

David Schwimmer was certainly quoted as looking unfavourably on the Aniston workload and its effect on *Friends*: 'No one can convince me that it doesn't harm the quality of the show that people have to fly on Friday to New York to shoot for two days and come back late Sunday night to be back at work Monday.'

Once again Jennifer came out undamaged by a flop, but she would be under much greater pressure when *Picture Perfect* was released in August 1997. Jennifer was on a losing wicket before she started the film, at least from the critics' point of view, because a romantic comedy was exactly what everybody expected her first starring role to be. Within the confines of the genre Jennifer gives an impeccable performance, playing advertising executive Kate Mosley who misses out on promotion at her company because she is a single, carefree girl. The misogynistic premise is that she would be more stable if she were married. She would be more of a 'company man'. At a friend's wedding she meets a 'nice guy' called Nick, a handsome Mister Ordinary, played by Jay Mohr, who works as a wedding videographer. Back at the office her best friend concocts a story that Nick is Kate's fiancé (this is exactly the BF role that the old Jennifer would have taken), and suddenly Kate's career takes off. She even gets to sleep with the office lothario, played with relish by Kevin Bacon, who gets his kicks from bedding women who are spoken for. The plot develops when her boss insists on meeting Nick and she has to pay him $1,000 to pretend that they are engaged and then stage-manage a furious row so that they can break up. As it's a romantic comedy, she realizes that she has fallen in love with him and they end up together.

The director, Glenn Gordon Caron, had expected Jennifer to be an accomplished sitcom star from a world where everything revolves around immaculate timing but he was pleasantly surprised that she found a depth and vulnerability in a character 'which could easily have been two-dimensional. The quality Jennifer brings to her comedic roles is that she is not completely nice. She can be bitchy, irritating and hurt in the same scene. In other words she can play normal. Caron observed, 'Everything Jennifer does as an actor has to do with the business of being a human being.'

He did his best to talk the film up and praise Jennifer: he told *TV Guide*, 'No matter what kind of ridiculous or morally questionable things Kate does, you can always hear her heart beating.' Caron had high expectations of the film which might have been for him the start of a new career directing movies. It is his last movie to date. Instead, he has returned to television as the writer–producer of the series *Medium*, which stars Courteney Cox's sister-in-law Patricia Arquette. Whisper it quietly but up to this point Jennifer Aniston seemed to be the kiss of death for directors. Her record to date was four movies, all with different directors, three of whom have yet to direct another movie.

In *Rolling Stone* Magazine, Peter Travers gave the film two stars out of four and commented, 'Jennifer Aniston is a friend in need of a movie script that will really let her talent blossom. *Picture Perfect* is too TV-ish and timid a romantic farce to do the trick.' Most reviewers latched onto the same point – Jennifer was not well served by a film which did not stretch her undoubted talents. Travers astutely recognized that Jennifer had a 'knack for skilled underplaying'. This is the whole nub of her acting style as perceived originally in New York by Anthony Abeson who described it as 'acting on inhale'. Travers also highlighted the Aniston look – not her beauty but the way she dumped a date for not wearing a condom with an 'eloquent arch of her eyebrow'. It was a point about acting skill previously well made by D. David Morin on her ill-fated sitcom *Muddling Through*. Jeff Millar in the *Houston Chronicle* thought *Picture Perfect* was 'a romantic comedy that's adequately romantic but a bit short on comedy.' It must have been frustrating for Jennifer realizing that everyone seemed to recognize her worth but wish for better material. She was not entirely pleased with *Picture Perfect*, dodging questions with an almost *Leprechaun*-like reply: 'Let's not talk about that movie.'

One highlight of the movie is when Jennifer's character is in the bathroom and says the word 'shit' ten times in a row. An exchange with an interviewer from *People* magazine nicely reveals the Aniston wit and why she is such a good companion. Jennifer said of the 'shit' sequence, 'Good line, huh. I came up with that one. There was one shit in the script but I improvised and nine of them were my shits.'

Jennifer looked sexy and fashionable for her starring debut. She filled her frocks and was also much curvier than in future films. She is notoriously critical of the way she looks on screen and may have thought she filled too much of it. More than one of her old friends noted that she changed shape around this time, becoming much more slender. One observed, 'Jennifer had a really healthy body shape at that time. Her body has changed since then – that bottom isn't there any more.'

In retrospect, *Picture Perfect* is nothing like as bad as critics maintained. Nine times out of ten romantic comedies get a bad press but when you rent the DVD a year or two later they are perfect for curling up on the sofa on a cold winter's night. Bellina Logan observes, 'I remember reading the script and thinking "Oh, that's very sweet," that's about it.' Jennifer almost certainly needed to do better next time if she was to avoid another Razzie nomination.

Jennifer has always been concerned with staying power. She does not want to make any wrong moves, and is forever trying to grasp the magic formula that provides actors and actresses with long careers. Her mother in *Picture Perfect* was played with a deft sardonic touch by Olympia Dukakis, the doyenne of Greek actresses. She was sixty-six when the film premièred and advised that stars have to keep reassessing their careers. 'Staying power is very mercurial,' she said. The proof of that was right on Jennifer's doorstep: having warned her many times of the fickleness of her chosen career, John Aniston was written out of *Days*

Of Our Lives just as he was about to celebrate his sixty-fourth birthday. His words of warning to Jennifer that in show business you 'get chewed up and spit out' came back to haunt him. At least he did not go the way of Joey in *Friends* whose spoof character Dr Drake Ramore was written out of *Days* by falling down an elevator shaft. Instead, Victor Kiriakis had a stroke rendering him catatonic but giving the option of a return if the character was needed again. John Aniston was therefore able to resume the role in 1999 on a recurring rather than a contractual footing.

Jennifer had to spread her support around in 1997. While her father was having his work problems, her friend and co-star Matthew Perry was struggling with his own personal crisis. After months of media speculation, fuelled by his dramatic weight loss, he finally acknowledged he had a problem with prescription drugs. In June 1997 he checked into a rehab centre in Minnesota revealing that he had become addicted to the painkiller Vicodin since a jet ski accident a couple of years earlier.

Jennifer said all the right things. She told a television reporter, 'He's doing great and we are really proud of him.' She also told *USA Weekend*, 'Unfortunately he's in the public eye, so his experimentation is out there, and I guess it went too far.' The ineffectual quotes do not convey, however, quite how seriously she and the whole *Friends* crew were taking Matthew's problems. It was only several years later when he seemed to have conquered his demons that they were able to talk freely of their concern. Jennifer was probably hit hardest. She has always adored Matthew and clucked about after him, playing with his hair on set and sitting in his lap. She revealed in *Friends . . .'Til the End* that they were worried that they were actually going to lose him:

'Forget the show. His life, that was our main concern.' Marta Kauffman said, 'It was terrifying watching someone you care about in so much pain.'

Matthew, himself, told David Wild of the extreme tensions on set during this dark time. 'The third season was very difficult for me and I made things very difficult for other people with my addiction problems and my behaviour.' Sadly, this would not be the end of Matthews's addiction problem. At its worst point, he was taking between twenty and thirty Vicodin tablets a day and washing them down with a quart of vodka. It would take another five years and several trips to rehab before he could declare himself to be drug and alcohol free.

SEVENTEEN

An Unhappy Ending

Romantic comedy has one fundamental rule that seemingly must feature in every film of the genre – the conquering of an insurmountable hurdle. In *Picture Perfect* Jennifer's character had the obstacle of barely knowing the man she was supposedly going to marry. Her next film, *The Object Of My Affection*, had a more tricky stumbling block – she was in love with a gay man. Normally that would be the end of the matter but not in Hollywood. Jennifer signed for another summer on location in New York for what would be her most challenging role to date.

Jennifer's own private obstacle was keeping her relationship with Tate happy and moving forwards. They kept separate homes in Los Angeles but this time they decided to find an apartment in Manhattan together for the summer, perhaps a reaction to the time they had spent apart the previous year. Jennifer found an apartment in Greenwich Village for the long, hot summer. It made a change to be living in a real New York apartment again instead of just pretending. Despite being set in New York, *Friends* was definitely the Californian view of Manhattan. The only genuine element was the exterior shot of the apartment block where they lived. The building at the junction of Grove and Bedford Streets in the Village became a minor tourist attraction. Everything else connected with the show could be found at the Warner Bros studios in Burbank. Even the fountain where they frolic at the start of every episode was there. The street outside Central Perk was, in the earlier episodes, a painted backdrop.

One of the commonest gripes against *Friends* is that there would be no way a chef (Monica) and a waitress (Rachel) could afford the large and comfortable apartment they share stacked with product placements like a state-of-the-art Bang and Olufsen sound system. That's slightly missing the point of fiction. Jennifer, however, could afford it in real life and the apartment she rented was very much in the image of her own home in the Hollywood Hills, bursting with antiques and the smell of fresh roses. Superficially at least it was a perfect summer interlude. Jennifer was working. Tate walked Enzo and washed the dishes.

Jennifer liked *The Object Of My Affection* and enjoyed making the film. During her time on set, she discovered all the fun of a fart toy which became her pride and joy. The toy simulated the sound of flatulence and Jennifer, exercising the skills she had acquired through years of drama classes, would go through an array of embarrassing gestures which would have everyone around her dissolving into fits of giggles. Her co-star Paul Rudd observed, 'Farts are funny and they never get old.' Jennifer kept the toy for use on the set of *Friends* where she became the queen of mock flatulence.

Jennifer needed something to keep her amused making the *The Object of My Affection* because she had to pretend to be pregnant in the heat of a Manhattan summer. For weeks she was strapped into a pregnant belly, a padded bottom and stitched breast implants. To make her feel even less comfortable she had to wear sweaters and jackets to fit in with the plot. It was only make believe and Jennifer actually quite enjoyed the experience: 'It was a fun fantasy for a time plus the fact that I got to take the whole thing off at night.'

For the first time in a film she was under the guidance of one of the finest modern theatre directors, Nicholas Hytner. At the time Hytner was in great demand in the film world because of the success of the BAFTA award-winning *The Madness Of King George* (1994). That same year he had won a Tony for directing the revival of *Carousel* on Broadway. He would later confirm himself a leading figure in contemporary theatre when he won another Tony, in 2006, for his direction of the masterful Alan Bennett play *The History Boys*. He is currently Director of the National Theatre in London and, also in 2006, was ranked number twelve in the *Independent on Sunday's* 'Pink List' of the most influential gay men and women. He also courted much controversy in 2007 when he called veteran London theatre critics 'dead white men' for their misogynistic treatment of plays directed by women. Jennifer and her feminist friends from The Hill would have cheered him on for that. Hytner makes very few films – *The Object Of My Affection* was the third of only six he has ever made.

Hytner handled the comedic possibilities of gay relationships with a deft touch, avoiding the use of gay stereotypes. 'There are no limp wrists and no slit wrists,' said Hytner. Barbra Streisand songs are also missing. The film was based on a play by Pulitzer Prize winner Wendy Wasserman who said that she had the real experience that some of her best friends and men that she had loved most in her life had been gay.

Jennifer played Nina, a New York social worker who offers a spare room in her apartment to George, played by future *Friends* star Paul Rudd, and then falls in love with him. He returns Nina's love in every way except sexually. He also supports her when she becomes pregnant by her Neanderthal boyfriend. *The Object Of My Affection* is an intelligent film which starts out Doris Day and ends up Woody Allen.

While filming, Jennifer also had to fulfil publicity duties for *Picture Perfect* which was released in August 1997. On one occasion she was interviewed at her rented apartment by a writer from *TV Guide*. Halfway through Tate came in having taken Enzo for a walk. The ensuing snapshot of their life together more than anything else summed up where their future problems might lie: Jennifer is the centre of attention while Tate does not really know what to do with himself; he goes into the kitchen and comes back to announce there's no water, he puts a CD in the music centre and it turns out to be the *Hercules* soundtrack. Jennifer buries her head in her hands when the interviewer asks how they are different and he volunteers, 'She's a lot wealthier than I am'.

During that interview they were both asked if they would be moving in together when they returned to Los Angeles. Tate started to say, 'Yes' but Jennifer interrupted with a firm 'No'. That may or may not have been a desire to keep that personal information to herself. Somehow they managed to get out of sync. The easy psychology is that they wanted different things in their lives at a crucial time. (Popular opinion identified that as the root cause of her subsequent split with Brad Pitt.) Perhaps one was a precursor of the other. In an interview in July 1997, Jennifer, then twenty-eight, was asked, as ever, about children:

Jennifer was the perfect foil for two of Hollywood's most popular and funniest men – Jim Carrey in *Bruce Almighty* (*above*; 2003) and Ben Stiller in *Along Came Polly* (*below*; 2004).

A little matter of a broken toe was not going to stop Jennifer smiling when she arrived at the People's Choice Awards in Pasadena in January 2003, where she was named favourite female.

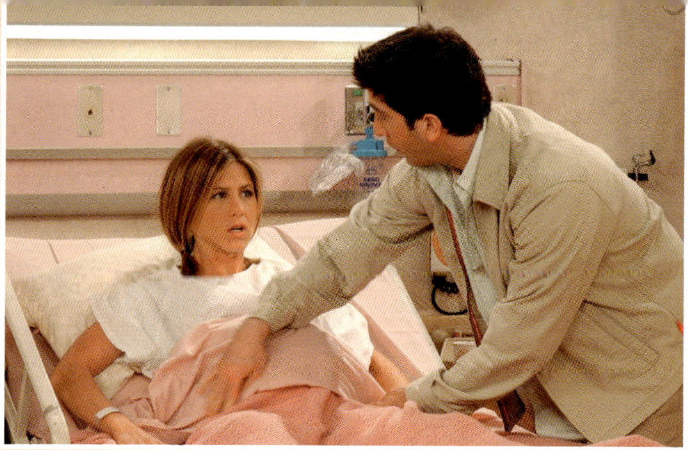

100% Aniston – Rachel gives Ross her 'you cannot be serious look' as she prepares to give birth.

What a swell time they had: one of the final shots of the six 'Friends' together in February 2004.

Even though she's in the lion's den – the media room – Jennifer can't help grinning with pleasure when she wins the Golden Globe Award in 2003.

At least Brad Pitt hasn't changed, just the beautiful woman on his arm in Beverly Hills. With Jennifer in March 2000; seven years later Angelina Jolie has taken her place at his side.

Friends forever: the women who helped her through the bad times. With Andrea Bendewald at a breast cancer charity show (*left*), clowning Kathy Najimy (*centre*) and co-star Courteney Cox (*right*).

Her on-screen chemistry with Vince Vaughn won them a Teen Choice Award.

Her father's daughter: John Aniston posing proudly with Jennifer at the première party for *The Break Up* in Los Angeles, May 2006.

Her off-screen chemistry with Vince made them the centre of attention at the French Open Tennis Championships in Paris, June 2006.

Post Brad, Jennifer is constantly surrounded by protection and paparazzi: leaving a Paris hotel.

Trying not to look bothered when cornered on a Manhattan street in May 2006.

Arriving in Los Angeles after visiting Vince in London.

Rumor Has It (*above*; 2005), with Kevin Costner as her romantic interest, was not Jennifer's finest hour, but *Friends With Money* (*below*; 2006), in which she dressed up as a French maid, was a return to form.

The secret of Jennifer's appeal: even when dressed like a Hollywood superstar, she always looks completely natural.

Jennifer is proud to be godmother to Coco, daughter of Courteney Cox and David Arquette, here walking on Malibu Beach in May 2007.

I'll be there for you: Jennifer Aniston and Courteney Cox.

Jennifer today – walking on the beach in Malibu with Dolly, her white German Shepherd puppy, while her faithful old dog, Norman, a Welsh corgi cross, trots along behind.

The ultimate Jennifer Aniston picture: her beautiful eyes reveal a hint of vulnerability.

'I've always said I'd like about three. I love everything about them. I want to be a young mom too. I'm not ready now but in a couple of years.' The response is illuminating for future reference.

Within a relatively short time things were not so good, although neither blamed living together under one roof in New York. They appeared together in a short comedy film to support their friend Grant Heslov in his writing and directorial debut, *Waiting For Woody* (1998). The Woody in question was Woody Allen and the plot revolved around an unlucky actor securing an appointment with the great man. Woody does not actually appear but Jennifer played herself, as did George Clooney. The film was well received and won three awards including Best Short Film at the New York International Independent Film and Video Festival.

Jennifer's relationship with Tate was already unsteady when, a short time later in early 1998, he appeared as a guest star in several episodes of the fourth season of *Friends*. For this fourth year of playing Rachel, Jennifer was earning $100,000 an episode so that after the twenty-three-episode run she had banked $2.3 million. The season had begun with Ross and Rachel breaking up again when she wants him to admit that the original split was entirely his fault. Ross has a new girlfriend for the season, a British girl called Emily played by Helen Baxendale, a role originally turned down by Patsy Kensit. During the previous season Rachel had moved on from her job at Central Perk to Bloomingdales. Emily is her boss's niece and Rachel inadvertently brings her and Ross together.

Tate plays a well-to-do customer called Joshua who Rachel has a crush on, starts dating and then eventually frightens off by moving too fast and asking him to marry her, although she is just reacting to the news that Ross and Emily are getting married after just six weeks together.

One of the most ironic segments in the whole ten seasons occurs in Season Four, in 'The One With Rachel's Crush' – Number 86. Ross and Joey compile a list of actors that have met on a film and then got together afterwards. They think of Susan Sarandon and Tim Robbins (*Bull Durham*, 1988) and Kim Basinger and Alec Baldwin (*The Marrying Man*, 1991). If that episode were written today the most famous by far, much to Jennifer's chagrin, would be her future husband Brad Pitt and Angelina Jolie (*Mr and Mrs Smith*, 2005).

Phoebe probably has the best storyline during the fourth season, acting as a surrogate mother for her brother and ending up expecting triplets. Unlike Jennifer in *The Object Of My Affection*, Lisa Kudrow was actually pregnant in real life. Her son Julian was born on the same day the final episode of the season was broadcast, 7 May 1998. Lisa, initially, was the most critically acclaimed of the *Friends* stars. She was nominated for an Emmy in 1994 and 1996 as Outstanding Supporting Actress in a Comedy Series before winning the award in 1998. Jennifer, by contrast, was relatively unheralded and yet to be nominated for any prestigious award. Perhaps they could not see past her hair after all. Quietly, however, she emerged as the most three-dimensional character, a tribute to her restrained acting.

As Rachel, Jennifer's storyline with Ross again provided the cliffhanger for the fourth season finale which took place in London during a much publicized trip to the UK by the cast of *Friends*. Ross and Emily are getting married when Rachel slips unnoticed into the church. During the vows, Ross accidentally says Rachel's name instead of Emily's.

By this time any prospect of a wedding between Jennifer and Tate Donovan was finished. She had moved on. They had worked together twice more before their final split, first in a television episode of *Hercules* which transferred from the big screen for two seasons with Tate reprising his role as the voice of the hero. Jennifer was the guest voice as Galatea, Hercules' dream date in the episode of the same name, ironically as that was not exactly the case when it was broadcast in November 1998.

More curious was their appearance in the cast of a film that is arguably the biggest failure of Jennifer's career. Not surprisingly it is glossed over when her work to date is appraised. The offending movie was called *The Thin Pink Line* (1998) which had one ingredient that one might have thought guaranteed more than a straight-to-video result. Both Ross and Rachel were in it. At the height of their *Friends* fame, both Jennifer and David Schwimmer were in a movie together. The mere fact that this important event for fans has been buried suggests the film did not fulfil expectations. The clue is in the title – a gay parody of the multi-award-winning quasi-documentary *The Thin Blue Line* which examined the conviction of a prison inmate on death row.

The Thin Pink Line is a film about the making of the making of a documentary about a prisoner on death row, a tortuous idea. The condemned man is flamboyantly gay which is supposed to be the cue for a number of the film's jokes. It must have seemed like a good idea in the pub. The cast list of cameos reads like an ensemble that Woody Allen or Robert Altman would have been pleased to put together. Jennifer, David and Tate were joined by Mike Myers, Will Ferrell, Jason Priestley and Janeane Garofalo (another bad move on her part) and Illeana Douglas who had been Jennifer's best friend in *Picture Perfect*. Even Jennifer's real best friend Andrea Bendewald had a role. Nobody formed a line, pink or any other colour, for this venture because it failed to get a theatre distribution although it was released in Japan in 2000. *The Thin Pink Line* was soon forgotten when Jennifer pressed on with starring roles.

Tate and Jennifer's split was made even more painful by being drawn out like a bad toothache. They no longer had enough in common to make it work. Tate suggested that they had different personalities: 'She likes top-notch hotels and luxury, and I like bed and breakfasts and riding my bike. That's the most shallow version of it but it's indicative of our personalities.' The communication, which she had said was the cornerstone of their relationship, was breaking down. Jennifer never confirmed Tate's version of the principal reason for their split. They finally acceded to the inevitable in the spring of 1998, going their separate ways after two and a half years together. Tate's father J. Timothy Donovan graciously commented, 'Sons don't always tell their parents why they broke up. Jennifer and Tate are both nice people, but nice people don't always get married and live happily ever after.'

Jennifer denied very strongly that the breakdown in their relationship had anything to do with a clash over marriage and babies. Five years later she would have to repeat those rebuttals.

As was the case with Daniel McDonald, several years passed before Tate finally tasted the success he craved. He also found fulfilment on Broadway appearing with the formidable Judi Dench in *Amy's View*, a play by David Hare, which had transferred to New York from the National Theatre in London. Dame Judi won a Tony Award for her performance. Tate was not so lauded but was voted one of the ten sexiest stars on Broadway in 1999.

His small-screen break came at last in the hit series *The OC* in which he had a recurring role as Jimmy Cooper, father of Marissa Cooper played by Mischa Barton. After years of trying to make it as a leading man he finally became a recognizable face playing a dad. He was forty and the popular Mischa was seventeen. Tate was happily surprised, fearing that *The OC* would be just another pilot doomed to failure after twenty years of similar endeavours. His luck continued to change with a substantial role in the Oscar-nominated drama *Good Night and Good Luck* (2005), written by his old pals George Clooney and Grant Heslov. He is also the star of a film titled *Neal Cassidy*, about the legendary, larger-than-life roadmate of Jack Kerouac. The upturn in his career coincided with a more stable romantic situation. He had dated, among others, actresses Lauren Graham and Whitney Allen as well as socialite author Plum Sykes. He met Lauren when he appeared at a theatre festival in Williamstown, Massachusetts, the hometown of Matthew Perry. Coincidentally, stage actress Whitney Allen is from Evanston, Illinois, where David Schwimmer went to college at Northwestern University. Tate finally settled down, at the age of forty-two, with a virtually unknown actress, Corinne Kingsbury. They married in Malibu in November 2005. Her only film to date is a minor role in *Old School* (2003), starring Vince Vaughn.

Splitting up with Tate coincided with Jennifer's health being at a low ebb. She generally felt unwell, had no energy and was not her usual happy self – in other words classic symptoms of emotional upset. For a while Tate Donovan had been the real deal and Jennifer was allowed to take their break-up badly. She was broken-hearted. She did not say so at the time but later hinted that he had grown progressively more resentful of her success and had been stuck in a 'you're there and I'm not mentality'. Perhaps he foresaw a lifetime of taking Enzo for walks in the park while Jennifer held court before an endless gaggle of photographers and interviewers. She also said, 'It's not my fault that I'm a star and he isn't. If I could switch places with him I would.' The impression with Tate and Jennifer is that they missed their moment but as Jennifer observed honestly about herself, 'I am not a spokesperson on relationships'.

She was much more candid about her break-up with Tate than she would be in the future about Brad Pitt. It always seems to be part of her personality, however, to talk something through from every conceivable angle. During one interview at a hotel in Beverly Hills she confided, 'He said he wasn't going to marry me because he didn't want to be Mr Aniston for the rest of his life. I told him that was a stupid reason. It was him I loved, not his career.'

Poignantly Jennifer also said, 'It was a very difficult time for me because I so desperately wanted to have children, a subject Tate was never enthusiastic about.' Perhaps she needed to date a much more successful actor.

Part Three

A Soap Opera

When GQ *magazine named Jennifer 'Woman of the Year' in 2005, the accompanying article began with this quote about her and Brad Pitt:*

'Look. I'm not defined by this relationship. I wasn't when I was in it and I don't want to be in the aftermath of it. And that's really important to me. Let's let everybody move on and live their lives, and hopefully everybody will be really happy.'

EIGHTEEN

In The Footsteps Of Jennifer

It had to happen. I'm sitting in Swingers restaurant in Santa Monica when my devastatingly pretty waitress announces, 'Actually, I'm an actress.' Sadly, Swingers is not as wild as it sounds but a popular LA-based chain presenting bistro and burgers served by young waiters and waitresses, glowing with good health and California sunshine. 'How's it going?' I enquire, as she whizzes off to get my Heineken. 'Good,' she lies. I seem to remember Jennifer did an advertisement for Heineken which kept on being shown on TV during football, as if she would be the least bit interested in the game Americans call soccer. I wonder if the young, ambitious Jennifer ever told a world-weary Englishman that, actually, she was an actress. I bet she did.

Just along the coast from Santa Monica is Malibu where, in recent years, Jennifer has spent her summer weekends in a rented seafront villa next to David Geffen's mansion. You can access the beach down a narrow passageway next to his house. Apparently Geffen tried to make the whole beach private and keep prying eyes and long lenses well away, but the local residents objected. As a result, I can walk out straight towards the sea and stand around looking a bit stupid. This area is called Carbon Beach and it's lovely, with sandpipers darting busily about as the surf hits the shore. I can just imagine how relaxing it must be for Jennifer to walk along the shore throwing sticks for the dogs. The only problem is, of course, that post-Brad she doesn't do that. Her minder or bodyguard is the dog-walker. It would have been nice to have met Norman, her beloved Welsh corgi cross. Norman is a great name for a dog. He was an actor dog who Jennifer found through the animal trainers on *Friends*, the same people who provided the show with the duck, the chick and the unforgettable monkey. Apparently he was so lazy that he gathered a bad reputation and was not getting any work. Norman sounds great. These days Jennifer also has a beautiful white German shepherd called Dolly.

Half a mile along the beach, Courteney Cox and David Arquette have a house. They also live in Beverly Hills, just down the street from where Jennifer has bought her new home. I am told it would cost about $30,000 a month to rent a house next to the ocean in Malibu. Jennifer can afford it. She made – give or take – $35 million in 2002 when she topped the *Forbes Celebrity 100* list. It's an odd list based on money earned and magazine covers. Does making the cover of *Vanity Fair* equate to a million dollars? *Forbes* calls it a combination of earnings and sizzle.

The big issue for Jennifer is privacy and the way the paparazzi abuse it. She has a team tracking her 24/7. It must be truly ghastly; to have more money than you ever dreamed of and all you can do is close the curtains and spend your days inside a luxury prison. The moment you step outside in an old T-shirt and headscarf to take Norman to the vet, your picture is taken and ends up all over the news-stands. It's a Catch-22 situation because by staying out of sight, the bounty on a picture goes up.

Jennifer is increasing the price on her head, but what can she do? How do you become less famous?

On the freeway back into LA there used to be an enormous poster advertising the movie *Mr and Mrs Smith* starring Angelina Jolie and Brad Pitt. I wouldn't have blamed Jennifer for finding another route back into the city. At least she isn't still rattling around the huge house on Ridgewood she shared with Brad. It can't have been a very happy home, and neither of them stuck around to live there after they split, selling it on to Ellen DeGeneres and Portia de Rossi for close to $25 million.

Michael Jackson used to live a few doors down at one time and Danny DeVito lives next door. He got on well with Brad and Jen and would pop in for dinner or a hand of poker from time to time. 'Hey Brad, Danny's here.' Well, it is Hollywood. I loved that episode of *Friends* when DeVito played a fat, old stripper called Roy – 'The One Where The Stripper Cries' – and had to strip in front of an audience of millions.

The Anniston–Pitt mansion is beyond huge – some 28,000 square feet. Brad loved the challenge of the grand design. I was chatting to someone who knows him who told me that, after children, architecture is his great passion. He loves the history, studying and absorbing other people's ideas. If he had to answer the fanzine question of what he would have liked to have been if not an actor, I am sure he would have said architect. I wonder if he married the wrong 'Friend'; – Courteney Cox studied architecture and spends her free time doing up houses. On second thoughts, they are both very strong characters and would have spent the whole time arguing about the shape of the pool.

Brad did a lot of work on the house including putting in an

English-style pub and a turret from where he and Jennifer could stretch out, look up and gaze at the stars. All that money, time and effort; and the grand plans they must have had. How can two people live in a place like this, behind massive brown wrought-iron security gates with CCTV cameras scanning any cars that go by? It would be even worse if your partner was away a lot, filming in some far-flung location. I would be happier in the old place in Blue Jay Way and I am sure Jennifer was as well.

I decide to go and talk to a photographer about Jennifer – not one of the 24/7 hired guns but a proper California-based British photographer. He tells me, 'The problem is she is surrounded by a bunch of sycophants. They take it on themselves to protect her, causing a scene and a big fuss. People in LA worship the stars so even passers-by interfere if they think a star is being harassed. If she goes out to a restaurant in Malibu, she will call for a police escort.'

Times have changed quickly for Jennifer. When she and Brad were together they never seemed to bother with all that malarkey and would just slip out together for a quiet dinner at one of their favourite restaurants. I am told they particularly liked a couple of places in West Hollywood where it was ok for diners sitting outside on the terrace to light up a joint between courses. I have no idea if Brad and Jen liked to do that but I can think of a few actors who would.

Jennifer's life seems to have changed so much since her break-up with Brad. She is a much bigger target for the paparazzi now than she ever was as one half of the golden couple. I try to imagine calling the police in West London and asking for a Panda car to escort me to the Taj Mahal or the Mandarin Garden.

I am with friends and we join a line queuing to get into a trendy bar in Venice. It's December and the temperature has dropped considerably from the daytime. We aren't moving and the crowd is getting restless. Jennifer would have got the cops to drop her round the back. A young woman comes up: 'Excuse me, Sir. Is this the line for the bar?' I am not sure I like being singled out and called sir in a line of fifty people hopping up and down to keep warm but I tell her it is. This seems to get the conversations going generally and the guy next to me tells me it's a really good place. 'Mean burgers,' says another. When I mention what I'm doing in town I get the impression everyone is a bit bored with Jennifer and Brad, and now Jennifer and Vince. She is in danger of being defined, in the eyes of the public, by the men in her life. 'She never does anything,' says the burger connoisseur. Someone suggests she should appear in a British reality show – then we would all be sick of her or, as Chandler Bing might say, 'Could we BE any more sick of her!'

Next morning I turn on the TV and it's official: 'Jen and Vince have broken up.' Vince has apparently been seen partying with strippers in Budapest. Vince doesn't seem to mind photographers as much as Jennifer or Brad. He used to wander around Malibu when he was staying at the beach house. I suppose it's all a matter of degrees. Britney Spears, in the long ago past, used to be ok about having her picture taken, but look at her now. She ends up beating a car like Basil Fawlty. It's going to get to you in the end. Some stars have a built-in radar for photographers. Cameron Diaz always seems to be able to hide her face with a hand or a hat or just gives the finger. When Jennifer is snapped, she likes to smile because she hates seeing pictures of herself with a scowl on her face.

This morning I am driving out past Long Beach to meet Michael Baroni, a company lawyer who dated Jennifer back in her New York days. This is not a leisurely drive through Beverly Hills or a rally exercise around the hairpins of Laurel Canyon. This is the freeway – a dirty, slow, desert of a drive, an hour to do twenty miles. Michael is charming and polite with a genuine affection and respect for Jennifer and those New York days. He takes me to a local Italian restaurant and over some fantastic lasagne tells me how wonderful the Californian lifestyle is and how the sun keeps a smile on your face. I have to say the drive back to Santa Monica was more agreeable.

Jennifer has talked in the past of becoming bi-coastal and dividing her time between New York and Los Angeles – she still regards herself as a New Yorker. I think it all depends on memories. In the end I suppose the home she loved in Blue Jay Way had too many memories as well, even though she and Brad were happy there. Her new home in Beverly Hills cost a cool $15 million. I won't go up and take a look in case she's home. I can't very well sympathize with her lack of privacy and then loiter outside her front door. I am told it has six bedrooms and seven bathrooms which seems a little excessive unless you like sleeping in the tub. Perhaps Norman has his own bathroom. It's a one-storey property. So, it's a bungalow. $15 million dollars for a bungalow.

NINETEEN

Brad

Jennifer's answerphone had an important message. It was from Brad Pitt suggesting he drop by with some coffee and help her pack for a trip to London to film the Season Four finale ('The One With Ross's Wedding'), parts one and two. Brad Pitt! The message was typical of Brad's easygoing approach to life. He and Jennifer had yet to go on a date but he was already offering skinny latte.

The popular story goes that they were set up by their managers on a blind date, a perfect way to start a fairy-tale romance. The alternative version is that Brad fancied Jennifer and asked his people to discover discreetly if she might like to have dinner. He favoured a low-key getting-to-know-you approach – his first date with Gwyneth Paltrow had been dinner at an Italian restaurant. Jennifer, it was ascertained, was agreeable to something similar. The next step, as protocol dictates, is for the gentleman, Pitt, to call the lady, Aniston. That's when he left the message. Endearingly Jennifer was seized by nerves. She may have been Jennifer Aniston but this was *the* Brad Pitt. She later confided to Oprah Winfrey, 'I was so nervous I never called him back. When

I got back from England we had a date.' You can do this in Hollywood when you are very famous – my people will call your people and we'll take it from there. Jennifer also told Oprah, 'I fell in love on our first date.'

Ironically when Jennifer was in London she had to spend much of her time answering questions from the British media about Tate Donovan, mostly denying they were engaged. A jaundiced press might have been forgiven for thinking that her denials were confirmation of an engagement but that was not at all the case and, in reality, Tate was already history.

Presumably Jennifer and Brad did not spend too long over dinner discussing their past relationships. Jennifer's dating history might have been worthy of a main course but Brad's needed a twelve-course banquet. Jennifer might also have noticed that she was almost unique in that she had never co-starred with Brad. He was notorious for dating actresses he worked with and that fact alone might have set some alarm bells ringing. Or perhaps not. He was Brad Pitt and he had beautiful, smouldering blue eyes.

The Brad on-set conquests reputedly included, in chronological order, teenage beauty queen Shalane McCall, who he met on *Dallas* when she played Jenna Wade's daughter Charlie and he played Randy, her older boyfriend; then there was Robin Givens, before she married Mike Tyson; they appeared together in a sitcom called *Head Of The Class*. Next came horror queen Jill Schoelen who he met in the forgettable movie *Cutting Class* (1989); they were rumoured to be briefly engaged. He also proposed to the precocious Juliette Lewis who was seventeen when they co-starred in a TV movie called *Too Young To Die* (1990). Three years later they co-starred again in *Kalifornia*

(1993) in which Pitt played a serial killer by the name of Early Grayce. The Amazonian Geena Davis, six feet tall in her stockinged feet and one inch taller than Brad, was the star of *Thelma and Louise* (1991) in which Pitt first made his name. In the film she falls for his good looks, especially in his boxer shorts, and this attraction continued briefly off screen. The lovely Thandie Newton acted alongside Pitt in *Interview With A Vampire: The Vampire Chronicles* (1994) and she, as well as the beautiful English actress Julia Ormond with whom he starred in *Legends Of The Fall* (1994), was said to have briefly dallied with Brad.

His most famous pre-Jennifer romance, however, was with Gwyneth Paltrow, a mere five feet nine and a half inches tall. For a while they were Hollywood's golden couple after they met filming the scary thriller *Se7en* (1995) and Gwyneth is proof that Jennifer was not the first person left devastated by Pitt. Some or all of these actresses may have succumbed to his charm, but clearly no leading lady was safe from Brad's charms and, anyway, few would want to be.

Brad, born in December 1963, is a touch more than five years older than Jennifer. He was from the town of Shawnee, Oklahoma, but was brought up in Springfield, Missouri, where his family still live. *The Simpsons*, of course, is set in the fictional town of Springfield but which state that's in remains a mystery. He was raised a Southern Baptist although Missouri is more of a midwestern or central state. Bradley is his second name. His real first name is William, after his father who worked as a manager in a transport business. (Jennifer liked to call Brad 'Willie'.) He dropped out of college where he was studying journalism to try his luck in California. It was quite spontaneous and the sort of behaviour one might expect from the hero in a road movie. He was twenty-two, had a couple of hundred bucks in his pocket and was at the wheel of his trusty Datsun, known affectionately as Runaround Sue, the title of a great early-sixties number one by Dion. Brad explained his sudden move: 'In my head I was done with college. I was on to the next thing.'

He had done just a little acting, certainly not the intensive study that Jennifer had put in by the same age. Surprisingly, considering the heart-throb status he would later achieve, he had done practically no modelling either, a campus calendar being the extent of his camera work.

In those carefree days Brad really lived a drop-out life, sleeping on floors and taking any dead-end job that came along, including dressing as a chicken to advertise a restaurant aptly named El Pollo Loco. The superstar of the future had to stand on the corner of Sunset Boulevard in scorching heat to try and entice customers in. He also drove strippers, sold cigarettes and delivered fridges. During that time he met up with the lesbian singer Melissa Etheridge and slept on her couch. Theirs would become a great and enduring friendship. His first acting job was as an uncredited extra in *Less Than Zero*, a small-budget adaptation of the Bret Easton Ellis novel. He wore a pink and white striped tank top, cool sunglasses and stood around in a doorway. His fee was $38.

Like many before him, Los Angeles inspired Brad to try and break through as an actor. He had the looks but none of the skills and *Less Than Zero* was as low as he wanted to get. He started taking lessons with the well respected, avant-garde drama coach Ray London, who had taught, among others, Sharon Stone, Forest Whitaker and Geena Davis. London advocated the approach that actors should utilize their current feelings rather than try and create an emotion from a bank of memories. He died in 1993, aged fifty, from AIDS-related causes. Later in 2005, Brad would show his appreciation of his former teacher in a special tribute to him. He has also been a long-time supporter of research into AIDS.

In the eighties, however, Brad was scratching around in *Dallas* and a variety of TV episodes but getting nowhere. The slasher movie *Cutting Class* was his *Leprechaun*, and eventually he was third choice for a small role in *Thelma and Louise*. His brief on-screen appearance as hitchhiker Adonis, J.D., who gives Thelma her first orgasm, was all it took to propel him to instant stardom after four years of trying. Brad used to joke that he had given Thelma a $6,000 orgasm, the amount his character stole from her purse.

Jennifer fleetingly met Brad socially in 1994 at Guy's, a bar on Beverly Boulevard. She thought he was a 'sweet guy from Missouri', but neither was free to pursue a friendship. That was the year he was named 'Sexiest Man Alive' by *People* magazine, just one in a succession of similar nominations and awards over the years. He still receives this type of accolade well into his forties. By the time Jennifer met Brad again, he was transformed from a pin-up, a persona he profoundly disliked, to an award-winning and Oscar-nominated actor. These days you can seemingly win an award for being able to tie your bootlaces but Brad had been noticed for two of the most prestigious: he won a Golden Globe for Best Supporting Actor for his performance as a mental patient in Terry Gilliam's sci-fi thriller *Twelve Monkeys* (1995), and he was nominated for the Oscar but lost out to Kevin Spacey, who won for *The Usual Suspects* (1995), although he, more fairly, should have been in the Best Actor category.

The MTV Movie Awards encapsulate the appeal of Brad Pitt and why he has risen to the top in a crowded market place. In 1994 he won two awards for his role in *Interview With A Vampire: The Vampire Chronicles*. He won Best Male Performance and Most Desirable Male. He almost did the double again the following year but only won in the most desirable category for *Twelve Monkeys*. Exceptionally good-looking men and women are everywhere in Hollywood but Brad Pitt is also a fine actor who can shine in the right role. In that respect he is similar to Jennifer. Being loved by the camera is not enough for longevity, especially as you grow older.

Thelma and Louise broke the magic $100 million box office barrier which guarantees a star's bankability. But, on screen for no more than fifteen minutes, Brad was not the star. Other films like *A River Runs Through It* (1992) and *Legends Of The Fall* (1994) did good but not great business. Anthony Hopkins who starred with him in the latter observed, 'Brad is very light-hearted and has a great sense of humour,' revealing just how easy it was to get along with him. *Kalifornia* performed poorly. *Interview With A Vampire* was successful, but was primarily a star vehicle for Tom Cruise. But everything changed with *Se7en* when Brad and Morgan Freeman played detectives hunting a serial killer in one of the best and grizzliest thrillers of the nineties. Again, he was only second choice for an important career role (this time it was turned down by Denzel Washington). The success of *Se7en* allowed his salary to increase from $4 million up to a reported $10 million for his next film, *Sleepers* (1996). Brad's work on *Se7en* deserved to be taken seriously but, while he was acting his socks off on set, he could not escape being 'Brad Pitt' – outside some 2,000 young girls would stay all day screaming and trying to catch a glimpse of their hero.

At this stage Brad had begun a relationship with Gwyneth Paltrow, the ethereal actress who played his wife in *Se7en*. They both claimed it was 'love at first sight', the same sentiment later echoed by Jennifer after her first date with Brad. Gwyneth rose from being a relatively unknown actress to a leading star. In the mid-nineties they were the king and queen of Hollywood. When he accepted his Golden Globe Award, Pitt thanked Paltrow calling her 'the love of my life, my angel'. They were one of the first celebrity couples of the modern era whose every move was chronicled for the readers of glossy magazines. Pitt even had to take legal action to prevent the publication of some risqué photographs of the two together.

Pitt proposed to Paltrow in Argentina in December 1996 while filming *Seven Years In Tibet* (1997). She took the trip to Springfield to meet his family, a journey Jennifer would make a couple of years later. 'Brad's the one good one and I got him,' said Gwyneth. She only had him for another six months before they abruptly broke off their engagement. No definitive explanation has ever been given which has led to many theories, but Paltrow was clearly and demonstrably upset. 'My heart sort of broke that day and it will never be the same,' she said. In the publicity maelstrom that surrounded the break-up between Jennifer and Brad, it is easy to forget that he had 'previous'. There has never been any suggestion of third-party involvement in the split between Brad and Gwyneth. Paltrow had seemed keen to have children but she also had a career which was about to move up a gear with her Oscar-winning role in *Shakespeare in Love*

(1998). By the end of 1997 she was dating her co-star in that film, Ben Affleck. She and Brad have kept their own counsel on the reasons for their break-up but the intense media scrutiny and speculation prompted him to build a wall around his private life. The problem with conducting a love affair in public and saying such gushing things about one another is that you look a bit silly when it's all over.

Brad and Jennifer shared a common bond: a belief that their acting abilities were seriously undervalued as a result of the pre-occupation with their looks. Jennifer remained distinctly unhappy about the coverage of her hair while Brad wanted the world to know there was more to him than being voted Sexiest Man Alive. In some respects he faced the same dilemma as Robert Redford two decades earlier – namely, how to be taken seriously with such movie-star looks. Perhaps it was no coincidence that Redford recognized there was more to Pitt than looks when he cast him in *A River Runs Through It*. For both actors their face had been their fortune as well as their albatross. Redford observed, 'He had an inner conflict that was very interesting to me.'

The first date went so well, it was quickly followed by a second. Jennifer told *Vanity Fair* that from then on they just 'huddled' in her little house, sitting on the couch, smoking, watching television and ordering steak and mashed potatoes. 'It was a little love nest,' she said. They used to order takeaway a lot because, as Jennifer freely admitted, she is better at thawing than cooking. As a result of finding each other such easy company, their love affair moved ahead rapidly. Jennifer's dog Norman loved Brad from the start which was reassuring. She observed, 'This was very much meant to be.' They were not, however, ready to declare their love to the world which may have had something to do with the fact that Tate was such a recent relationship, as well as reflecting Brad's growing antipathy towards press intrusion in the wake of the coverage of his break-up with Gwyneth.

The *Friends* episodes featuring 'boyfriend' Tate were not shown until April 1998, the same month their relationship was said to have ended. It had been late March when she filmed in London and came back to start dating Brad. There is no suggestion of an 'overlap' but rather like the Angelina Jolie–Brad Pitt situation a few years later, it was very tight. Neither Jennifer nor Brad seemed the least bit reluctant to plunge head first into another serious relationship after Tate and Gwyneth respectively. Jennifer later told *Vanity Fair*, 'Gwyneth is a lovely person but I didn't worry about their past relationship. Once this began, those previous relationships were done.'

In May, at the end of her commitments to the fourth season of *Friends*, Jennifer flew to Austin, Texas, to film *Office Space*, an offbeat comedy, as might have been expected from Mike Judge, creator of the animated shows *Beavis And Butthead* and *King Of The Hill*. Having 'starred' in *Picture Perfect* and *The Object Of My Affection*, Jennifer was now languishing down the cast in an undemanding role, playing a pretty waitress (once again). She observed, 'I play Joanna, a waitress at TGI Friday who's a stoner chick . . . It's a dark comedy, not romantic at all.' Within a couple of years, Jennifer would have to read in the press stories alleging that she was a stoner chick in real life. Brad followed her to Austin and the two of them were seen acting affectionately together at the Four Seasons Hotel. They maintained they were just friends but that was not true and Jennifer was thrilled to see him. As one eyewitness remarked, 'They looked very together.'

Office Space was a funny satire on the inanity of office life and the frustration engendered by the simplest of everyday things that govern ordinary jobs – the computer that takes an age to shut down, the malfunctioning photocopier that tells you there is a paper jam before you put the paper in. The film perhaps starts too well. In the opening scene, the leading character Peter Gibbons, played by Ron Livingstone, is stuck on the freeway, moving slower than a man walking on the sidewalk. Eventually the next lane speeds up so he switches lanes just as it slows down. The lane he has left then speeds up so he changes again and so on with predictable results: he ends up moving just a few feet.

Office Space boasts a piece of dialogue that brilliantly sums up the agony of soulless work. Peter tells his therapist, 'Since I started working, every single day of my life has been worse than the day before, so that every day you see me is the worst day of my life.' Unfortunately, Jennifer does not deliver any of the movie's best zingers although she does have one memorable line for women in general to remember. She tells Peter, who is in love with her, 'Why don't you call me when you grow up. Oh wait, you know what, that's probably not going to happen, so just don't call me, ok?' Jennifer could have used the line on a few men in real life. She is under-used as the waitress, Joanna, but does display her comedic skill by making as much as she can of a running gag about her uniform. Marjorie Baumgarten in the *Austin Chronicle* noted, 'Aniston is delightfully un*Friends*-like in her downplayed role as Peter's love interest.' The critic has inadvertently drawn attention to one of Jennifer's motivations in taking a role like Joanna. In films, she was moving progressively further away from Rachel Green. Within four years she would have firmly put Rachel in the bin and shut the lid when she made *The Good Girl*.

Jennifer's other motivation was that she had been introduced to the talents of Mike Judge by one of her best friends in Hollywood, Kathy Najimy, who had been one of the lead voices in *King Of The Hill* throughout its nine-year run. Kathy, a familiar face on television, was also one of the stars of the sitcom *Veronica's Closet* which was filmed at the studio next to *Friends*. Most days, she would join Jennifer and the girls for lunch. She is a self-confessed feminist and gay rights supporter who, like Courteney Cox, started a family later in life and was thirty-nine when her daughter was born.

Although a small movie, *Office Space* is never less than adroitly observed and built up a cult following. Who could fail to be impressed with a movie that names one of its office drudges 'Michael Bolton'? Judge turned down the opportunity to direct a sequel, but with Kathy's help he did persuade Jennifer a few years later to be the voice of Pepperoni Sue in an episode of *King Of The Hill* entitled 'Queasy Rider'. Jennifer had acquired a taste for voice-providing in 1999. She voiced the character of Mrs Stevens, the choir teacher, in an episode of the irreverent *South Park* entitled 'Rainforest Schmainforest'. More significantly she led the vocal cast of *The Iron Giant*, an animated feature film and, ironically, considering Jennifer was only a voice, probably the most critically acclaimed movie of her career to that date.

The movie was an adaptation of the Ted Hughes' bedtime story, *The Iron Man*, and featured a nine-year-old boy called Hogarth who befriends a one-hundred-foot robot – the Iron

Giant – who crashes to earth during fifties' America. Jennifer voiced his mother, waitress Annie Hughes. The film, which refreshingly was not a Disney release, worked beautifully on two levels. For children, mainly boys (for there are no princes in this story), it is an exciting adventure as Hogarth struggles to hide his new friend from the pursuing G-Men. For adults, it is a witty swipe at the 'reds under the bed' paranoia which beset the US during that period. Rob Blackwell of *SPLICEDwire* called it, 'A Norman Rockwell meets *War of the Worlds* story wrapped around simple, heartfelt themes.' He also thought it a 'visual masterpiece'.

The project was first pitched to Warner Brothers by Pete Townshend of The Who, and Des McAnuff who had directed the group's masterpiece *Tommy* on the London stage. Townshend had already released a concept album based on the book in 1989 and was disappointed when his original idea of an animated musical was dropped. The film's director, Brad Bird, a former artist on *The Simpsons*, explained, 'Pete was disappointed that the thing he wanted to make wasn't what I had in mind but he was very supportive of our film.' Bird's next feature would be the huge hit *The Incredibles* (2004), which grossed more than $261 million in the US alone, ten times more than *The Iron Giant*.

When Jennifer had finished her short stint in Austin, she and Brad headed east in June. They were seen together 'in public' for the first time when they attended the Tibetan Freedom Concerts at the RFK Stadium in Washington. Brad's role in the film *Seven Days In Tibet* had led to him being banned from China. They did not make any announcements or talk about each other but the mere fact that they were together at such a high profile event was enough for the whole world to know they were a couple. On the Saturday they watched REM and Radiohead from the VIP balcony, while on the Sunday they were seen being 'all cuddly backstage'. When questioned by the media, all Pitt would say was, 'I've no idea what to tell you'. Jennifer gave the impression that she wanted to shout her love for Brad from the rooftops but knew that she would be for the high jump if she did. Her caution over saying too much was illustrated when she told an interviewer that she was not 'withholding' but that she just wanted to 'preserve something that's mine'. She did tell *Rolling Stone*, 'This is the happiest time of my life. I'm not saying why, it's for a lot of reasons: work, love, family, just life – all of it.'

Brad and Jennifer were also together at Kathy Najimy's wedding before Jennifer had to report back for the fifth season of *Friends* for which her salary had now risen to $125,000 an episode. For once the Ross-and-Rachel saga was not the principle ongoing plot interest. While in London, Monica and Chandler had slept together and the season followed the development of their relationship, in particular their efforts to keep it secret from the others. The writers wrung every yard of comic mileage out of that plot culminating fourteen episodes later in 'The One Where Everybody Finds Out' – Number 111. Courteney Cox, in particular, was delighted that Monica had a better storyline at last: 'I have a new love for the show since I've gotten into this relationship.' Phoebe, meanwhile, had given birth to triplets in the one hundredth episode, a landmark that would guarantee a lifetime of revenue from syndicated repeats. On set, they marked the occasion with a large, gaudy cake and David Crane said, 'Contrary to popular opinion it doesn't feel bad to hit one hundred'.

On screen, Phoebe marked the occasion with one of the greatest lines when Ross tells her everything is going to be all right: 'That's easy for you to say. I don't see three kids coming out of your vagina.'

Jennifer accompanied Brad to New York in November 1998 for the première of his new film in which he played Death. The three-hour-long, hugely expensive *Meet Joe Black* never remotely looked like recouping its $90-million budget. Once again they stayed together at a hotel called The Four Seasons, this time on the Upper East Side just a few blocks from the Steiner School. Brad, however, walked the red carpet alone while Jennifer was escorted in through a back door. Afterwards, the press were not invited to the première party at the Metropolitan Club so that Brad and Jennifer could be relaxed in each other's company without having to worry about eavesdroppers.

They had been dating for little more than six months but Jennifer's life was starting to change irrevocably with the realization that fame confined and restricted behaviour rather than opening up a brave new world. Individually, Brad and Jennifer were hugely famous but together they were instant royalty, Hollywood's version of Charles and Diana. Jennifer was the sweet girl who had bagged a prince. From the very beginning, of course, public perception was confused. Mark Frith, editor of *heat* magazine explained, 'It wasn't Jennifer who pulled Brad. It was Rachel who pulled Brad and I think it gave hope to every girl sitting on the sofa watching *Friends* that they could pull the local pin-up.'

TWENTY

Turning Thirty

Brad passed the scrutiny test. He was given an excellent approval rating by the old gang as a prospective boyfriend for Jennifer which was something that was still very important for her. She wanted her close friends to like her boyfriend. She told *Rolling Stone* that her friends were all supportive, adding gushingly, 'especially when they found out what a loving human being Brad is.' More realistically, she added, 'At first they're like, "I hope he's not an asshole, some conceited fuck or whatever." But you get past that in five minutes.'

Kathy Najimy recalled that they knew immediately that he was the one. She was impressed that Jennifer was able to be one hundred per cent Jennifer when she was with Brad, not changing herself for him. Kathy said, 'That's all I really wish for my friends.' This viewpoint is interesting because it reflects the general desire for female empowerment among Jennifer and her friends – why should women compromise their lives for men? Kathy also observed, 'I saw how much he loved her. I went home and was weepy about it.'

Jennifer celebrated her thirtieth birthday on 11 February

1999. One of those television programmes charting a life's progression would have been interesting at this point. At ten, Jennifer was adjusting to life without her father in a rough neighbourhood on the Upper West Side. At twenty, she had no job, no boyfriend and was debating whether to leave New York for Los Angeles. At thirty, she was a multi-millionairess, one of the most popular stars in the world and the girlfriend of a man to die for. The man in question was determined to make her thirtieth birthday a memorable one. A week before the big day he threw a party for 500 of her 'closest' friends at the fashionable Barfly restaurant on Sunset Boulevard. For her actual birthday he and Jennifer chartered a private jet to fly nine of her real closest friends down to Acapulco in Mexico. This was the height of luxury and not one of those old Hill trips. They were there for Valentine's Day and went out for a romantic dinner and danced into the wee small hours. Romance does not get any better.

By the time they returned to California, Brad and Jennifer were engaged. They have tended to be confusing about the exact time they became engaged. In 2001, Jennifer said they decided to get married five months after they started dating which would suggest Brad asked her before she returned to the *Friends* set the previous September. Brad, however, said they were engaged for eighteen months before they married which would place the date in early 1999. The more romantic version would have Brad popping the question as fireworks lit the skies of Acapulco on Valentine's Day. The less inspiring would have been following an episode of *EastEnders* – which they both loved – at the house on Blue Jay Way. Either way, they successfully kept the news a complete secret, something precious just for them.

In the world of fairy tales and rom-coms, marriage is the

embodiment of happy ever after. Jennifer, however, had never seemed set on marriage as a life target. It did not feature as a particular ambition. She explained, 'I didn't have a fantasy of what marriage would be like. I had no idea.' Her desire was perhaps more for a partner, a best friend or a buddy to share her life with, someone with whom she was totally in tune. If that included marriage, then fine. Looking back on when Brad asked her to marry him, she recalled, 'I went "Oh ok. Well that makes sense, yeah."' Perhaps keeping the engagement a secret, an intimacy shared with just each other, was what made it particularly special.

While they were away a young, aspiring actress faced trespassing charges, having broken into Brad's home in Los Feliz – an unwelcome by-product of fame.

She was discovered by a caretaker, allegedly wearing Brad's clothes including a blue hat, green sweatshirt, black tracksuit trousers and shoes – hopefully not a red-carpet ensemble. Police found her carrying a book on witchcraft, a note to Pitt and a large safety pin decorated with ribbons. She was placed on probation for three years and ordered to take psychiatric counselling.

If Brad had an unwelcome stalker then Jennifer had an even more troublesome incident. A 'stalkerazzi', as a particularly unpleasant form of paparazzi are nicknamed, scaled her neighbour's eight-foot-high wall and took pictures with a telephoto lens of Jennifer relaxing in her garden. She was sunbathing topless. When the offending pictures showed up in magazines in both the US and Italy, an outraged Jennifer embarked on a four-year crusade for legal redress.

More happily, Jennifer had a season of *Friends* to finish.

Rachel, still a twentysomething, was not doing quite as well as Jennifer. She did have a new job at Ralph Lauren although her love life was in need of perking up and nothing much was happening with Ross – until they went to Vegas for the season finale. In the closing scene Rachel and Ross emerge drunkenly from the doors of a wedding chapel, newly married. Rachel had beaten Jennifer to the altar.

Brad was already popular on the *Friends* set at Burbank. An insider explained, 'Everybody wanted to hang out with Brad.' Compared to Brad's easygoing charm, Arquette was an acquired taste. Brad would drift down to the set in the afternoon and hang out with the boys, playing video games and talking cars. By contrast, even Courteney Cox conceded that David Arquette could be off the wall, the type of guy, she said, who 'liked to put a trench coat on and run through the set and flash people'. Fortunately, she added that he was wearing underwear at the time. Cox, who has acknowledged she was a commitment-phobe, spent the season planning her wedding.

When the season ended Brad and Jennifer travelled to Europe for a holiday, not bike riding in Provence or visiting ancestral haunts. Instead they visited the Alhambra Palace in Grenada, Spain, where they reportedly booked their hotel room under the pseudonym Mr and Mrs Ross Vegas.

They were back in California by 12 June 1999, for Courteney and David's wedding at the historic Grace Cathedral on Nob Hill, San Francisco. It was three days before the bride's thirty-sixth birthday. They exchanged rings inscribed with the words 'A deal's a deal'. As a couple they were undoubtedly more wacky than Brad and Jennifer. Their wedding invitations showed them dressed for Halloween in mock homage to *Scream*, the movie where they met. Together they just clicked. Courteney said, 'I can't just be with someone because it's great sex – because orgasms don't last long enough.'

Quietly, during that summer Jennifer helped out at a Rape Treatment Centre in Santa Monica. She did not make a big deal of it: 'It's too easy to call out all these charities you're part of. So many people want to stand up for something, but it can be dangerous. We have a voice, but you have to educate yourself first. Truthfully, I would do it all if I could but I've just been finding things I'm moved by.' Kathy Najimy observed, 'She's always been very supportive of me and my activism. Whether it's AIDS things or choice issues, you name it, she's done it.'

In September, as the millions of *Friends* fans wondered if Ross and Rachel would stay married for the sixth season, Brad and Jennifer stepped out together as an official couple for the first time. For most of the year they had spent their time as far away from the cameras as possible but now they happily posed for photographs on the red carpet at the Emmy Awards at the Shrine Auditorium. The appearance of the hottest couple in show business diverted attention away from yet another disappointing night for *Friends* which again failed to win Best Comedy Series, losing out, as ever, to *Frasier*. Brad, tanned and fit, sported a little goatee beard and blond streaks in his hair. He looked remarkably like one of the incarnations of David Beckham. He was still in good shape from all the training he had done for the controversial film *Fight Club* (1999) which he had filmed in LA and which, it just so happened, was due to be released in a couple of weeks. Jennifer revealed a hairstyle light years away from the sleeky smooth Rachel. She was also blonde, full of braids and more than a little unkempt – the Worzel Gummidge shag. That style was history, however, when she was on Brad's arm at the *Fight Club* première in the first week of October. From being absolutely nowhere, suddenly Brad and Jennifer were everywhere.

The strange events at a Sting concert in New York on a cool night in November 1999 further undermined their pursuit of secrecy. Sting was playing the last of five consecutive nights at the Beacon Theatre on the Upper West Side, a neighbourhood full of old haunts and memories for Jennifer. The former Police singer had recently begun his *Brand New Day* World Tour promoting his album of the same name which would win a Grammy award the following year.

Sting was launching into a new song called 'Fill Her Up' when Jennifer suddenly appeared on stage. Nobody even knew she could sing. The lyrics caught the attention of all Brad and Jennifer watchers because the song tells the story of a couple going to Vegas to be married. One line actually referred to the 'real diamond' she was wearing. Later down the chorus is the advice to 'fill her up with babies' and 'be her loving husband'.

With twenty/twenty hindsight the song was not the best choice for Jennifer and Brad. 'Fill Her Up', a sort of country-gospel song, is not one of the familiar, timeless classics like 'Every Breath You Take' or 'Roxanne' – Jennifer must have practised hard. The 'spontaneous' moment was then capped off by Brad Pitt strolling on stage, affectionately putting his arm around Jennifer and holding up her ring finger to the wildly applauding audience. The ring finger was certainly sporting a sparkly new ring. Afterwards, representatives played down the significance suggesting it *was* a ring but not an engagement ring. Nobody was fooled, especially when Jennifer let slip that it was all true at the after-show party at the Shark Bar. The speculation that they might be getting married had been going for at least a year. *People* magazine even reported that Jennifer had been shopping for her wedding dress. Now, it could move on to the details: when and where.

Jennifer has always been a sociable and gregarious woman, a trait her friends have confirmed, from teenage times right through her twenties. The constraints of fame have tended to suppress this, so, ironically, her 'Hey, people, look at me I'm marrying Brad Pitt. He's hot,' type of behaviour was probably far more the real Jennifer Aniston. She was clearly very much in love and chuffed to bits.

Now that everyone knew it was all true and Brad and Jennifer were set to be crowned the new king and queen of Hollywood, attention could return to Burbank and the sixth season of *Friends*. Jennifer may have been engaged to Brad but would Rachel stay married to Ross? The short answer was no and they decided to seek an immediate annulment in 'The One After Vegas' – Number 122. This is the episode which acknowledges that Courteney Cox is now Courteney Cox Arquette by having everyone add David's name to their own for the closing credits – Jennifer becomes Jennifer Aniston Arquette and so on. The episode ends with a dedication, 'For Courteney and David who did get married'. One of the high spots of the season was the three guest appearances by Bruce Willis, playing the father of a student Ross starts dating. He takes a shine to Rachel and they, too, start dating. Willis had become friendly with Matthew Perry when they co-starred in the comedy *The Whole Nine Yards* (2000) and had agreed to donate his fee for playing Paul Stevens to charity after he lost a bet to him on set. He did, however, win an Emmy for 'Outstanding Guest Actor in a Comedy Series'.

Nothing, it seemed could make 1999 anything other than a special year. One major problem in Jennifer's life, however, became considerably worse – her relationship with her mother Nancy. After their earth-shattering bust-up in 1996, things appeared to have mellowed a little although there had been no reconciliation, even when Johnny became a father and Jennifer an aunt in 1998. Her attitude to Nancy, perhaps influenced by her own happiness at this point, had softened sufficiently for her to tell *Rolling Stone* magazine that her mother was 'warm, loving, nurturing, wise, funny and old fashioned'. She also expressed a desire to tell her mother to lighten up sometimes and just hang out. That certainly did not sound like a daughter who had decided to cut her mother out of her life for ever. But, at this stage, she had not read *From Mother And Daughter To Friends*.

Some journalists jumped to the conclusion that Nancy was 'cashing in' on her daughter's fame. The ghastly title alone certainly pointed to that. *Vanity Fair* called it 'appallingly self-serving'. Commercially the book would have been viable only if it contained as many personal memories of Jennifer, one of the biggest stars in the world, as possible. The book, however, is not really about Jennifer at all. It is a 278-page therapy session for a woman who has had a troubled and unhappy time. Nancy also appears to offer an excuse or explanation for the events which first caused a rift between them in 1996 when she appeared on a tabloid television show and was, she claims, duped into talking about Jennifer. If she thought that Jennifer would read her book, understand what happened and extend an olive branch then she was completely mistaken. Divulging Jennifer's tears and private moments of vulnerability was never going to tempt her daughter to pick up the telephone.

Jennifer was engaged to one of the most famous men in the world but her mother had yet to meet him. An interesting side effect of this rift was that it provoked an argument between Jennifer and Brad. Unlike his bride-to-be he came from a stable background and the family unit was something he valued highly. A friend confided, 'Brad is totally family orientated. He didn't like the fact that she didn't talk to her mother. They had big fights about it.'.

By contrast, Brad's family welcomed Jennifer. His mother Jane, in particular, became a close friend of her prospective daughter-in-law when Jennifer joined them for a family Christmas in Springfield in December 1998.

At least Jennifer was able to introduce Brad to her father. The two men – both actors – got on well and John would join them for dinner out. He said, 'We just walk in some place and it's not a big deal.' John, it was amicably agreed, would have the honour of giving Jennifer away at her summer wedding.

Rachel and Ross, for once, were not the focus of attention for the finale of *Friends* in May 2000. The two-part episode 'The One With The Proposal', Part 1 and 2, centred on the romance between Chandler and Monica and the circumstances of their decision to marry. The scenes were moving and funny with Courteney Cox bringing the same sense of vulnerability to Monica that Jennifer brings to her comedy. She told David Wild, 'I loved the episode where I asked Chandler to marry me. I hadn't had the chance on this show to play a dramatic, comedic moment quite like that before.'

While Jennifer was fully occupied in planning her wedding she still found the time to quietly and with no fuss visit the troubled Robert Downey Jr in prison. The talented Downey Jr had been having a rough time in jail since he had been sentenced to three years for probation violation relating to a 1996 drug charge. He had been beaten up and choked by inmates unimpressed by his star status. His close friend and former agent Jerry Goldstein had asked around Hollywood to try and find someone to cheer him up. According to Goldstein only Jennifer responded even though she was not a personal friend.

After her two-hour visit, Downey Jr told Goldstein, 'Jennifer was there for me when other so-called friends turned their backs. Thanks to her I have hope, a way out. Before, there was none. I'd even thought of doing myself a favour by ending it all.' The emotive words were endorsed by Goldstein: 'He's like a frightened rabbit. Overtures were made to several Hollywood stars to go to see him. Only Jennifer did and it's just about saved his life.' The shifting sands of fame and stardom were never better illustrated than by contrasting Downey's circumstances with those of the wedding of the year just two months later.

Jennifer Aniston married Brad Pitt on a glorious summer's day on 29 July 2000, in Malibu. It was the first superstar wedding of the new millennium. Part of the Pacific Coast Highway was closed, the skies above the Malibu cliffs were declared a no-fly zone to prevent photographers buzzing the ceremony, and security guards brandishing machine guns menacingly patrolled the perimeter. This was a fairy-tale wedding for the twenty-first century.

For the venue, Brad and Jennifer chose the grounds of the luxurious estate belonging to *Roseanne* producer Marcy Carsey.

It was a perfect choice. More than 50,000 blooms turned the setting into a floral paradise. Brad apparently wanted the venue to resemble a Zen garden while Jennifer requested lots of candles and lanterns. Jennifer finds a spiritual quality in candles and in the calmness a flickering flame can bring to any environment. Her house on Blue Jay Way was full of candles and her 'chosen family' would light candles when they bonded in the woods of Laurel Canyon. The effect was beautiful. A canopied bridal walkway hid Jennifer in her moment of joyful anticipation as she lightly clasped her father's arm.

Jennifer admitted to being edgy the day before: 'I had those typical jitters, but on the day I was just excited in a good way.'

The wedding was of the top-secret variety. Everybody knew it was about to happen but even the guests had to await a telephone call to tell them when and where. It was like an episode of *Mission Impossible*. Having accepted their mission for 29 July, 200 guests congregated at Malibu High School before being shuttled to the wedding venue five miles away. It was reported in the press, though cannot be substantiated, that all the staff had to sign a document that made the Official Secrets Act seem like a parking ticket. They were warned not to speak to the press or they could be liable to pay a huge $100,000 fine.

The evening ceremony, timed so that nobody would keel over from the heat of the day, began with Jennifer walking down the aisle to the song '(Love Is) The Greatest Thing'. She wore a dress by a then little-known Milan-based American designer, Lawrence Steele. Of course, he was not little-known after he designed Jennifer Aniston's $52,000 wedding dress – a backless, long white silk tulle halter dress encrusted with tiny pearls. Her circular veil was topped off by a tiara interlaced with pearls and

Swarovski crystals. Fashion reports said that Jennifer wanted a pretty but sexy look. She wore a pair of four-inch-high Manolo Blahnik ivory suede sandals with tiny ankle straps. Brad looked every inch the matinée idol in a Hedi Slimane dinner jacket, although he spoiled the Clark Gable effect a little by wearing a conventional tie instead of a more smooth bow tie. He had joined Jennifer the day before to have matching blonde highlights done, although on the day her hair was specially styled by Chris McMillan. *Friends* make-up artist Robin Siegel was also on hand to help with what Jennifer called a team effort.

The two bridesmaids, Andrea and Kristin, fussed over their dearest friend. They also wore Lawrence Steele – pale green silk chiffon tunics over white silk slips. The flower girls wore cream silk. Brad's brother, Doug, was his best man and amused everyone by dropping the ring, although he claimed it was actually his father who dropped the ring during the pre-vow relay. Brad had helped design the rings. They were both white-gold bands embedded with diamonds. Jennifer's was inscribed 'Brad 2000' and his, 'Jen 2000'. Despite her nervousness, Jennifer showed she had lost none of her comic timing by fluffing her lines and then declaring that she was sorry but she had never done this before. The couple wrote their own vows. Brad promised to 'split the difference on the thermostat' while Jennifer said she would continue to make his favourite banana milkshake.

The whole occasion was rumoured to have cost $1 million although these figures are usually plucked from thin air. It was, however, an extravagant occasion with a forty-strong gospel choir singing before the ceremony, a six-tier wedding cake and a thirteen-minute firework display being just some of the highlights. A Greek bouzouki band gave the reception a boisterous flavour and the singer Melissa Etheridge, an old friend of both Brad's and Jennifer's, gave a rousing rendition of 'Whole Lotta Love' by Led Zeppelin. Matthew Perry described the night as the most romantic of his life, and Brad was moved to tell Jay Leno in a later interview on *The Tonight Show* that it was an amazing night. He also revealed that at the eleventh hour the paparazzi had vanished, leaving the ceremony remarkably free of upset and ill feeling. He recalled, 'When the ceremony started the press backed off and I really have to thank them. They were so cool with us. They let us have our moment. They let us have what turned out to be the highlight of my life.'

All the *Friends* cast were there, except for Matt LeBlanc who was filming abroad, as well as other co-stars from their acting past including Cameron Diaz, Edward Norton and his then girlfriend Salma Hayek. Old friend Kathy Najimy was also among the two hundred or so guests. Jennifer's mother Nancy was not one of them. Nobody had known for sure the depth of feeling that had led to mother and daughter becoming estranged but here was the proof. Superficially it seemed harsh that hatchets could not be buried for one day but Jennifer had decided that having Nancy there would ruin it. Ironically, her father John, who had deserted the family when she was nine, gave Jennifer away, while her mother, who lived half an hour away in a modest apartment in Toluca Lake was not sitting in the front row, nervously craning her neck to see her daughter walk down the aisle with her still-handsome dad.

Jennifer was very upset about the course of events that resulted in her mother not being at her wedding. Not only had Nancy not been invited to the big day, she had never actually met Brad Pitt. Nancy wrote a whole book revealing her hurt and anguish. Jennifer is as revealing in just one paragraph in *Vanity Fair*. She said that although it broke her heart because of her mother's own childhood and dreams of family life, Nancy 'didn't know where she ended and I began'. In Jennifer's eyes, Nancy was trying to live her own life through her daughter's.

TWENTY-ONE

Post-Nuptial Depression

Something strange happened to Jennifer Aniston during the year after she married Brad on that wonderful evening in Malibu. She was not filled with great joy at her new status as Mrs Brad Pitt, Queen of all Hollywood. She did all the things a newly married woman might want to do like ordering stationery and cards emblazoned with her new name, Jennifer Pitt. She expressed her delight when she was sitting in her dentist's surgery waiting to have a wisdom tooth extracted and the nurse opened the door and politely enquired, 'Mrs Pitt?' And yet, when a television reporter asked a banal question about married life, she responded, 'There's a new feeling now that you're married and it's just better. You have just got your bud there with you for ever.' She may have been taken unawares but describing the 'world's sexiest man' as your 'bud' seemed low-key and flat.

Nine months after the wedding, Jennifer gave a soul-searching interview to Leslie Bennetts for *Vanity Fair* in which she described her turmoil: 'This has been the hardest part of my life, as well as the best year of my life. The period after the wedding was extremely intense, for a lot of reasons.' Jennifer revealed that she faced a Pandora's box of doubts, insecurities, fears and mistrust. Married life, it would appear, was not the fun-packed voyage one might have expected for someone blessed with all the superficial trappings of wealth and happiness. Surely Rachel Green would have been turning handsprings at becoming Rachel Green Pitt? Incredibly, Jennifer revealed that she was so disturbed after the wedding that she chopped of her hair which, thanks to the Rachel, had become a symbol of the empty and trivial world of stardom and celebrity. 'I hate it,' she cried, adding, 'I did it mainly to relieve me of the bondage of self.'

The article is a fascinating deconstruction of a troubled woman who perhaps internalizes far too much for her own good, reflecting the penchant for self-analysis so prevalent in modern American society. Reading between the lines it's easy to play amateur psychiatrist and identify the chief areas of Jennifer's inner struggle. First and foremost was the relationship with her mother and the trauma engendered by not inviting her to the wedding. When she spoke of it her eyes filled with tears. Then there was the as yet unsuccessful search for a marital home, the responsibility of being a role model, the curse of being judged on your looks and your weight, and the prospect of starting a family. She also still seemed to be dwelling on her parents' divorce which did not sound that healthy when you were only just married.

Jennifer seemed all over the place in the interview, forever firing out words like 'shame', 'low self-esteem', 'bullshit' and 'mess'. The impression was of someone going through a process who, one hoped, was on her way out to the other side. Ordinary folk crowding into sweaty train carriages every day to jobs they hate might suggest that this was a multi-millionaire superstar needing to get a grip. But that view does not make Jennifer's torment any less real. Unintentionally, however, her friend Kristin Hahn, while seeking to praise Jennifer, put her privileged world into perspective: 'She [Jennifer] gets excited by a flower in her back yard. Most people let the gardener take care of that stuff.'

Jennifer herself mentioned a new initiative she had begun on the Internet to help 'empower' and 'encourage' young girls. The idea, originating from a friend, was to give the kind of advice to teenage girls that Jennifer herself had been denied growing up. Jennifer was hosting her own session called Jen XX on *voxxy.com* – 'where a new generation of girls speak out'. Melissa Etheridge was also involved. Girls could actually go online and receive advice from Jennifer Aniston. The mantra she promoted was 'just be happy with who you are', advice she herself continually struggled to follow. Jennifer's social concerns always appear focused more on the individual rather than the wider global issues. She receives an enormous amount of satisfaction from helping just one person, as in the case of Robert Downey Jr. Her husband may have embraced a wider picture, the whole jigsaw, but Jennifer was more concerned with finding one piece.

Professionally, Jennifer Aniston Pitt had begun married life on the crest of a wave. The *Friends* contract had been up for renegotiation for the first time in five years and the last collective had stood their ground and bartered a deal whereby each of them would receive $750,000 an episode. Jennifer's salary for making twenty-four episodes in the seventh season would be $18 million. The gang were already doing well but this took them up several divisions in the pay league.

Jennifer chose to find time to make a new film. Her own personal troubles might have been improved if Brad had played the lead role in the film *Rock Star* as he originally intended to do when it was called *Metal God*. Jennifer was not attached to the project at the time but joined later when Mark Wahlberg had been cast in the lead. He had nearly achieved rock-star status when, as rapper Marky Mark, he had a few hits before concentrating on his acting career in which he was much more successful. Wahlberg played a Xerox machine repairer who fronts a tribute band until he is recruited to become the singer with the actual band. Jennifer played his girlfriend/manager who he eventually dumps on the road to success. As a teenager Jennifer had fancied herself as a rock chick and this was the closest she was ever going to get. Set in 1985, the screenplay was partly based on the true story of Ripper Owens who fronted a Judas Priest tribute band before being chosen to take over from original member, Rob Halford. 'I liked the story because it was a fun period of the eighties,' she explained, revealing that she still had a pair of leather trousers in her wardrobe from that era.

Jennifer found she could identify with her character in terms of being someone who stood outside the main action: 'Pretty much I was an observer.' She asked Brad for advice about how to play her role and he told her, 'Be Sting,' in the way that Sting was cool and sexy without even having to try. Jennifer said, 'I remember thinking, "Be Sting, huh? All right. Yeah. I'll try it."'

She also shrugged off criticism that she was again choosing a supporting role, rather than the lead role a star of her stature could command, by pointing out that she had not been offered a major role that appealed to her. And, anyway, 'It's too much responsibility,' she laughed.

George Clooney was an executive producer on the film. He was also very gracious about Jennifer's abilities as an actress, in particular the way she could transform a scene: 'Whenever you're in trouble, you throw it to Jennifer and she makes the lines sing.' Clooney is the best possible proof that a television star can 'break out' and make it as a movie star. He is box-office gold and critically acclaimed. He acted in one of the great sitcoms, playing the factory boss Booker Brookes in *Roseanne*, and Jennifer was greatly impressed by Clooney's ability to hold down his breakthrough role in *ER* while making the film *Batman and Robin* (1997) at the same time. 'I don't know how he did it,' she said.

In the *Los Angeles Times*, Kenneth Turan summed up *Rock Star* as, 'classic Hollywood comfort food intent on delivering well-worn homilies about the pitfalls of fame, the attractions of a normal life, and how being yourself is just the most important rule.' Even though her role as Emily did not jump out as an Aniston character, he was not alone in praising Jennifer's 'convincing' performance. Perhaps the highlight of the film was Rachel Hunter, ex-wife of Rod Stewart, playing a drummer's girlfriend and advising Jennifer on the legal rights of an oft-spurned spouse. Jennifer's ironically bad eighties' haircut ran it a close second.

The highlight for Jennifer herself, was that she had got to see plenty of her brother Johnny. He was working as a production assistant on the film. The one disappointment, however, came when a proposed cameo by Steven Tyler, her all-time favourite from Aerosmith, fell through. She and Brad used to have a running joke that, if the opportunity presented itself, she could have a love freebie with Steven.

All this took place while Jennifer was coping with her chronic introspection without Brad. In a taste of what was to be their marital dilemma he had gone on location for three months, filming the thriller *Spy Game* (2001) in Morocco, London and Budapest. They did their best to ease the burden of absence which Brad had described prophetically as the 'beast'. For the most part though, Jennifer and Brad had to be content with communication via webcam which was marginally better than nothing. Jennifer flew to both England and Hungary during breaks in *Friends* but, while better than nothing, a luxury hotel was no substitute for a snuggly evening at home on the sofa. Jennifer had developed a fear of flying over the years so it was no small deal for her to jet backwards and forwards across the Atlantic. She even tried hypnotism to help alleviate the growing phobia.

Brad flew home to Los Angeles for Christmas but was away again on 18 January 2001, so Jennifer gamely flew the family flag alone at the LA première of his film *Snatch* (2000), a geezer heist movie directed by Guy Ritchie, who had become a member of Brad's new circle of close friends. Brad had approached Ritchie and asked for a part in the film because he had been so impressed with the director's *Lock, Stock and Two Smoking Barrels* (1998). His efforts at a decent Ray Winstone-style London accent did not go well and so he ended up playing an Irish boxer, a traveller called Mickey. Jennifer must have been as mystified as everybody else by her husband's totally incomprehensible accent.

A week after Brad left, the couple had to face the first reports of a much discussed topic – that they were a 'stoner' couple who were overfond of smoking dope. A 'concerned friend' was quoted in the US tabloid, *The Star*, as saying that they had told pals their idea of a perfect night was getting high together at home. There was also unsubstantiated talk that they were high when they met President Clinton. Brad has never commented on alleged drug use but Jennifer has been refreshingly candid. She told *Your Life*,

'I enjoy it once in a while. There's nothing wrong with it. Everything in moderation. I wouldn't call myself a pot head.'

The following month *Friends* reached a milestone. In 'The One Where They All Turn Thirty' – Number 160 – Rachel struggles to adjust to her thirtieth birthday while the other five characters recall their own feelings that landmark. Creeping middle age might ultimately spell the end for the quintessentially twentysomething comedy. Lisa Kudrow was already thirty-seven when the episode was aired, Courteney Cox was thirty-six, and Jennifer herself was just three days off her thirty-second birthday. Three days after that was Valentine's Day. Brad was still away and Jennifer was facing an ordinary day at the studio. When she walked into her dressing room, however, there were more than a thousand red and pink roses. On the wall, red rose petals spelled out the words, 'I Love My Wife'. She loved the romantic gesture.

Rachel and Monica spent much of the series sorting out plans for Monica and Chandler's wedding which was another case of art imitating life. To make matters even more confusing Andrea Bendewald, who had been Jennifer's matron of honour, turned up as a guest star in 'The One With The Cheap Wedding Dress' – Number 163 – in which she played a girl called Megan who battles with Monica for the same bridal dress. They literally fight for it. Andrea, keeping in the marriage mood, had become engaged to actor Mitch Rouse just a week before she got the part. They had met on the set of a short-lived comedy series, *The Secret Lives Of Men* in which he starred. While Rachel helped Monica with wedding arrangements, in real life Jennifer was looking at wedding dresses with her best friend. She would be maid of honour at two weddings, one fictional, one real.

Jennifer's most talked-about scene in the series, however, was nothing to do with weddings. Instead the full-on kiss she gives guest star Winona Ryder garnered the most attention. Jennifer was an old hand at acting out lesbian snogging. In 'The One With Rachel's Big Kiss' – Number 166 – the elfin Winona played an old college friend of Rachel's who pretends not to remember that they had once made out while drunk. Rachel has to kiss her again to jog her memory which was quite titillating material for primetime Thursday nights. Winona was reportedly complimentary about Jennifer: 'When I saw the episode, all you see is hair and you don't see lips. I was kind of bummed out because we got a couple of chances to do some pretty nice kisses. She's a very good kisser.'

Jennifer's lesbian kiss generated enormous publicity for the seventh season of *Friends* which needed a boost, having been overtaken in the ratings by the reality show *Survivor*. It was also about the only good thing that happened to Winona Ryder that year. Winona is a consummate actress, who impressed the *Friends* cast as much as any other guest star, but she could give Jennifer a run for her money in wrestling with internal demons. Winona, however, will always be best known for her shoplifting arrest in December 2001, at Saks Fifth Avenue on Wilshire Boulevard in Los Angeles. At the time of her arrest she was found to be carrying a potpourri of painkilling drugs – Demerol, Endocet, Vicodin and Vicoprofen.

Ironically Winona was reinforcing the pitfalls of celebrity that had so plagued Matthew Perry. He again had been suffering badly throughout the seventh season of *Friends*, culminating in another spell in rehab. He had been treading the familiar path of working on a movie while making the TV show. Perry was in Dallas shooting a comedy, *Servicing Sarah*, with Elizabeth Hurley when he complained of severe stomach pains and was advised to go into rehab immediately. His father, John Bennett Perry, and a private specialist checked him into the Daniel Freeman Hospital in Marina Del Rey where he began detox. *US Weekly* described his situation as 'serious, potentially life-threatening'. His condition was not helped by a compulsive predilection for vodka. The magazine reported that sources blamed a demanding schedule which kept him half the week in Los Angeles and the other half in Dallas: 'He was taking certain medications that made him drowsy, and then someone gave him speed to get him through his work. He was really trying, poor guy, but he didn't have a chance.'

Perry, himself, had appeared contrite the previous year when he said, 'You play, you pay,' after being hospitalized with pancreatitis, a screamingly painful stomach complaint which can be brought on by alcohol and drug excess.

For the most part Matthew has preferred not to give the public a blow by blow account of his problems. In September 2002, however, he was quoted in *People* magazine as saying he had at one stage downed an 'insane number of pills' as well as drinking 'probably a quart of vodka a day'. 'I've been through a very dark time,' he admitted.

Matthew was able to count on the support of his friends including Jennifer. The movie was shut down and at Burbank scenes not featuring Chandler Bing were filmed first to give him the chance to recover. Amusingly there would be stories suggesting that he was the father of Liz Hurley's child which, like many others concerning Matthew, turned out to be false. The father, however, did turn out to be someone called Bing in real life – millionaire film producer Steve Bing.

Shortly before Matthew went into rehab the *Friends* gang, including Marta Kauffman, David Crane and Kevin Bright, gathered in front of a cake to celebrate the 150th episode. The photograph of the occasion is revealing. A gaunt Matthew is sandwiched between Lisa and Jennifer. His arm is around Jennifer's waist and she is clutching his hand in a manner displaying genuine affection and reassurance. They may, as she once put it, have had 'brother-and-sister fights' but they also demonstrably shared a brother-and-sister bond.

When Brad flew back from Europe he was straight off to Las Vegas to start filming *Ocean's Eleven* (2001). George Clooney and Brad had become great friends and, instead of *Rock Star*, he had agreed to accompany him in remaking the famous Frank Sinatra heist movie. Jennifer would make the trip to join Brad on set when she could. George thought the couple very 'homely'. Clooney and Guy Ritchie were Brad's drinking pals, poker partners, two of the boys, the lads, the posse – just the guys whose company Brad enjoyed in much the same way as Jennifer had Courteney, Andrea and Kristin.

Season Seven of *Friends* ended in May 2001 with what had become a customary two-parter, this time 'The One With Monica And Chandler's Wedding'. The cliffhanger was that one of the gang was pregnant. Wrongly, it was thought to be Monica but, in fact, it was Rachel who had left the positive pregnancy test in Monica's bathroom. The storyline would put Ross and, in particular, Rachel back in the spotlight. It would also, perhaps inevitably, raise the question of whether in real life Brad and Jennifer were going to start a family. Here she was being provided with the ideal window of opportunity by the writers of *Friends*.

Even though *Friends* is fiction and
would have been very hard for Courten
been Monica who was pregnant. Befor
confirmed that she had suffered a miscar
have been the first for her and husband D
reports in the US suggested that she and Jen
to be pregnant at the same time. Fanciful
was very upset for her dear friend and s
thought it heartless to try for a baby at a time o
news. A miserable summer for Courteney was made wo
news that her father, Richard Cox, was suffering from can
and only had a short time to live. After his death, as a mark of respect, she once more called herself Courteney Cox, dropping the Arquette professionally.

One of the fascinating aspects of Jennifer's life at this time was that when she came through her troubled time, stronger, she produced the best work of her career, both in a film and in *Friends*. She had summed up her journey by telling *Vanity Fair*, 'I think I'm just starting to feel I can stop apologizing to myself, to my family, to my friends, to the world.' As a demonstration of that she accepted by far her most challenging role to date in the small, independent film *The Good Girl*. The director of *Rock Star*, Stephen Herek, offered the opinion that Jennifer could be the female romantic lead in just about any film. In *The Good Girl* she was certainly the lead but there was little romantic about what Jennifer called, 'a pretty dark little slice of life'. She was so surprised to be offered the role of Justine, a working-class Texas housewife trapped in a marriage to a pot-smoking couch potato, that she thought they had called the wrong person. Jennifer explained, 'She's fed up with her life and doesn't feel any passion more and tries to shake it up and get into some s.'

…ations included Jennifer's first naked love scenes, in … with the younger actor Jake Gyllenhaal which added …pice: Jennifer, at thirty-two, was the older woman. Her …cter Justine is a lost soul, working in a local supermarket …ere she meets the young, tortured college dropout with a drink …roblem played by Gyllenhaal and embarks on a torrid and tragic affair. Her husband's best friend discovers her secret and is soon blackmailing Justine into giving him sexual favours. And then she falls pregnant without knowing who the father is. Justine was definitely not Rachel Green.

Jennifer was typically thoughtful and methodical in preparing for the role of downtrodden Justine, perhaps aware that it was by far her biggest acting challenge to date. She drew on her own experience and observations of how easy it is not to achieve one's hopes and dreams in life and be stuck in a rut with no obvious means of changing things.

Jennifer was a little nervous about the sex scenes and Brad was able to reassure her and tell her not to worry about it. At least he did not tell her to 'Be Sting' – following the famous tantric sex enthusiast would have led to the steamy bits taking a week to finish. Jake Gyllenhaal, at twenty-one, was the new heart-throb on the block. He had dark, brooding looks in addition to being a clearly talented actor – as he would later prove in *Brokeback Mountain* (2005). He thought Jennifer brought an 'interesting compassion' to her role: 'You follow her character through this maze and you should hate her. But because of the charisma that Jennifer brings to it, you love her somehow.'

Casting Jennifer was the brainwave of the writer Mike White.

He said, 'Who wouldn't want to see America's Sweetheart get blackmailed for sex and try to institutionalize her boyfriend and cheat on her husband.' The director Michael Arteta agreed, sent her the script and received a call the very next day to go and see her at the house on Blue Jay Way. He told her he thought she would be perfect because of the work she had done in *Office Space*.

Arteta was particularly impressed with Jennifer's physical approach to her role, for which she adopted a Charlie Chaplin walk, with little steps and hunched-down shoulders, carrying the cares of the world just as the comedian's immortal character of the Little Tramp had done. He perceptively described the Aniston appeal as playing regular, approachable people while remaining glamorous. More than that, however, Jennifer could bring her emotional depth to the role, layers from within which she had been exploring through her post-wedding agitation, 'the bondage of self'.

Jennifer prepared for the most challenging role of her career by taking the advice of an acting coach and tying weights to her wrists and ankles to prevent her from using any 'Rachelisms', the cute comic gestures which worked so well in *Friends* but would be inappropriate for the downtrodden Justine. She also made sure her hair was scraped back in a most unflattering fashion – little chance of the Justine becoming a must-have style.

When she finished shooting *The Good Girl* in the summer of 2001 she had plenty of time to fret about what the critics would have to say when it was released the following year. She confided, 'I'm terrified for it to come out because it's different.'

In the meantime, Brad was back and they could concentrate on finding a suitable marital home. They had been married, a year and, during that time, home had been either a hotel suite or the house in Blue Jay Way. Although they had bought a $4-

million beachfront property in Santa Barbara the year they married they had never lived there. Eventually they settled on a house that used to belong to the great star of the thirties and forties, Fredric March, who had won Oscars for *Dr Jekyll and Mr Hyde* (1931) and the post-war classic *The Best Years Of Our Lives* (1946). March, whose real name was Ernie Bickel, was also a fine stage actor, one of the few to win two Tony awards. His house in Beverly Hills had been specially designed for him by Wallace Neff, the renowned Californian architect. Neff was held largely responsible for the homes of the great movie stars bringing a distinctive Spanish or Mediterranean flavour to the developing city. He designed Pickfair, the twenty-two room mansion of Douglas Fairbanks and Mary Pickford and, possibly, the most famous of all Beverly Hills homes. Jennifer's new house could not match Pickfair but Brad had grand designs for their 'family' home.

The March house, which spanned 10,000 square feet, had six bedrooms and cost the couple about $14 million. They began with a few minor alterations but plans spiralled into a two-year, $1-million project. They ended up having to bus building crews to the home so as not to clog up the cul-de-sac for other residents. Renovation and restoration would almost symbolically drag on for most of their married life. During that period, while making her next film *Bruce Almighty*, in which Jim Carrey's character is granted God's powers, Jennifer observed, 'If I was God for a week, I would have the house finished.'

TWENTY-TWO

A Good Year

Brad Pitt's comment on the joys of married life was that he enjoyed being able both to break wind and eat ice cream in bed. He would now have two years to sample those delights before leaving once again for an extended period of location work when he was filming the epic flop *Troy* (2004). During that time he and Jennifer could establish what seemed to be a strong foundation for a lasting marriage. They had yet to move into their family home, but life appeared to be sweet. Jennifer's friend Kathy Najimy observed, 'She's very affectionate with him. He makes her feel grounded and whole and smart. She makes him feel like Fred Astaire.' It was almost as if their married life was just beginning and Jennifer was now feeling better about things, especially as Brad was there to listen to any problems. In a television interview, he revealed, almost bashfully, 'With Jen and I, everything is on the table. We discuss everything.'

Brad finally agreed to appear as a guest star on *Friends*. The eighth season had begun with the dark despair of 9/11 hanging over America. Surely, Rachel's pregnancy would be the last thing anyone could be bothered about in the wake of such a cataclysmic event in the nation's history? Nobody would watch, would they? That, however, that would have been the wrong assumption; everybody wanted to escape into Central Perk. As Marta Kauffman explained in *Friends . . .'Til The End*, 'I think people wanted to laugh more than they wanted to see the awful images of the Towers coming down again. After a time people were ready to laugh, *needed* to laugh again.' She was entirely right and the episode starring Hollywood's royal couple together for the first – and only – time attracted some of the highest ratings the show had ever received and cemented a return to its number-one position.

Jennifer, who still thought of herself as a New Yorker, revealed that people were actually coming up to her in the street and thanking her for providing half an hour of escape from that awful reality. She agonized over how pointless and banal a sitcom seemed to be and wondered what she should be doing. The answer came in the very first episode of that season, 'The One After "I Do"' – Number 171 – when Rachel takes another test which confirms that she is pregnant. The audience laughed so hard they were almost crying: 'I realized people desperately needed that release.'

Brad appeared in 'The One With The Rumour' – Number 179 – in which he played Will (his real, first name), an old, formerly fat friend from high school who Monica invites round for Thanksgiving dinner, not realizing he hates Rachel for the way she treated him. He reveals in the show that he and Ross formed the 'I Hate Rachel Green Club'. The plot neatly exploits the fact that the audience all know that in real life Jennifer and Brad are married.

Brad was allowed to share his wife's dressing room where

one of their wedding photographs had pride of place. Usually he kept his visits to the set very low-key so as not to divert too much attention from the regular stars of the show. On this occasion he was the star and was suitably nervous, telling Jennifer that he knew he was going to blow his first line in front of a live studio audience. For a change, it was Jennifer's turn to reassure.

When it came to Brad's opening line, inevitably, he messed it up and had to do a retake. Having eventually cleared that hurdle, he proved to have an unrealized flair for comedy, so much so that his performance earned him an Emmy nomination for Outstanding Guest Actor in a Comedy. The other high point of the season was the acting tour de force from Rachel as she went through nine months of pregnancy, during which she learns that Joey has fallen in love with her while she and Ross, the father of her baby, remain resolutely apart. The ability of the general public to confuse fact and fiction continued with Jennifer being congratulated on her pregnancy by people she did not know. She made light of it: 'I got a lot of free desserts.'

Rachel gives birth to a baby girl called Emma in the end-of-season two-parter 'The One Where Rachel Has A Baby, Parts 1 and 2'. Jennifer cried when a real baby was put in her arms. She admitted, 'I'm an emotional person. My husband calls me a leaker.'

Jennifer Aniston's acting talents were finally recognized when she was nominated for an Emmy as Outstanding Leading Actress in a Comedy. She later recalled, 'It was a great honour but frankly it was more exciting to be married.' *Friends*, was nominated yet again as Best Comedy Series. Normally the show would expect to be beaten by *Frasier*, but that acclaimed comedy was surprisingly not nominated that year. Jennifer, it would seem, was on a roll: when *The Good Girl* was released in August 2002, the praise was almost unanimous. For once, Jennifer positively enjoyed talking about one of her films and was clearly proud of it. She told *Flare* magazine, 'It was a good sign for me that I was able to watch it through without cringing.'

The critics particularly enjoyed Jennifer's performance. *Village Voice* reviewer J. Hoberman noted, 'She holds her crinkly, eye-batting television-honed mannerisms in check – perhaps focusing her calculated sitcom presence on the care and maintenance of a flat, nasal delivery. *The Good Girl* is a small movie, but surrounded as it is by more extravagant hamming, the star's constricted performance gives it a particular pathos.' Duane Byrge in the *Hollywood Reporter* thought the film an 'absorbing, slice-of-depression life that touches nerves and rings true'. He also called Jennifer's performance 'smartly solid'.

Jennifer, while pleased at the positive reaction, summed up her frustration at needing to take a role that was such a radical departure before she was properly appreciated: 'Suddenly, they're like "Hey, she's really an actress," as if I was just some bullshit comedienne before.' Some even suggested she might be nominated for an Oscar, although that proved elusive. She was, however, named Actress of the Year at the Hollywood Film Festival in October 2002. Brad was visiting his family in Springfield so missed his wife's big speech in which she forgot to thank her castmates. 'I understand the whole crying thing now. I have stage fright unless I have something written for me to say. I couldn't speak. I'm a blithering idiot.' She was nominated for several other film awards but in the end won just one more, the Teen Choice Award for Best Movie Actress which was a reflection more of her popularity than of critical regard. Jennifer has won more of these awards – eleven to date, in one category or another – than any other female. She has some way to go, however, to match Justin Timberlake who has eighteen.

Ironically, the number-one box-office smash when *The Good Girl* was released was a rom-com, *My Big Fat Greek Wedding*, a film which might easily have cast a previous incarnation of Jennifer Aniston as the best friend. In some ways the praise for her performance in *The Good Girl* detracts from her worth as a comic actress. Although a naturally amusing companion she is not a comedienne and is acting full throttle in everything she does – whether it's *Friends* or *The Object Of My Affection*. At least her Emmy nomination was proof that a wider world was starting to appreciate the qualities her former drama teacher Anthony Abeson had recognized all those years earlier.

Brad and Jennifer may have been destined never to appear in a film together but, quietly, they had become involved in production, setting up their own company. Jennifer had already been encouraged by Kristin Hahn to become involved in projects away from the mainstream. Initially they called the company Bloc. Jennifer had played the word in Scrabble during one of the games nights she and Brad held every week. Checking the dictionary, they discovered the definition suited their ideas perfectly – a group of persons, parties or nations, united for common action or by a common interest. They joked that their company should be called Blocheads.

The best news was that Brad was home for the important things like her thirty-third birthday and Valentine's Day. Roses in her dressing room were lovely but a party at the sushi bar Katana on Sunset Boulevard was unbeatable, especially when Brad gave her a Harry Winston charm bracelet and toasted his wife: 'You're my best friend, my soulmate, the one I'll spend eternity with.' Interestingly, Brad was now echoing Jennifer's previous sentiments that they were buddies. She continued to maintain, 'You have to be friends, first and foremost.'

Originally they had planned to move in to their new house in March 2002 but that date was soon seen to be wishful thinking. Similarly the weekend retreat in Santa Barbara was still practically a construction site.

Jennifer's mood at this time was definitely a happier one than when she had suffered post-nuptial blues. She loved staying at home with Brad, spending their days at the house on Blue Jay Way, just hanging out, listening to Radiohead, reading scripts and books and learning lines. Jennifer also liked to hike in the hills or sometimes just sit smoking and watching the sunset. The overriding impression was that here was a couple who enjoyed the simple life.

They seemed happiest living a slightly hippy-esque existence, a cursory nod to their old lives – he as a college dropout and she as an out-of-work actress. While they set about gutting their new palace, they lived at Jennifer's house until it flooded and they had to move into another bolt-hole in the Hollywood Hills. Jennifer used it as a studio for painting and sculpture while Brad jammed with pals or worked on his designs for their home. Brad was keen for Jennifer to join in the jam sessions and so had given her a course of guitar lessons as a birthday present, but she was never going to be Eric Clapton. In the evening they would order takeaways – he would eat pizza and she would eat corn chips and salsa, providing neither was weight-watching that day – and watch a movie together or their favourite reality TV shows; Brad loved *Survivor*. Jennifer said, 'They are our guilty pleasure. We can't *not* watch.' At their weekly games nights they would invite friends over and play dominoes, charades or table tennis. Poker nights were taken a little more seriously. On Sundays the girls would come over. Jennifer observed in O, the Oprah magazine, 'We're so boring'.

Jennifer was on a diet most days or, more precisely, being careful about what she ate. She tended to favour a high-protein regime, having the same thing for lunch every day when filming *Friends* – a salad with garbanzo beans (chickpeas), turkey and a lemon dressing made with pecorino cheese.

Surprisingly, Jennifer seemed to enjoy more privacy as Mrs Pitt than she would later be allowed as the ex-Mrs Pitt, when everyone wanted to know how she was coping. She and Brad would take in restaurants like their favourite Italians, Il Sole and Orso, in West Hollywood. They also liked Japanese food. They were always very informal and enjoyed a good reputation for being unpretentious. A friend recalled, 'They used to eat out a lot. Nobody bothered them much.' They would also drive over to Malibu to spend the evening with Courteney Cox and David Arquette. Courteney recalled, 'We would just eat and talk and have glasses of wine and enjoy ourselves.' Every so often Jennifer would go on a girls' night with a mixture of her closest friends including Courteney, Kathy Najimy, Andrea, Kristin and Mandy Ingber, who taught her exercise and meditation. Sometimes Melissa Etheridge or Catherine Keener would join them. They originally had both been Brad's friends but had since adopted Jennifer. Keener had starred with Brad in the little-known *Johnny Suede* (1991) and she and her husband, actor Dermot Mulroney, had been regular guests at the Pitt home.

As major celebrities, currently the golden couple, Brad and

Jennifer were not intimidatory, pretending to be something they were not. Kristin Hahn described them as being 'very graceful' about their fame and position. Jake Gyllenhaal observed, 'Everyone's like, "They're so nice and perfect together". But who is the person who established that two very famous people who are a couple have to be jerks?'

The big question would be: was this amiable drifting companionship enough to sustain a marriage?

Brad had two preoccupations at this time – redesigning the house and growing a beard any hobo would be proud to have for the movie *The Fountain*, which, in the end he never made, with Hugh Jackman eventually playing the role earmarked for Brad. Jennifer maintained that she did not mind the beard when it had grown softer, although she was fast out of the blocks to help him shave it off.

Brad accompanied Jennifer to the Emmy Awards in September 2002. Thankfully he had shaved his mountain goat-beard by then and was sporting a fashionable goatee. Jennifer looked dazzling in light pink Dior. Surprisingly, Brad was pipped for his award by Anthony LaPaglia who had demonstrated one of the worst English accents of all time when he appeared as Daphne's brother, Simon Moon, in *Frasier*. Jennifer, however, won and, just a little emotionally, thanked her husband and *Friends*. Brad almost missed it all when he scooted off to the men's room during a commercial break. Next up came the moment *Friends* had waited eight years for – the programme won the Emmy for the first time. Everyone seemed to notice how close and affectionate Brad and Jennifer were at the after-show celebrations at the renowned Zucca restaurant in downtown Los Angeles.

Jennifer copied the Brad Pitt/George Clooney approach to movies by not attempting to follow *The Good Girl* with another worthy film but, instead, taking on a big budget, box-office cert. It was all about sustaining a career and not getting too pigeon-holed. For every *Babel* (2006) or *Syriana* (2005), there was *Ocean's Eleven* (2001), *Ocean's Twelve* (2004) or *Ocean's Thirteen* (2007). For one thing the blockbuster kept the salary up and enabled one to act in better movies for a fraction of that amount but with the possibility of winning an award. Clooney earned $20 million for *Ocean's Eleven* but worked on *Syriana* for just $350,000 and won the Oscar for supporting actor in it. Similarly Brad Pitt made at least that figure for *Ocean's Eleven* but won the Golden Globe for *Babel*, whose entire budget did not exceed his salary for the former film.

Jennifer co-starred with Jim Carrey in *Bruce Almighty* and for the first time broke through the $100-million box-office barrier. A Jim Carrey film, however, is all about the man himself and Jennifer had no illusions about who was the star of the movie. Up to that point practically everything he touched in movies had turned to solid gold. He was paid a reported $25 million for *Bruce Almighty*.

In the movie Carrey plays Bruce Nolan, a disgruntled television newsman in Buffalo, New York, who blames God for his failure to win a promotion. God, played by Morgan Freeman, is unimpressed and grants Bruce his powers to teach him the lesson that it is not as easy being God as one might imagine. Jennifer is Nolan's fiancée, Grace Connelly, a sweet and devoted kindergarten teacher, who he is worried about losing. One of his first acts as Bruce Almighty is to make Grace's breasts larger. The scene itself, schoolboy humour at its best, has Grace examining her pneumatic chest before declaring, 'It's weird. I woke up this morning and I swear my boobs look bigger. Do they look bigger to you?'

One scene that did not make the movie's final cut was when Jennifer's character is in a grocery store with her sister. Picking up a tabloid magazine she notes the fictitious actress on the cover and says, 'She's so talented but all they want to talk about is her hair,' a funny but not-too-subtle reference to Jennifer in real life.

Bruce Almighty, as Jennifer acknowledged, is a Jim Carrey vehicle and the enjoyment of the film ultimately rests on whether the audience likes his 'act' – neatly described by one critic as a toothy smile with a hint of the demonic. Jennifer once again displayed her skill of maintaining a presence while another actor is centre-stage. It harks back to those days at her New York drama class when she was able to lend support and not steal anyone's thunder. In the movie Carrey's character is told by his producer, 'There's nothing wrong with making people laugh,' a sentiment echoing the words of Anthony Abeson when Jennifer was in high school.

The film probably begins better than it ends, the early laughs being preferable to the slightly preachy last thirty minutes when the novelty of the idea has worn thin. Once again Jennifer was reviewed positively, described by Kevin Thomas in the *Los Angeles Times* as 'lovely and down to earth' – qualities which are in fact quite difficult to act. Owen Gleiberman in *Entertainment Weekly* observed, 'She has grown into a winsomely spunky and appealing movie star, with the ability to put her tenderest feelings right up on screen.' At last she was being described as a real movie star and not a *Friends* wannabe one. Roger Ebert in the *Chicago Sun-Times* affirmed that she really would have a movie career.

Jennifer's role in *Bruce Almighty* was never likely to win her any serious awards but she and Carrey were nominated for an MTV Award for best screen kiss. *Bruce Almighty* proved to be a phenomenon at the box office, reaching number one in the US and taking an estimated $562 million worldwide – then the highest-grossing comedy of all time. Some astute publicity helped. They could not use the stand-by of an on-screen romance between Carrey and Jennifer, so instead we were treated to the old 'cheat death' story in which Jim was a hero for pushing her out of the way of a toppling giant crane. Carrey, who thought Jennifer 'totally cool', topped a poll as the biggest money-making star of 2003. More interestingly from Jennifer's point of view, he once said he spent too long in interviews being 'really angry at my parents'.

Jennifer was filming *Bruce Almighty* at the same time as the ninth season of *Friends* was shooting. During the eighth there had been rumours that the show was coming to an end but this just seemed to be a salary-negotiation gambit when it was announced that the *Friends* gang of six would be receiving $1 million an episode. Nevertheless, Jennifer asserted that she was certain the ninth season would be the last. She was not alone. The whole cast thought the end was near. After the superb eighth season, which reached a crowning moment with the Emmy awards, the ninth proved an anti-climax. David Schwimmer echoed a general view that 'we were done'.

Jennifer spent much of the series, as Rachel did, coping with being mother to a young baby. Jennifer noted that Rachel was growing up, maturing a little with the responsibility of parenthood and the realization that it was no longer a fantasy. The close friend guest starring in Season Nine was Dermot Mulroney, Brad's buddy, who appeared in three episodes as Gavin, the man who has been Rachel's temporary replacement at Ralph Lauren while she is on maternity leave and wants her job when she returns.

Friends may have been work, but it was fun and reassuring to welcome actual friends into 'work'. Paul Rudd who had clicked so well with Jennifer on *The Object Of My Affection* became established in the regular cast as Mike, boyfriend of Phoebe. He had once been linked to Jennifer to spark some publicity for the film, a liaison which was news to the woman he was actually living with at the time. As Mike, he seemed to have been around in the show for ages but in fact only appeared in seventeen episodes out of a grand total of 236. No wonder Jennifer described *Friends* as a 'comfy pair of shoes'.

At one point while making Season Nine, Jennifer was spreading herself very thinly. Before the last frame of *Bruce Almighty* had been shot Jennifer had signed on to make *Along Came Polly* with Ben Stiller, another highly bankable star. She ended up making *Bruce Almighty*, *Along Came Polly* and *Friends* all at once. Trying to cope with the workload was not made any easier when she broke her toe. She smashed it into an ottoman while rushing to answer the phone at home.

Along Came Polly is an archetypal date movie, light, inconsequential with some terrible gags which are very funny. Jennifer had to share some scenes with a ferret, an animal which seemed to get along with a nervous Jennifer but took an instant dislike to Stiller. He played the wonderfully named Reuben Feffer, risk assessor and loser whose wife goes off with her scuba instructor on their honeymoon. Jennifer is the offbeat Polly, a girl from school who comes back into his life as he tries to pick up the pieces. Stiller had once played Jennifer's boyfriend in an episode of *Friends* entitled 'The One With The Screamer' – Number 70 – in which he did the screaming.

Polly, a slightly dim cocktail waitress, is the opposite of Reuben. She loves salsa dancing and her blind pet ferret. She is not a weak person and comes across as someone spending time with Reuben for the good reason that he is a nice guy, nothing more. She is the sort of woman Jennifer might have become if she had stayed in Laurel Canyon – Ann Hornaday in the *Washington Post* called it 'bohemian fecklessness'. Polly is extroverted where Reuben is painfully not. She is a free spirit whereas he is a risk assessor who takes no risks. No Ben Stiller film would be complete without the obligatory gross scene and this time it involves his character's inability to digest spicy food and the ensuing overflowing toilet.

Reviews for Jennifer were more mixed than usual. Ann Hornaday described her as 'characteristically warm and adorable'. Bruce Westbrook in the *Houston Chronicle* thought, 'Her Polly tempers a lustful, reckless bent with earthy honesty and warm concern, without playing the vulnerability card.' Steven Rea in the *Philadelphia Inquirer* was disappointed that Jennifer did not do enough: 'Aniston's performance remains frustratingly muted, low-key and a little sleep-walky.'

Jennifer was a great fan of Diane Keaton growing up and more than one critic alluded to the Annie Hall traits of Polly Prince. The film, however, is much more like Stiller's previous gross-out hit *There's Something About Mary* (1998) and perhaps Jennifer's role would have been better suited to the more kooky persona of Cameron Diaz. The critics may have been expecting too much from an Aniston–Stiller dream combination. Despite the lukewarm reaction, the film made $27 million on its first weekend, securing number-one position at the box office. In total in the US it returned more than double its $40 million budget. As with *Bruce Almighty*, however, this was definitely not Jennifer's film. Jim Carrey and Ben Stiller films have both become almost a genre in their own right, certainly a subspecies of modern comedy. (The two appeared together in one film, *The Cable Guy* (1996) which Stiller also directed, but surprisingly it was a comparative flop compared with their other, individual hits.)

Both Jim Carrey and Ben Stiller are huge movie stars but Jennifer was a much bigger 'star' and one story from the set of *Along Came Polly* illustrates her status among the general public. Universal executive Mary Parent, who was overseeing the film, walked into her office one day to see a crowd of assistants looking out of the window: 'I said "What's so exciting in my office?" And they said, "Jennifer Aniston's down there." You, know, there are big movie stars on our lot every day, but I don't have a crowd of people in my office looking out the window.'

Mary also made a cogent observation about Jennifer's popularity: 'She's extraordinarily beautiful but at the same time I think she's just as appealing to women as she is to men, and women don't punish her for the fact that men think she's hot.'

In 2002 Jennifer had it all – critical acclaim, big box office, awards and a cosy home life with a romantic husband who was also her best friend. When asked if *Friends* would continue past the current ninth season, she was quoted in *Entertainment Weekly*, 'In my mind I'm done. I want to start my family.'

TWENTY-THREE

The End Of Friends

Jennifer was grinning back in May 2001 when she revealed that while she would be content with two or three children her husband Brad definitely wanted seven. 'He loves the idea of having a huge family,' she said. It was not the sort of remark one would take too seriously. When the prospect of seven kids was raised in an interview later that year, Jennifer joked, 'Not unless he gets a mail-order bride, but I'll give him the rest. I hope I'll be a good mom. I love kids.' The reality was that Brad genuinely loved children and wanted to be a real dad with a large family. When he and Jen eventually moved in to the March House, he would have the neighbourhood kids round to the mansion grounds and teach them soccer skills. He enjoyed joining in. The problem was that in December 2003 he would be forty years old with no prospect of children on the immediate horizon.

At no time has Jennifer publicly said that she did not want children. Also, there is absolutely no evidence that she has ever thought that in private. Her outpourings on the subject of children over the years have been almost heartbreaking in retrospect. She told *Cosmopolitan*, for instance, in August 1997: 'I've always said I'd like about three. I love everything about them. I want to be a young mom too. I'm not ready now but in a couple of years.' Then, she was with Tate Donovan in a relationship that would not last much longer. A 'couple of years' later, when she was planning a marriage to Brad Pitt, it was too soon to think about a family.

Five years after the *Cosmopolitan* interview she began the ninth season of *Friends*, convinced it would be the last and obviously a good time to start a family. It has been suggested that Brad wanted a family and Jennifer wanted to finish her career. She compromised by saying she would have children after *Friends*. To many people's surprise, however, it was announced in December 2002 that the cast collective had been persuaded to go on for a tenth season. Jennifer reportedly insisted on the season being a shorter one, eighteen episodes in all, with filming finished before the end of January 2004. It would mean each of the six picking up an extra $18 million as a nest-egg in case their careers did not survive the curtain call in Central Perk. Soon after signing the deal, Jennifer told *Flare* magazine that, yes, she and Brad did want children: 'We definitely want to and at some point, probably in the next year or two, we will go down that road.' The prospect always seemed to be a couple of years in the future.

In another interview, Jennifer told *Elle* magazine, 'We have time, so much time. Brad has said to me, "Listen, I'm ready now. But I'll wait. Two years." I'm like, "You're giving me a two-year window?"' Perhaps the most interesting of a plethora of observations Jennifer has given on the subject of children was when she was asked about the perceived difficulty of juggling a career and motherhood. 'Something has to give,' she said. 'That's why I'm going to do this [work] now and do it as much as I can.' Her mother Nancy, worth remembering, gave up her career to devote herself to her husband and family which was not necessarily something Jennifer wanted to copy.

Whispers began among Hollywood gossips that all was not rosy in the Aniston–Pitt household. The decision to continue on with *Friends* inevitably meant a further postponement of starting a family and the rumblings of disharmony can, in retrospect, be traced to this point in their married lives. Those rumours of discord, and they were nothing more than that, were given some substance when the couple travelled with Courteney Cox and David Arquette to Mexico for a New Year's holiday. The girls went for workouts in a nearby gym while the boys hired a fishing boat and went snorkelling. The thin evidence of distance between Brad and Jennifer was fuelled by various locals including a taxi driver who picked them up at San Jose de Cabo airport and remarked that they displayed no affection to one another when they were sat in the back seat of his cab.

On returning to Los Angeles, Jennifer attended the People's Choice Awards at the Pasadena Civic Auditorium alone, with an empty seat beside her. Inevitably she won, the third time in four consecutive years that she was voted Favourite Television Performer. *Friends* won Best Comedy. She also gave a most curious interview to *W* magazine in which, it was claimed, she hesitated when asked if Brad was the love of her life, before replying, 'I think you're always sort of wondering, "Are you the love of my life?" I mean, I don't know. I've never been someone who says, "He's the love of my life." He's certainly a big love of my life.' It was as if Jennifer had forgotten for a moment that she was giving an interview and not lying on the analyst's couch. A year later, she was asked by Diane Sawyer in a live television interview about the article and she resolutely denied hesitating, maintaining she was quoted out of context and said, 'I married him because he was the love of my life.' That may be so but the original interview was the one people remembered. She also revealed in *W* that they had arguments: 'We do fight. Well, we have discussions. I am not a fan of fighting when it is screaming.'

The Golden Globes ceremony was their next public outing to come under the spotlight. Jennifer had been nominated for the very prestigious award – perhaps second only to the Oscars – for her performance as Rachel Green. The couple were late arriving with Jennifer, blaming a 'dress dilemma' as they squeezed in a thirty-second interview on their way in. Jennifer, wearing a black halter-top ensemble and a ponytail, was still hobbling and using a cane because of her broken toe when she made her way onto the stage to accept her award as Best Actress In A Comedy Series. She began by thanking her five co-stars in *Friends* and said warmly, 'I love you guys. You started out as my colleagues, and you're my friends – and you're my family.'

Unfortunately she forgot to thank, or even mention, her husband. Looking on, Brad's sunny expression was caught on camera changing to one of disappointment. Afterwards, Jennifer was aghast at her faux pas declaring backstage to NBC anchor Matt Lauer, 'I forgot to thank my husband, like a nincompoop. And I love you Brad Pitt and I thank you so much.'

The chances of Jennifer omitting to thank her husband on purpose are slim to nil. It was undoubtedly a genuine mistake brought on by the sheer excitement of the occasion. Her acceptance speech at the previous year's Hollywood Film Festival had been almost as bad. Even if they *had* rowed in the limo on the way over, she still would have thanked Brad because this was a public event and she was a professional star. The Golden Globe was a huge accolade and, coming so soon after the Emmy, it could not get any better for Jennifer. The rumour-mongers immediately put two and two together and made five, missing the more important insight into Jennifer's character. The *Friends* crew were, in her eyes, her family and, as such, represented a hugely important factor in her life. Filming the last episode would be like attending a funeral. The aftermath would be a bereavement.

The last season of *Friends* would be one of three momentous events in Jennifer's life in 2003. The second would be leaving her happy home in Blue Jay Way and finally moving to the $14-million Pitt Palace, while the third would be waving Brad goodbye as he left for an extended period on location. The now penultimate series of *Friends* concluded with everyone in Barbados for a Palaeontology Convention. Ross ends up with Joey's girlfriend, the brainy and beautiful Charlie while Joey kisses Rachel. Charlie was played by the statuesque six-foot tall black actress Aisha Tyler which was significant because *Friends* had received some criticism over the years for not featuring any black roles.

By the time the episode was broadcast in mid-May 2003, Brad had flown to Malta and would be parted from Jennifer, with the exception of the odd break in filming, for five months. They had yet to celebrate their third wedding anniversary. The consequence of this long separation was that Brad was not there for Jennifer when she was particularly vulnerable. When it comes to thinking – or perhaps brooding – Jennifer was Olympic standard. And, to add to her problems at this time, the estrangement from her mother remained unresolved.

Jennifer had to go to this year's wedding alone. This time around it was the turn of Matt LeBlanc. He became the fourth member of the *Friends* gang to say 'I Do' in the off season when he married his long-term girlfriend, former model Melissa McKnight in Hawaii. Melissa had previously been married to Anthony Esposito, bassist with heavy-metal group Lynch Mob, and already had two children. At least Courteney Cox and Lisa Kudrow were there so Jennifer was not short on company. Both David Schwimmer and Matthew Perry were absent, appearing on stage in Chicago and London respectively. LeBlanc hit upon a novel way of foiling unwanted paparazzi by hiring out all the helicopters on the island of Kauai for the exclusive use of his guests.

In July 2003, more than two years after Brad and Jennifer had bought their marital dream house, it was at last ready for them to move in. The problem was that after spending $1 million and a great deal of blood, sweat and tears, Brad was not there, having travelled on to Mexico with *Troy*, and Jennifer had to pack up her two-bedroomed house on Blue Jay Way and venture down to the new home by herself. In the end she made a good decision not to sell her old house, preferring to rent it out to Sacha Baron Cohen, aka Borat and Ali G. It would prove to be a great comfort to her in the troubled times ahead.

Jennifer and Brad did not share the same taste in design, neither interior nor exterior. Brad was modern in outlook while Jennifer had a more classic, cosy inclination where decoration was concerned. She summed it up by saying that he did the outside while she did the inside. They both had strong opinions and would argue keenly about their different ideas for the house. By the time they had finished 'discussions', the property boasted a tennis court, a beautiful swimming pool and spa, an English-style pub and games room, a professional screening room, a stainless steel kitchen with a heated floor and black hardwood floors in the living area. Brad designed a nursery for the house which they decorated in green.

Jennifer had strong reservations about Brad's preference for cold, more masculine effects including the use of marble and stone floors. He also liked hard, clean edges and insisted on a glass table which Jennifer told *Allure* was 'not very kid-friendly'.

Jennifer compared the process of designing a house as a couple to 'the stories you hear about having babies together'. It was, she thought, 'a test of a relationship'. Later, when it came to sorting out possessions during their divorce, neither Jennifer nor Brad seemed remotely interested in continuing to live in the Pitt Palace. It was far too big for two people, let alone one. The house needed to be filled with the family of nine which Brad had wanted.

They actually spent very little time there together as a married couple, but when they were at home, Jennifer did her best to make it 'homely'. She even made one doomed attempt to learn to cook. For her first home-made dinner she chose to make, of all things, pizza. It was not *Masterchef*. Brad loved pizza but Jennifer's version was, according to a friend, a 'riot' – the Rachel Green school of cookery. They decided to order takeaway pizza in future.

Brad's new project in development was a comedy spy caper called *Mr and Mrs Smith* (2005), mimicking the theme of the superb *Prizzi's Honor* (1985) in which Jack Nicholson and

Kathleen Turner so memorably played a hitman and hitwoman involved in a relationship while trying to kill each other. Nicole Kidman was originally cast as Mrs Smith alongside Brad. Her marriage to Tom Cruise had been one of the first big celebrity casualties of the new century when they divorced in August 2001. She had been single since then and rumours circulated, ironically, that Jennifer was unhappy at the prospect of the willowy star being on location with her husband. These sorts of stories keep interest in an upcoming film ticking over. When it became clear that Nicole was not going to do the film after all, the next actress in the frame was Catherine Zeta-Jones. Jennifer, it was said, was happier about this because Brad did not really go for dark-haired women. In the end, the third choice, raven-haired Angelina Jolie was cast.

Jennifer met Angelina just once for a very brief but courteous conversation before filming began. She told Angelina that Brad was looking forward to working with her. 'I hope you guys have a really good time,' she said. It is not the conversation of someone eaten up with either jealousy or a sense of foreboding. She was more preoccupied with filming the last series of *Friends*.

Angelina Jolie – pretty little angel – enjoyed a reputation and image almost diametrically opposed to Jennifer's. She was not America's Sweetheart nor was she the girl next door, and she was not a woman's woman. Men may have dreamed of Angelina as some sort of comic supervixen but women were far more likely to suffer nightmares. Angelina, like Jennifer, was the daughter of an actor and a minor actress. Her father was the celebrated Oscar winner Jon Voight who left her mother, Marcheline Bertrand, when his daughter was just one year old, although she saw him regularly until she was seven. Over the years their relationship has been a volatile and strained one, culminating in some remarks Voight made on television in 2002 when he suggested she had 'serious mental problems'. They have not spoken since. Like Jennifer, Angelina started therapy while still at school. She too has said that her home circumstances while she was growing up made her determined to be an independent woman.

From the very beginning of her acting career Jolie seemed destined to become better known for her sexual charisma and predilections. She had a lesbian affair with Jenny Shimizu, a Japanese–American actress who she met on the set of *Firefox* (1996). Jenny observed, 'I was attracted to her mouth. I was also attracted to her body language – she moves very felinesque.' Angelina did not hide her lesbian light in the closet, revealing, 'I fell in love with her the first second I saw her.'

Angelina had already met and fallen for a British actor, Jonny Lee Miller, making the movie *Hackers* (1995) and, for a time, there was a ménage a trois, although Jenny said that they never had a threesome. Angelina, however, did gain a reputation for being an S&M enthusiast and also had a collection of knives and slept with a snake in a tank at the bottom of her bed. All in all she came across as a dangerous woman to know, but that did not deter Miller from marrying her in March 1996. Angelina wore black leather trousers and a white blouse with her husband's name scratched across the back in her own blood. They lasted nearly three years but were divorced in February 1999 when Angelina was twenty-three. In a later interview he admitted that he had sucked her blood, adding, 'She did that kind of thing.'

Such a first marriage would take some beating but Angelina topped it when she fell for the grizzly actor Billy Bob Thornton, again on set, this time making *Pushing Tin* (1999) in which he played an air-traffic controller and she was his beautiful and damaged wife. They first set eyes on one another in an elevator, a moment Billy Bob described as a 'bolt of lightning' while Angelina said she 'nearly passed out'. Her attraction for Billy Bob was so dynamic she thought it 'chemical'. At the time Thornton was living with actress Laura Dern, who was reportedly astonished to learn that Billy Bob had married Angelina in Las Vegas on 5 May 2000: 'I left home to work on a movie and while I was away my boyfriend got married and I've never heard from him again.' Billy Bob had already been married four times and had three children before Angelina, twenty-four, became his fifth bride. He was forty-four and when they were pictured together he looked like a mangy cat who had got the cream. Their wedding could scarcely have been more different from the celebrity extravaganza a couple of months later in Malibu at which Brad and Jennifer became Hollywood's golden couple. The official wedding picture of Mr and Mrs Pitt – taken by an old pal Michael Sanville – revealed Jennifer in her beautiful dress smiling happily at Brad, every inch a movie star in his tuxedo. They radiated glamour. Angelina and Billy Bob wore jeans in the Little Church of the West Wedding Chapel where they paid $189 for the twenty-minute ceremony.

Angelina and Billy Bob wore phials of each other's blood around their necks. They were also disarmingly honest about their rampant sex lives with Angelina claiming that Billy Bob was 'an amazing lover'. She enthused, 'He does certain things to me in bed that, well, they're beautiful'. The Thorntons were not a couple who did anything in the predictable, teeth-flashing way of Hollywood celebrities. At the MTV Awards in 2000 Billy Bob told an interviewer on the red carpet that he and Angelina had just f***ed in the limo on the way over. Also shocking, but of greater significance from the point of view of Jennifer's story, was Angelina's relationship with Billy Bob's two young sons. They triggered domestic and maternal feelings in her that up until then had remained resolutely hidden. Now she talked of adopting children and also said, 'I would love to have children with Billy.'

Angelina had Billy Bob's name tattooed on her left arm. She was such a devotee of body art that she could have been a living installation, a finalist for the Turner Prize. The first tattoo she had done was the letter H on the inside of her left wrist. At the time she was involved with actor Timothy Hutton who she met on the set of *Playing God* (1997), although she later said it also represented her brother Jamie Haven (they both dropped Voight from their names). She also had a Tennessee Williams quote on her left forearm – 'A prayer for the wild at heart kept in cages,' and, matching it on her right forearm, a quotation in Arabic meaning 'strength of will'. Her best known tattoo is a Latin phrase just below her navel – '*Quod me netrit me destruit*', meaning 'What nourishes me also destroys me'. She has various others dotted about including a tiger and a dragon and a Latin cross. Jennifer has no tattoos.

Angelina's film career, like Jennifer's, had also blossomed. She won a Golden Globe in 1999 for her performance in the TV movie *Gia* (1998), about the tragically short life of supermodel Gia Marie Caranga whose downward spiral of drug abuse ended in her death from AIDS-related causes at the age of twenty-six. Angelina followed that with an Oscar in 2000 (and another Golden Globe) as Best Supporting Actress playing opposite Winona Ryder as a mental patient in *Girl, Interrupted* (1999). At the awards, she famously gave her elder brother Jamie a kiss on the lips, before declaring, 'I'm so in love with my brother right now,' when she accepted the award. The sniggering response from the media was that Angelina was more shocking than ever, snogging her brother. The innuendo was that they must be conducting some incestuous affair which they most certainly were not. Angelina was outraged, 'For some reason people thought it was more interesting to focus on something that was sick and disturbing rather than the fact that two siblings support and love each other.'

Angelina became a star, however, playing the superhero Lara Croft in *Tomb Raider* (2001) which became the highest-grossing action film with a female in the lead. More than that, it cemented Angelina's position as a lad's mag fantasy pin-up, wearing figure-hugging costumes in which her breasts seemed to defy gravity. More interestingly, *Tomb Raider* was filmed in the UK and Cambodia and Angelina, removed from the artificial world of Hollywood, became socially responsible and aware of humanitarian problems. She was horrified at the plight of the Cambodians and became actively involved in the United Nations High Commission for Refugees, visiting refugee camps around the world. She was made a Goodwill Ambassador for UNHCR in 2001. In November of that year she travelled to an orphanage in Cambodia and found a three-month old baby who she decided to adopt and call Maddox. Initially, Billy Bob was on board but he went off touring with his rock-and-roll band instead of staying with Angelina and Maddox. Angelina said she had not planned on being a single parent. She would later have Billy Bob's tattoo removed by laser and replaced by the co-ordinates of where her adopted children were born.

Angelina had spent most of 2003 making the film *Alexander* (2004) in which she played Olympias, the epic hero's mother, in one of the most ridiculous pieces of casting in recent times. Angelina was just eleven months older than her screen son, Colin Farrell, with whom she was romantically linked. Farrell, who has a fearsome reputation as a hellraiser, accompanied Angelina and Maddox on a trip to the Pyramids in Egypt which helped to fan the flames of rumour, but nothing much came of it; perhaps Angelina thought Farrell too irresponsible to be involved with her adored adopted son.

Back in Los Angeles, when Angelina signed on to make *Mr and Mrs Smith* for $20 million, Jennifer had begun filming the last series of *Friends*.

The tenth season of *Friends* needed to resolve the Ross-and-Rachel situation, especially after she and Joey had decided it was never going to work out between them. The classic episode of the series was 'The One Where The Stripper Cries' – Number 229 – featuring a bravura guest appearance by Jennifer's next-door neighbour, Danny DeVito. He plays a short, fat and old stripper who is hired for Phoebe's hen party and bursts into tears when she says she doesn't want him. Jennifer found the time during the filming schedule to plan Brad's fortieth birthday. A week before Christmas, Jennifer persuaded Jamie Oliver to fly to Los Angeles and prepare a special private dinner to mark the occasion. For one of his presents she gave him a silkscreen on canvas by the fashionable artist Russell Young of one of his all-time favourite actors, Steve McQueen.

Jennifer and Brad's production company, meanwhile, continued to grow, especially as they had now been joined by renowned producer Brad Grey and been taken into the Warner Bros corporate embrace. They were now called Plan B Entertainment. Jennifer was especially excited when they won a bidding war to secure the rights to Mariane Pearl's memoir, *A Mighty Heart*, the moving story of how she lost her journalist husband Daniel to terrorist kidnappers. Jennifer, it was assumed, would play Mariane on screen.

The anticipation of the last recording of *Friends* was immense with wall-to-wall media coverage. Jennifer told Diane Sawyer, 'I should have a shock thing around my neck like those dogs, when they start to bark. When I start to cry, I just get electrocuted.' The night was an emotional and moving one for Jennifer, the 'leaker', but at least she had her 'chosen family' there. Courteney Cox, who was by now expecting again, observed, 'Her best friends were all in the front row and I just thought that was so great.'

Brad, surprisingly, could not make it because of commitments to *Mr and Mrs Smith* which had started filming in Los Angeles. He missed Jennifer looking distinctly tearful during the last bow in front of the studio audience. She explained how she felt losing the comfort of *Friends*, 'It's just hard, absolutely painful, in the weirdest way. Because it's the most fun and joyous place to be.'

The final two-part episode, 'The Last One, Parts 1 and 2', focused inevitably on Ross and Rachel. Rachel is leaving to take a new job in Paris but Ross races to the airport to tell her how he feels. Unfortunately he rushes to JFK when she is leaving from Newark. He finally gets to the right airport just as she is leaving and, movingly, pours his heart out. She decides to go anyway and, crestfallen, Ross returns to the apartment. A couple of minutes later Rachel arrives, having realized after 236 episodes that she really loves him, too. They kiss. It was a perfect feelgood way to end the story of their romance leaving the audience unsure whether to cheer or reach for the tissues. An audience of more than 52 million Americans were watching when the scene was broadcast on 6 May 2004.

TWENTY-FOUR

From *Rumor* to Reality

Sadly for Jennifer, the spark of romance, so bright for Ross and Rachel, seemed to be leaving her marriage rapidly. She was spending very little time with Brad and when she did they argued. Their work commitments seemed to be piling up. Brad was due to take a break from *Mr and Mrs Smith* to go on location to make *Ocean's Twelve* in Italy. Then he would resume *Mr and Mrs Smith*, also due to start location work in Italy. Jennifer was on the road promoting *Along Came Polly* and, incredibly, would sign up to make four films in the coming months, hardly the actions of someone who was going to find time to start a family.

Crucially, Jennifer's absence during the early part of the year drew Brad closer to Angelina and, specifically, her son Maddox. Angelina was, of course, a very beautiful woman but not every man would automatically step over Jennifer to get to her. Both women featured highly in the growing number of polls ranking 'most fanciable female' under some banner or other. Angelina, however, had something extra as far as Brad was concerned. She had a sweet little boy. It has been observed that as Brad was forty and in need of a family, Angelina *and* Maddox really appealed to him.

During his publicity push for *Troy*, Brad made a number of comments to reporters which suggested he was impressed by the company he was keeping. 'I tell you I've never seen someone so misperceived as Jolie,' he observed. 'Because she's a really decent human being, and very dedicated to her UN work, and very dedicated to her child. It's a daily thing for her. I was really surprised . . .' On another occasion he said of his relationship with Jennifer, 'Neither of us wants to be the spokesman for happy marriage, or coupledom. I despise this two-becomes-one thing where you lose your individuality.' Both remarks are taken out of context but, nevertheless, remain interesting.

The last time Jennifer and Brad spent an extended period of time together as man and wife was in May and June 2004 when Jennifer flew to Italy to be where he was filming *Ocean's Twelve* in Rome. She stayed for more than four weeks while Brad was working. They were also guests of George Clooney at his house on Lake Como in a party that included Brad's friends and co-stars Julia Roberts and Matt Damon. Over lunch one day, Jennifer told Julia that she had been offered a movie called *Derailed* co-starring Clive Owen. Julia, who had starred alongside Owen in the acclaimed drama *Closer* (2004) replied, in her lazy southern drawl, 'Well honey, if you can, you have got to work with him because he is dreamy.' The movie world was just as small as the television world, it seemed, because before that Owen had made another drama called *Beyond Borders* (2003) in which he played opposite Angelina Jolie, who adopted Maddox while she was making the film. That movie, less well received than *Closer* and a box-office failure was set in some of the places of war-torn Africa which Angelina had visited as a goodwill ambassador, including Namibia, a country which became dear to her heart.

Back in Los Angeles, Jennifer became a godmother when Courteney Cox gave birth to a baby girl, Coco, two days before her fortieth birthday. She was the third of the *Friends* gang to become a parent. Matt LeBlanc had become a father in February when his wife Melissa also had a baby girl, Marina. Rumours surfaced in June that Jennifer would join the parental group because she was at last expecting a baby and, according to MSNBC, an announcement was expected soon. Before she left for Italy Jennifer had said, a little oddly, 'We're absolutely in the process of having a baby. It's where we're headed.' She was also reported to be taking folic acid in preparation. Brad had also confirmed, 'We're heading that way. It's a natural progression for us and it's time.'

In July 2004 the *National Enquirer* newspaper claimed that Jennifer had suffered a miscarriage. The story said she had fallen pregnant the previous month and quoted 'sources' saying that the news had left both stars devastated. It alleged that Brad broke down and wept because he had 'wanted to become a father more than anything in the world'. The talkative 'source' continued, 'Brad was a total wreck over the miscarriage.' Unsurprisingly, there was no confirmation or even comment of any kind from the Brad-and-Jennifer camp.

Nothing more was ever said about it. From that time on, however, all the stories about Brad and Jennifer's marriage seemed to be negative ones. By the autumn, the name of Angelina Jolie would loom even larger when Brad resumed filming on *Mr and Mrs Smith* in Italy while Jennifer was engaged on the ironically titled *Derailed*. Jennifer seemed to be working so hard; it was as if she was making sure she did not have time to dwell on the disintegration of her marriage. She was due to make *Rumor Has It*, *Derailed* and *Friends With Money* in rapid succession. The fourth movie she signed for, a heist thriller called *Gambit*, has still to be filmed.

Rumor Has It, which she began in late July 2004, was not her finest hour. She told *Vogue*, with refreshing honesty, that it was 'the worst experience of my life, the worst experience, the worst film. It sounded like a great idea, an interesting backdrop for a romantic comedy. But it was never fleshed out, never fully realized. And for me personally, I was going through a horrible time. I wasn't at my best as an actor. I was unmotivated by it. Why talk about it? We can let that little train go by.' The quote reveals just what Jennifer was going through in the late summer of 2004, the dark side kept hidden from the public who only saw smiles and laughter. As she said, it was a 'horrible time' – but at least she was paid $8 million.

The 'great idea' for *Rumor Has It* was that Jennifer played an obituary writer who sets out to prove that she is the grand-child of the two lovers from the film *The Graduate* (1967) – Dustin Hoffman and Ann Bancroft or, in this case, Kevin Costner and Shirley Maclaine. The plot is a torture but needs the audience to believe that the dashing dot.com tycoon Beau Burroughs (Hoffman's original character was called Benjamin Braddock) played by Costner, sleeps with three generations of the same family.

Surprisingly, *Rumor Has It* was directed by Rob Reiner, who brought the sublime *When Harry Met Sally* (1989) to the screen. For once his sure touch deserted him and Jack Matthews in the

New York Daily News called the movie a 'lump of coal, sculpted from the kind of high-concept idea screenwriters find scribbled on bar napkins after nights of heavy drinking'. In Reiner's defence he was only brought in to rescue the film when the original director, Ted Griffin, who also wrote the screenplay, was fired just eight days into the shoot amid unsubstantiated reports that he and Costner had clashed repeatedly on set. Ironically Griffin, who later disowned the film, had earlier written Brad's hit movie *Ocean's Eleven*. Costner maintained that Griffin was replaced before he had even started work on the movie and he had no information regarding the 'mechanics' of his dismissal.

Jennifer, who normally survives bad criticism even when the film is tepidly received, was not immune on this occasion. Claudia Puig in *USA Today* said, 'Her performance seemed phoned in.' Philip Wuntch in the *Dallas Morning News*, observed, 'Ms Aniston performs in a constant state of whiney agitation.' It was part of a post-*Friends* backlash against Jennifer's film-star aspirations. One reviewer even meanly described her as an 'ageing anorexic TV actress'.

Romantic comedies are often enjoyed more second time around, when the DVD comes out and they can be sipped guiltily in the comfort of one's living room like a mug of milky cocoa. Unfortunately, that was not the case with *Rumor Has It*. The suspicion remains that it was another film relying on Jennifer's charm to make it work. She was not at her best and the movie was not made of strong enough material to survive without it. The film was a box-office disappointment.

Intriguingly, and probably because the film was not released until Christmas 2005, it was widely assumed that Jennifer's 'horrible time' was a reference to the period *after* her separation from Brad. The media made a mistake – she filmed *Rumor Has It* before they officially split and Jennifer kept her distress well hidden. Actor Mark Ruffalo, who played her long-suffering boyfriend in the film revealed that he had no idea of what she was going through at the time. The inference thoughout the whole of 2004 is that Pitt and Aniston were putting on a performance in public which did not tally with what was going on in private. Jennifer's general mood while filming was not helped by the set, which was just two stages over from Stage 24 at the Warner Brothers studios in Burbank. Inevitably she found herself drifting over to the old *Friends* stage to remember better times, especially when it came to August, when filming a new season would normally be about to start. One of the very few bright spots in the whole *Rumor Has It* experience for Jennifer was supplied by Mena Suvari, the actress playing her younger sister in the film. Mena has Greek relatives on her mother's side and the two actresses were able to swap stories about their families and their childhoods.

As soon as she finished filming in late October, Jennifer flew to Chicago to begin *Derailed* with Clive Owen. Speculation about her marriage was reaching crescendo point with stories in the British press of an alleged rift provoked by Brad's closeness to Angelina. His spokeswoman, Cindy Guagenti, was even moved to say, 'He is not having an affair with Angelina Jolie.' Angelina commented, 'I wouldn't sleep with a married man. I have enough lovers. I don't need Brad.' The *News of the World* claimed that Jennifer and Brad were leading separate lives, which, as it turned out, was a pretty accurate reflection of how things were. They were apart far more than they were together.

Derailed, which has nothing to do with train wrecks, provided

Jennifer with a much more interesting and challenging role than her previous movie. It was the first bona fide thriller she had attempted and the first time she was raped on screen – even if all was not as it seemed. The director Mikael Hafstrom called it 'a psychological thriller for grown-ups with grown-up themes.' Infidelity, blackmail and sexual violence were the grown-up themes in question. The film challenged the audience: are you ready to see Rachel Green become the victim of a nasty rape in a hotel room? Jennifer and Clive Owen play two married professionals, Lucinda and Charles, who meet on a Chicago commuter train and go to a hotel for a tryst only to be interrupted by a thief. He beats Charles up and rapes Lucinda. The film then concentrates on the moral choices faced by Charles who feels unable to report the crime because of the illicit circumstances in which it took place. He has been saving up for years to pay for medical treatment for his diabetic daughter, but has to decide if he should give up those savings to see off the thief who has proceeded to blackmail him. Owen is at the film's heart but Jennifer is riveting as the femme fatale, proving again that as an actress she is multi-layered and not a one-trick pony. The main criticism is that she features very little in the second half of the film. Realistically, her status deserved a bigger part but that has seldom influenced Jennifer's decisions about what roles to take. She explained, 'I just go by my gut rather than strategize. If it's good and I think I can do it well, then I'll do it.'

Derailed deserved a better reception, but ultimately lacked a little conviction to be a true film noir or even a Hitchcock thriller, although it did feature an excellent twist. Ty Burr in the *Boston Globe* noted, 'The plot is as pulp as the airport novel from whence it came.' He did, however, admit to having a 'pretty good time' watching it. Jennifer did not impress Mike Clark in *USA Today* who observed, 'Jennifer Aniston is an actress about as born to play femme fatale roles as fellow *Friends* alumni Matthew Perry would be to play Winston Churchill.' One critic suggested that if Owen had been cast as the new James Bond, then Jennifer would have been a good choice for Miss Moneypenny. Jennifer was in a no-win situation: when she makes a rom-com, everybody throws up their hands and wonders if she will ever shake off her Rachel Green persona; when she tries something completely different, the cry is that she should stick to being Rachel Green. Not everyone was negative though. Paul Clinton for CNN.com thought Jennifer and Clive generated believable sexual chemistry. He added, 'Aniston is excellent in a demanding role that requires her to switch gears at some pivotal moments.'

Jennifer herself had her doubts while filming: 'There was definitely a moment of "Oh gosh, I hope I can pull this off." I was starting to buy into my own stereotype in a way.' At least there was a 'friendly' face in the cast. Melissa George, who played Clive Owen's wife, had appeared in two episodes of the ninth season of *Friends*: 'The One With Phoebe's Rats' and 'The One Where Monica Sings' – Numbers 206 and 207. She appeared as Rachel's hot new nanny, Molly, who arouses Joey's interest, only to dampen his ardour when she turns out to be gay.

After Chicago, *Derailed* had moved location and Jennifer flew to London to film the interiors, including the rape scene. She could almost have waved at Brad's plane mid-Atlantic as he made his way back to the US to promote *Ocean's Twelve*. She missed the première of the film, but the European leg of the publicity tour gave them the chance to catch up with each other. They seemed friendly enough when they dined out in London's West End and Brad told one press conference that he was 'looking forward to spending Christmas with his wife'.

Some reports suggested Jennifer had stopped wearing her wedding ring and, again, the British press theorized that it was the friendship between Brad and Angelina that was putting a strain on the marriage. They did not travel home to Los Angeles together and Jennifer missed Brad's birthday. She also received the traumatic news that her therapist had died suddenly and she flew back in time for the funeral.

After what would prove to be their last Christmas together, Brad and Jennifer flew to the Caribbean island of Anguilla with Courteney Cox, David Arquette and baby Coco. Mistakenly, expectations were raised that this was a romantic holiday to rekindle the flame of their marriage. The true reason was that they were saying goodbye in a good way, as the best of friends, reassuring each other that they were coping. Their every move was being watched by the world's media.

They were seen walking along the beach for the last time to go to their villa, Jennifer in a navy blue sarong and Brad in a grey sweatshirt emblazoned with the slogan 'Trash'. They kissed tenderly, strolling as if they were two young lovers enjoying a dream holiday in the sun. They had been so very much in love.

The end came abruptly, the very next day on 7 January 2005 with the following public statement read by Brad's publicist, Cindy Guagenti: 'We would like to announce that after seven years together we have decided to formally separate. For those who follow these sorts of things, we would like to explain that our separation is not the result of any speculations reported by the tabloids. The decision is the result of much thoughtful consideration. We happily remain committed and caring friends with great love and admiration for one another. We ask in advance for your kindness and sensitivity in the coming months.' They had written the words together.

Nothing in the couple's behaviour suggested that they broke up over another woman. Instead, it had all the hallmarks of a couple who still had great affection for one another but were out of sync and had realized their futures lay elsewhere. A source close to the couple observed simply, 'Initially they were really good together. Jennifer is very sweet and a delightful person on her own but they were fighting such a lot, way before *Mr and Mrs Smith*. Sometimes people just don't make it together.'

Three days after the announcement, Jennifer reported for work on *Friends With Money*, her third movie in six months. The film, an independent ensemble piece, was shot in just three weeks in and around Los Angeles. While they were filming at the Santa Monica Farmers' Market, Jennifer needed to blow her nose and was offered a tissue by her make-up lady. Jennifer declined, demonstrating that she had at least grown savvy in understanding the ways of the tabloid press: 'If I hold a tissue they're going to take a picture of me and print that I'm crying.' Nothing, however, could have prepared her for the pandemonium in the media following her separation from Brad. It literally became the biggest story in the world, fuelled by speculation over Angelina.

Three theories were put forward by the British media for the split. The first and most popular was that they clashed over starting a family. The second, as suggested by the *Daily Star*, was that the marriage collapsed because Brad adored playing father to Maddox. The third reason, as claimed by the *News of the World*, was that Jennifer had caught Brad indulging in phone sex with Angelina. They, apparently, were always talking to each other in hushed tones but Jennifer found out when she listened in on a conversation. Angelina described the story as 'bullshit'.

Both the first and second explanations, backed up by sources close to the couple, appear to tell at least part of the story. The third is straight out of the soap opera that the whole saga was fast becoming. Angelina was perceived as rather like a Joan Collins figure in *Dynasty*, the bitch who wears red when everyone else is dressed in black or, as she herself said, 'the Wicked Witch of the West'.

The key unanswered question was whether Brad and Angelina were actually having an affair before Jennifer and Brad split. Jennifer, at the very least, was well aware that her husband was attracted to Angelina. Two of her closest friends endorsed that. Kristin Hahn, who would prove to be very outspoken on the subject of Brad, observed, 'She's not suggesting she didn't know there was an enchantment, and a friendship'. Courteney Cox also said, 'I don't think he started an affair physically, but I think he was attracted to her. There was a connection and he was honest about that with Jen.'

Jennifer chose to believe Brad about Angelina. They had spoken so often about their openness with each other and the strength of their friendship. He was 'her bud' so why would he lie to her? The affectionate and poignant scenes during their farewell in Anguilla strongly suggest a mutual agreement that they needed time and space – or perhaps a mutual agreement that *he* needed time and space. They do not depict a wife who knew her husband was cheating on her. It was all very civilized. Sadly, from Jennifer's point of view, Brad appeared to have just needed time and space to pursue his infatuation with Angelina.

After their joint statement of separation, Brad was in effect handed a green light to pursue his new love, guilt-free.

The 'connection' with Angelina was evident in pictures published before the end of January that had been taken the previous October on the set of *Mr and Mrs Smith*, and one in particular appeared to show Angelina snuggling up to Brad. In the coming months photographs of the couple around the world were going to be enormously painful for Jennifer who said, 'It's hard to be the abandoned one.'

In the short term, Jennifer was busy shooting a movie. *Friends With Money* is the sort of film that will pop up on television in years to come when nobody will recall that Jennifer was in it and then declare that they had forgotten what a good actress she is. Jennifer was understandably attracted to the theme: a circle of friends, all women and all with the hand of middle age upon them, deal with the myriad problems of their lives – money, love and the future – and talk about them a great deal. Jennifer excels in an outstanding female cast that included Oscar winner Frances McDormand, Joan Cusack and old friend Catherine Keener. Keener later acted like the protective friend, supporting Jennifer when they travelled to the Sundance Film Festival in Park City, Utah, when *Friends With Money* opened the 2006 event. Keener's own career has taken off with good roles in the unexpected hit *The 40-Year-Old Virgin* (2005), which also featured Paul Rudd, and *Capote* (2005), in which she played Harper Lee. In her latest film *Into The Wild* (2007), she plays opposite Vince Vaughn. She knows all the players in the Jennifer saga; if it was a long-running soap opera Catherine would be one of those characters who never seems to take centre-stage but is always in the bar or the café chatting with the more important protagonists.

In real life, Jennifer would have been the friend with the *most* money, but in the film she plays a school teacher, Olivia, who quits her job and becomes a cleaner. She is broke, a pot head and man free. Jennifer did not have to go further than some of her old friends on The Hill to research the role. While admitting that she had 'lived' and thus could make no judgement on the casual pot smoker, she told *US Elle* that she had a bunch of friends who were pot heads and were genius and wonderful but could not motivate themselves: 'They'll spend days trying to figure out how to make a birthday card.' She modelled Olivia on a particular friend, who she did not identify: 'I have my wonderful group of girlfriends and there is one who is younger than all of us, who hasn't quite figured out exactly what she wants to do, slightly unmotivated but trying to motivate and we're always giving her clothes and footing the bill and loving her.'

The subtlety in *Friends With Money* is that the three successful women have just as many problems as their poor friend. The overall effect is a subdued film. Wealth, luxury, acclaim, a glamorous marriage and all the trimmings do not make problems and anxieties any less real or significant.

After the lukewarm reception to her efforts in her last two films, Jennifer's portrayal of Olivia was acclaimed by many as her best performance yet, or certainly since *The Good Girl*, the last time she made an indie film. Some of the downtrodden characteristics she brought to Justine in that film she brings to Olivia in *Friends With Money*. Peter Travers in *Rolling Stone* applauded her 'gift for giving a character shades of light and dark'. He also observed, 'It's a kick to see Aniston cut loose and break her losing streak.' The view was echoed by Kirk Honeycutt in *The Hollywood Reporter*: 'Aniston excels at suggesting women unhappy with their lives and uncertain how to rectify the situation.' He also thought her well served by the director and writer Nicole Holofcener whose previous films *Walking and Talking* (1996) and *Lovely and Amazing* (2002) were also well-received, strong films about women and the intricacies of their friendships. Holofcener had originally written the role of Olivia with someone older in mind but changed her mind when she talked to Jennifer about it: 'I just felt she could be subtle and funny at the same time.' She also thought Jennifer would quit the movie when her separation from Brad was made public just a few days before shooting began. She recalled, 'That didn't happen and she was completely professional, available and friendly.'

Jennifer's performance is amazing considering what was going on in her personal life. She was perhaps calm and relieved that at least she had taken the right action over her marriage. That, however, was before the Angelina-and-Brad saga moved up a notch.

TWENTY-FIVE

Team Aniston

As soon as she had finished the shoot for *Friends With Money*, Jennifer was out having dinner with a man who wanted to persuade her to be in his new movie. He was Vince Vaughn and he had been the forgotten co-star of *Mr and Mr Smith*. At the time, nobody realized that they were discussing a new film and that their evening was no more than a friendly business meeting to talk about the project. Jennifer did later admit that there was a connection between them at the beginning, which is the customary way in which her relatively few important romances have begun. Jennifer was caught in a whirlpool of attention, far greater than when she was actually with Brad, and was wary of being seen in a rebound situation. She hated the level of scrutiny, describing it as 'awful'.

Vince was like a breath of fresh air and could scarcely have been more different from Brad. At least Jennifer would never face accusations that she had gone for a Brad clone. Vince was not going to top any poll for the most beautiful man in the world but, at six feet five inches tall, he was fun, charismatic, his own man and, right from the start, he made Jennifer laugh. Vince once said, 'If I'm not interested in a woman, I'm straightforward. Right after sex, I usually say, I can't do this anymore. Thanks for coming over.' The girls on The Hill would have choked on their margaritas. Vince Vaughn was a man with a six-pack in his hand, not underneath his polo shirt.

Surprisingly, Vince, a year younger than Jennifer and one foot taller, is from a very wealthy background in Chicago, brought up in the city's opulent Lake Forest suburb. His father was a self-made businessman and his mother, a well-respected money manager and investor. His parents were divorced but they were both millionaires. As a young man, however, Vince was a drifter who seemed to share none of his parents' ambition. He travelled west to Hollywood with nothing more to his name than a high-school diploma and a minor role in a Chevy commercial. He later revealed that he suffered learning difficulties as a child and this hampered his academic progress. He did not have the benefit of Jennifer's progressive and artistic education. Growing up he had not properly filled out his huge frame so was surprisingly skinny and not much good with sports or girls. He made up for that when he reached Los Angeles.

In Hollywood, he became one of the leading members of the 'Frat Pack', an informal group of friends and actors who often appear in the same movies together. Everybody loves labels and this one sticks because the films in question mostly achieved great success. Other frat-pack members include Ben Stiller, Will Ferrell, Owen and Luke Wilson, Jack Black and Steve Carell. Vince, for instance, has been in three films with Stiller and another three with Ferrell.

Over a ten-year period, this group has become the most bankable in Hollywood. Vince himself was first noticed in the cult hit *Swingers* (1996), a semi-autobiographical comedy about out-of-work actors in Hollywood, written by his friend and co-star Jon Favreau. Steven Spielberg was impressed when he saw the film and decided to cast Vince in *Jurassic Park: The Lost World* (1997) but it did not immediately lead to A-list parts. Playing Norman Bates in the mediocre remake of the Hitchcock classic *Psycho* (1998) did not help and Vince languished until he joined Will Ferrell and Luke Wilson in *Old School* (2003) in which they played three disillusioned guys trying to recapture their college days. After re-establishing himself, he was offered good parts in *Starsky and Hutch* (2004) and *Dodgeball: A True Underdog Story* (2004). These films were huge successes but owed more to the popularity of Ben Stiller than anything else.

Vince made it without Stiller and turned into a major star with *Wedding Crashers* (2005), an irreverent comedy about two men who gatecrash weddings to pick up women. The film was phenomenally successful, earning more than $200 million in the US alone. When he met Jennifer to discuss his movie, he was the more bankable of the two at the box office, although she was 'Jennifer Aniston' and, arguably, in 2005 the most famous woman in the world.

Jennifer filed for divorce on Good Friday, 25 March 2005, barely two months after the separation announcement. The ink was barely dry on speculative stories that her split from Brad would not be permanent and that it was only a trial separation: Brad's grandmother, Betty Russell, was quoted saying they would get back together; another story suggested they were undergoing marriage-guidance counselling. The reality of their situation was spelled out in the divorce petition filed at the Los Angeles Supreme Court which cited 'irreconcilable differences'. The progress of the divorce over the coming months ran smoothly, unhindered by legal bickering. They were both hugely wealthy and independently so. Their affairs only entwined where the house and Plan B Entertainment were concerned.

Coincidentally, as Jennifer filed for divorce, Brad and Angelina were together at the Parker Meridian Hotel in Palm Springs. They had apparently finished a magazine shoot promoting *Mr and Mrs Smith* and then had decided to stay on, with Maddox, for a few more days. An obligatory eye witness revealed, 'They were kissing and holding each other. He was rubbing her back. It looked romantic.' A hotel employee observed, 'It was obvious they were a couple.' They had checked into the hotel using false names, a move guaranteed to encourage gossip and innuendo. Brad's busy publicist, Cindy Guagenti said, 'Brad stayed on one side of the property and Angelina was on the other.'

Opinion in the media, it seemed, was drifting towards blaming Jennifer for the split because it was claimed she put her career ahead of family, thus denying her husband the baby he so obviously craved. Jennifer's supporters were robust in her defence. Kathy Najimy declared, 'Jennifer would never compromise a relationship for her career.' Leslie Bennetts, whose interviews provided such insight into Jennifer, thought the tendency to blame the 'victim' was 'amazing'. The idea that Jennifer, as a wife, should have produced children on demand was not one to appeal to the empowered women of today. The British writer Chrissy Iley described it as 'misogynistic'. Jennifer seemed on top of things, telling *Access Hollywood*, 'There is always going to be the tough and the nasty. You just tune out to that.' She was, however, unable to 'tune out' from what happened next.

Pictures were published around the world on 29 April showing

Brad building sandcastles with Maddox and Angelina on the beautiful Diani Beach in Kenya. They were of a relaxed and happy 'family' enjoying a day together at the seaside. Brad looked laid back and scruffy with an untidy beard. They appeared for all the world like a million other young families on holiday. They were only photographs but they revealed a paternal bond between Brad and Maddox while a smiling Angelina looked on approvingly.

Back in Malibu, where she had just rented a small beach house, Jennifer was flabbergasted. Here, for the first time, was incontrovertible proof of a relationship. She declared, 'The world was shocked. I was shocked.' 'It was a huge shock,' confirmed Lesley Bennetts. Many wondered how the photographer knew they were there. Andrea Bendewald said, 'It was extremely hurtful to Jen that he was seen with another woman so quickly after they were separated.'

Brad had turned into some sort of 'earth father' figure trailing his beautiful, maverick companion to all parts of the globe. He had always had a social conscience but it had previously been obscured by the Hollywood facade. Now he was a celebrity ambassador for DATA, the campaign founded by Bono to promote AIDS awareness and economic reform in Africa. Since meeting Angelina, he had travelled to South Africa to meet Nelson Mandela and support his AIDS initiatives, he had actively lobbied in Ethiopia and in the US he had fought for stem-cell research and supported the unsuccessful presidential campaign of democrat John Kerry.

Jennifer, meanwhile, packed for a summer in Chicago filming with Vince Vaughn. Her beloved dog Norman went too. A wonderful urban myth sprang up that she checked into her hotel under the name Mrs Smith but this turned out to be untrue. The movie was called *The Break-Up*, which Jennifer thought was a joke when she first heard it. It was a marketing brainwave, however, because it would inevitably lead to a huge raft of ironic publicity. In any event, it was a good move for Jennifer to leave Los Angeles because Brangelina, as they were now dubbed by the media, were coming to town for the première of *Mr and Mrs Smith*, which was neither artist's finest work but became a monster hit on the back of the public fascination with the 'Brad, Angie, Jen' soap opera which Jennifer once described as a 'sick, twisted Bermuda triangle'. It would not be long before Vince's name was thrown into the mix.

As part of the publicity campaign, Angelina was featured in *Vanity Fair*, usually Jennifer's magazine of choice. She gave absolutely nothing away regarding her and Brad, revealing she was in the African country of Niger when he and Jennifer announced their separation. 'I know nothing about their marriage,' she said. 'All I know is they seem like wonderful people and wonderful friends.' No word has been used more in the whole saga of Brad and Jennifer than 'friends'.

At the première itself Brad – now sporting a bleached blond look – and Angelina arrived separately and subsequently acted as if they had only just met. Later the same evening, Brad was interviewed by Diane Sawyer who asked him directly, 'Did Angelina Jolie break up your marriage?' 'No,' he snapped. He also explained, 'I don't see my time, certainly my marriage, as any kind of failure.' *Mr and Mrs Smith* proved to be anything but a failure, earning an estimated $186 million at the box office in the US alone.

Until he met Jennifer, Vince had managed to keep his own private life secret. He had become close to the distinctively voiced actress Joey Lauren Adams who starred with him in the film,

A Cool, Dry Place (1999) – a touching drama in which Vince played a caring, single parent of a five-year-old son. They remained good friends and she was the second female lead in *The Break-Up*. He has also been associated with co-stars Ashley Judd from *The Locusts* (1997) and Janeane Garofalo, the actress with the uncanny knack of making bad choices, with whom he made a comedy thriller called *Clay Pigeons* (1998). Part of the game in Hollywood is to romantically link actors and actresses together when they are in movies. They may or may not have had a fling but only rarely does a real-life liaison survive the final credits. They are like holiday romances – good fun but you hope the Greek waiter does not follow you back to Clapham.

Superficially, Vince would not have seemed Jennifer's type. He enjoyed a reputation for hard living and in days gone by would probably have been a great buddy of Richard Harris and Richard Burton, or, before that, Errol Flynn. He was a latter-day hellraiser with the record to prove it. After a brawl in 2001, he was banned from all bars in Wilmington, North Carolina, fined $250 and ordered to undergo alcohol assessment. In the brawl at the Firebelly Lounge, actor Steve Buscemi, with whom he was filming *Domestic Disturbance* (2001), was stabbed several times.

Vince does not own a mobile phone, never sends e-mails, smokes too much, likes a drink and loves to go out and have a good time. His weight fluctuates up and down depending on whether or not he is currently giving up smoking. He is disarmingly normal. After the nightmare of speculation surrounding Jennifer's desire to have children, she would be left in no doubt as to Vince's outlook: 'If I had kids maybe I would have a cell phone, but I would prefer not to have kids.' One trait Vince did share with Brad Pitt, however, is the desire to take his acting seriously.

Like Brad, he may have drifted into Hollywood but, once there, acting became a much bigger priority in life than drinking.

As usual, public perception is never quite on target. Vince is by no means the world's biggest extrovert bozo and Jennifer is not a wallflower. Anybody who expected her to sit around like a martyred broken reed was wrong. Jennifer is friendly, outgoing, gregarious and, socially, a leader. She is funny and witty and great company. Any assumption that she was the boring one in her marriage depends, to some extent, on how much you enjoy two years of constant home improvements.

At some point Jennifer and Vince became more than just good friends, although they vigorously denied it. The guessing game only served to fuel interest in them and the film. When they dined together at the fashionable Italian restaurant Coco Pazzo, the manager, Marco Mendoza, observed, 'Miss Aniston was a nice lady. You wouldn't have known they were movie stars.' The scrutiny of Jennifer was intense. Her meal choices were itemized to make sure she was eating properly and not pining for Brad. She drank Chardonnay and ate chicken and a mixed salad and for dessert they shared panna cotta, gelato and tartufo. Clearly her appetite was unaffected.

Jennifer also took Brad's mother, Jane, to the restaurant when she came for a visit in August. The two women had become good friends and Jane found Jennifer terrific company. Here is a week in the life of Jennifer Aniston's 'star track' log:

1 August – took Jane to see Chicago from the Hancock Observatory.

2 August – rented a 48ft yacht for an architectural tour down the Chicago River.

3 August – dined with Jane at Coco Pazzo.

7 August – took Jane to the Shedd Aquarium.

7 August – dined with Vince and five friends at the Japonais restaurant where she ate strip steak. Afterwards, a fan on the street allegedly shouted, 'You don't need him [Brad] Jen.'

9 August – went to see Buckingham Fountain with Vince before strolling over to Millennium Park where the *Daily Mirror* reported they were caught smooching.

14 August – invited the cast and crew of *The Break-Up* to a sunset dinner cruise and dined on chicken, salmon and a chocolate dessert.

The media only had eyes for Jennifer and Vince, however, reporting every time they came within five yards of one another. Even if they were in a group of half a dozen friends relaxing after a day's filming, it was always made to sound as if it was an intimate date. Jennifer was reportedly seen sneaking back to her suite at the Peninsula after spending the evening with Vince at the Four Seasons Hotel. Vince was decidedly prickly about the publicity declaring, 'I know people would love it if we were dating. But we're not.' Eventually the weight of evidence rendered these denials silly, especially when photographs surfaced a couple of months later of the two of them kissing passionately. Jennifer's spokesman helpfully observed that 'Jennifer hugs everybody', while she herself complained of the press, 'They really need boundaries.'

Vince had helped devise the original story of *The Break-Up* and wanted to set it in his old stomping ground of Chicago. The story was almost anti-rom-com – a bickering couple with little in common decide to break up and then continue to live in the same apartment. At this point, the plot was playing out like an old Cary Grant/Irene Dunne movie or, latterly, something starring Meg Ryan. In *The Break-Up*, however, the couple stay broken up, a twist that defies all the rules of romantic comedy. Vince always had Jennifer in mind for the role of Brooke, who works in a Chicago art gallery and falls for his character, Gary, a brash tour guide. Their relationship founders on the trivia of cohabitation – his refusal to do the dishes and his desire for a pool table. She asks him to bring home twelve lemons for a table centrepiece. He only brings three and it's downhill from there. Vince explained, 'They're not really arguing about the lemons. It's never about the lemons.' Jennifer, like Brooke, insists on a clean kitchen before she goes to bed. She always does the dishes, or loads the dishwasher.

Vince wanted Jennifer for the role for the same qualities that she had been developing throughout her acting career – good timing and understatement. She was exactly the type of actor who would bring out the best in Vince. She knew how to 'feed' him. As a result he observed, 'She is the heart of the movie.' The story was developed by Vince and two buddies and so they solicited Jennifer's feminine input. She had always liked to offer ideas to the scriptwriters in *Friends* but they were not always that welcome. But here they genuinely wanted to know what the female response would be. She may or may not have recalled one of the many rows she had had with Brad, although it's amusing to speculate that they may not have seen eye to eye over the pool table. She admitted that she found filming *The Break-Up* therapeutic. One of the funniest 'in' jokes is when her character Brooke admits to having a Telly Savalas wax job, an affectionate reference to the shaven head of Jennifer's much-missed godfather who had died in 1994. In front of the mirror Brooke admires the results with the line, 'Who loves ya, baby.'

Back in the real world, the problem for Jennifer was that whenever she walked past a news stand she, Angelina or Brad would be on the cover of most of the glossy magazines with a variety of hurtful headlines, 'Did Brad secretly propose to Angelina?' or 'Is Angelina pregnant with Brad's baby?' That was all speculation but the reality was just as hurtful. Brad joined Angelina in Ethiopia in July, where she visited the Horizons for Children orphanage in Addis Ababa and collected a baby girl for adoption who she called Zahara Marley Jolie. Brad's presence dispelled any lingering doubts that he was firmly part of this family unit.

It was even more distressing when Brad and Angelina posed for a bizarre sixty-page photo shoot depicting the light and dark side of marital life in *W* magazine. Called 'Domestic Bliss' it featured them as man and wife with a number of children made up to look like little Brad lookalikes. Brad had apparently come up with the concept of exploring the 'unidentifiable malaise' that wrecks apparently perfect marriages. The photo essay, with virtually no text, was set in fictional suburbia at the time of Kennedy's assassination in 1963, the year Brad was born.

As part of a publicity campaign for *Mr and Mrs Smith*, it was a master stroke. Whether intentionally or not, it gave the impression of sticking a knife into Jennifer and twisting it. The plight of her friend moved Kristin Hahn to memorably observe, 'This woman is basically having a root canal without anaesthesia.' Public sympathy for Jennifer was overwhelming in the months following her separation. The Hollywood boutique Kitson produced two sets of baseball shirts, one with the logo Team Aniston and the other Team Jolie. Jennifer's shirt was said to have outsold Angelina's by twenty-five to one. Many more women in the world felt they could be like Jennifer Aniston. Very few could imagine themselves as Angelina Jolie, however much they might fancy Brad Pitt.

The defining moment of post-Brad Jennifer came in the notorious interview she gave to Leslie Bennetts for the September 2005 issue of *Vanity Fair* at the bungalow in Malibu, just down the beach from where Courteney Cox had a weekend house. It was a beautiful bolt-hole, although Jennifer complained she was becoming trapped there by the 'ratzies' as she called the paparazzi who dogged her footsteps. When she opened the door to Leslie, she smiled and then promptly burst into tears. The ensuing interview was a heady cocktail of distress and anger. Jennifer was especially angry at the suggestion that the marriage had ended because she had refused to have Pitt's baby: 'That really pissed me off. I've never in my life said I don't want children. I did, I do and I will!'

Jennifer told Leslie that some evenings she would walk to the edge of the ocean and just scream. She also admitted that she had days when she would throw 'a little pity party' for herself. 'I would be a robot if I said I didn't feel moments of anger, of hurt, of embarrassment.'

She was at pains not to blame Brad but, somehow, her refusal to point a damning finger made his actions seem even less acceptable. She even shrugged off the *W* feature: 'He makes his choices. He can do – whatever. We're divorced and you can see why.' Memorably she condemned him with the killer remark, 'There's a sensitivity chip missing.'

Most interestingly, however, having dismissed the suggestion that the question of children lay at the heart of their split, Jennifer explained that Brad was emotionally unavailable to her when she most needed him at the time *Friends* ended: 'It was a family and I don't do great with families splitting up,' she revealed.

One of the more heartening things Jennifer talked of was the re-establishment of contact with her mother Nancy. They had, she confirmed, exchanged messages. It was a very small step but a start. They still have very little contact and, despite all the paparazzi following Jennifer nobody has ever captured a picture of her with her mother. They continue to lead separate lives, but she remains close to her father, John.

If this interview was therapy then it was a long and painful session on the couch – perhaps that was the point: hit rock bottom and then move on. The worst moment of the interview was when she wept, tears running down her cheeks, unable to talk about the rumours that Angelina was already pregnant with Brad's child. Kristin Hahn did the talking for her, 'My worst fear is that Jen will have to face them having a baby together soon because that would be beyond painful.' In the subsequent fallout Kristin left Plan B and Jennifer also gave up her interest in the company shortly afterwards, thereby missing out on involvement in the Oscar-winning *The Departed* (2006) and *A Mighty Heart* (2007).

The 'beyond painful' moment duly arrived in January 2006 when it was announced that Angelina was pregnant. She had already changed the surnames of her adopted children to Jolie-Pitt and Brad was looking into legally adopting them. Jen heard the pregnancy news and then went out to dinner with Vince at La Velvet Margarita Cantina in Hollywood. *Grazia* magazine reported that she said, 'Obviously I wasn't the woman Brad wanted to have a family with and Angelina is. That's all there is to it.'

At least Jennifer had a busy schedule lined up to take her mind off things. Having made four films in twelve months, she now had the task of promoting them. The most excruciating episode came when she visited London in July 2006 to promote *The Break-Up* and appeared on *Richard and Judy.* Finnegan gushed, 'I honestly don't know of anybody we've interviewed who has inspired so many of our friends and teenage children to say, "Please tell her I love her."' Jennifer replied, 'You've got me all kerplunked.' She also told them that Vince was a 'great friend'.

Reviews of *The Break-Up* were a little mixed although it did well at the box office, taking more than $118 million in the US. James Christopher in *The Times* called it a 'slick anti-romantic comedy'. He also thought it funnier and spikier than the equally hyped *Mr and Mrs Smith*. Jessica Reaves in the *Chicago Tribune* enthused, 'Aniston really shines when Brooke is alone, particularly in one scene that feels almost uncomfortably intimate. It's Aniston's return to the emotional authenticity that surfaced too briefly in *Friends With Money* and made *The Good Girl* such a revelation.'

Back home in Los Angeles Jennifer went house hunting and found a new property, again near Courteney Cox, in Beverly Hills. Her relationship with Vince was still going strong in 2006, although he was decidedly a man's man. 'Nobody's ever treated her like that before,' said a friend. Vince was very much the kind of man who would prefer to go and watch a ball game with his pals than chat cosily over a glass of wine. He was fun though. When he went to pick her up from a yoga class she was attending, he insisted on joining in. All the ladies dissolved into fits of giggles at the sight of six-foot-five-inch-tall Vince trying to stand on one leg.

Jennifer's new life as a single woman – her divorce having been finalized in October 2005 – did not revolve around Vince Vaughn. They would spend time together at her house on Blue Jay Way or at the beach house she rented in Malibu. Vince would sometimes take the dogs for a walk or pop out to buy cigarettes and groceries, while Jennifer was more withdrawn, finding strength and motivation in friends like Mandy Ingber.

Mandy taught Jennifer yoga and her bright green Beetle was often seen parked outside Jennifer's house. Jennifer had never been a yoga person, preferring a disconnected exercise regime to keep trim, pounding the treadmill for hours. Mandy Ingber changed all that and Jennifer has said that feeling fitter physically has helped her to feel fitter emotionally. Ingber told *Self* magazine, 'Emotions are energy. When you channel them physically, they're fuel.' Mandy helped Jennifer to look inwards and resolve her inevitable crises of confidence and identity after her marriage breakdown.

Jennifer explained that under Mandy's guidance she found an emotional release, admitting that she cried while doing the moves: 'You feel like you're having a therapy session, a workout and a meditation at the same time.'

Most days she would pop in to see Courteney Cox and her daughter Coco. Courteney's husband David Arquette also proved a great support. He was surprisingly forthcoming in an interview with the famous broadcaster Howard Stern in which he revealed that they knew all about the split with Brad but it was 'pretty much a surprise' when they found out he was sleeping with Angelina: 'I love Brad. He's a great guy. He did some stuff that hurt our friend.' He also said quite candidly that he did not think Jennifer hated Angelina because she was not like that. His tribute to Jennifer is touching: 'She's the greatest, she's a sweetheart, and she's so funny. She's a very strong woman, she's totally solid and she's got a great attitude.' He, personally, had never seen her shed one tear over Brad.

She still had to deal with the worldwide interest in the birth of Shiloh Nouvel Jolie-Pitt in Namibia on 27 May 2006. Brad was there at Angelina's side and cut the umbilical cord of his first child. *Heat* magazine reported that Jen heard the news when watching television in a Chicago hotel room. She was in the city promoting *The Break-Up* with Vince.

After the success of *The Break-Up*, Jennifer finally did what she should probably have done after *Friends* finished – she properly took time out to top up her tan, her favourite occupation. She did not totally forsake work though, joining her best friend Andrea in their first directing venture, *Room 10*. Starring Kris Kristofferson and Robin Wright Penn, it was about the relationship between a nurse and an emergency-room patient. Penn observed of Jennifer, 'She's not aggressive but she's assertive with her vision. She was very loving and calm and knew what she wanted.' Jennifer had other plans for diversifying her career which she had to reassess post-Brad when she was no longer involved with Plan B. Together, for instance, she and Brad had bought the rights to the acclaimed novel *The Time Traveller's Wife* but she will now not be associated with the project when it finally makes it to screen.

Jennifer made her Broadway debut in October 2006, nearly eighteen years after she had taken her final bow on *For Dear Life*. Like her very first starring role in *Dancing on Checkers'*

Grave, years before in St Mark's Church, the play, *Three Girls and Bob*, was just ten minutes long. Jennifer was one of the three girlfriends who go to an intimacy workshop and then try out its lessons on a hapless young man. The *New York Post* was complimentary and it was a light and happy experience.

The play was part of the sixth annual '24 Hour Plays' festival to benefit the Working Playground Inc., an organization that aims to bring the arts in to the classrooms of New York. Not every child can go the Fame School, but as many as possible should be able to benefit from exposure to the arts and the ability of music, drama and dance to inspire and energize those who come from poor, underprivileged communities. Jennifer liked the concept. Her co-star Rosie Perez, Oscar nominated for *Fearless* (1993), said of Jennifer, 'She was as sweet as pie. I really appreciated her coming because she raised the profile of the event and that is going to help so much.'

The hat-trick for Vince Vaughn of *Wedding Crashers*, *Mr and Mrs Smith* and *The Break-Up*, all of which were phenomenally successful, pushed his salary into the $20-million bracket for the 2007 release *Fred Claus*. When he travelled to Europe for filming in the autumn of 2006 stories soon began to circulate that he and Jennifer had split up. The denials followed and Jennifer flew to London where she stayed with Vince at the Dorchester Hotel. They did then, however, agree to end things amicably and issued a brief statement to that effect before Christmas. They said they would continue to be good friends. Speculation abounded as to who dumped who and why. A favourite theory was that Jennifer was too needy. They were certainly nice about each other when they attended the 2007 People's Choice Awards at the beginning of the year. Jennifer made everyone laugh when she accepted the award, again, for best female film star and said, 'Thank you for enjoying *The Break-Up*; I did.'

The new year, 2007, began poorly for Jennifer. Angelina featured in the January issue of *Vogue* saying she would welcome a real sit-down-and-talk kind of meeting with Jennifer. She put the onus on Jennifer saying, 'That would be her decision.' As Chandler Bing would say, 'Like *that's* going to happen.' Jennifer's new home was not yet ready. She was officially single, although that was not a surprise. David Arquette confirmed that she and Vince had really cared about one another, putting the relationship firmly in the past tense, although Vince did turn up at her thirty-eighth birthday party so perhaps all was not lost. She did not have the appetite for the Oscars where the former Plan B partners were set to celebrate the success of the Martin Scorsese film *The Departed*, which the company had co-produced. All these irritants paled into insignificance, however, with the news from New York on 15 February that Daniel McDonald, one of the loves of her life, had died from brain cancer at the wretchedly young age of forty-six. He had been gravely ill for some time but that did not make his death any easier to bear. They had remained on good terms and she had been delighted at his professional success and private contentment with his wife and two children. Daniel was Jennifer's first adult love and she always described him as 'a very dear friend'.

In May Brad and Angelina were at the Cannes Film Festival to promote their new films, *A Mighty Heart* and *Ocean's Thirteen*. Only three years earlier, in 2004, Jennifer had been on Brad's arm at Cannes and, to make matters worse, Angelina was being tipped for an Oscar nomination for her role in the film which Jennifer had expected to be hers. Brad looked in great shape but Angelina appeared thin and drawn, which did not escape media attention.

He had learned a lesson from his time with Jennifer and had not allowed absence to interfere with this relationship. He joined Angelina when she was filming in Prague, helping to look after the children and teaching local kids how to play soccer. He was in his element as the family man and he loved watching baby Shiloh fall asleep in Angelina's arms. A friend of the couple confided that Angelina had finally agreed to have a second baby. They were also seeking to adopt another African child so Brad would then have five children – well on the way to the seven he wanted.

Jennifer did very little acting in the two years following *The Break-Up*, although taking a sabbatical had no effect on the general public's desire to hoover up any information about her life. She was still very much the number one 'cover girl' for glossy magazines and the US tabloids. In this very competitive world, editors have to be certain the cover girl will boost sales and Jennifer is one of a handful guaranteed to do just that. Angelina Jolie is another, while in the UK only Victoria Beckham could be considered a serious rival. The mere fact of their perceived rivalry seems to have given Jennifer and Angelina an extended shelf life that shows no sign of slowing down.

Two magazines sat side by side on the news stands in June 2007. *New* magazine carried a picture of Angelina Jolie with the banner 'Angelina's Breakdown'. The other, *Look*, displayed a picture of Jennifer with the words, 'Jen's Shock Breakdown'. She can expect more 'breakdowns' when and if Brad and Angelina marry. For some reason the media are labouring under the impression that Brad and Jen talk all the time, remain close and still harbour feelings of love for each other. This is not the case, although it continues to be a good story.

Jennifer can expect the public to remain completely fascinated by her love life. Every time she comes within coughing distance of a man it will make the front page. Within days of her 'shock breakdown' she was linked to a 'former Essex bricklayer'. Paul Sculfor was not really a brickie but a thirty-six-year-old male model who had once worked on a building site when he left school. He was very handsome, was once in an ad for Levi's jeans and looks worryingly like Brad. As a friend observed, 'Paul is a man's man rather like Brad and Vince in that regard and that seems to be the sort of man Jennifer goes for.' Poor Jennifer was reported to be talking babies with Paul before she even knew how he liked his coffee. They certainly had dinner together and his Range Rover was parked all night outside her house, according to people who like to keep a round-the-clock check on these sorts of things.

At the time Paul lived with a pal in a modest apartment off Wilshire Boulevard and much was made of his lack of A-list credentials. The implication was that he would merely use Jennifer as a stepping stone to improve his alphabet rating. As it is he never really had the chance. No sooner had the Sunday papers picked over the bones of his past than the brief dalliance was over. The funniest aspect of his friendship with Jennifer was when he was photographed leaving her house clutching a bottle of Smart Water, which Jennifer advertises. It was suggested that it was all an elaborate stunt to plug the product. Hopefully that was not the case, because Jennifer is a single woman who is allowed to date good-looking men.

In the Autumn, Jennifer was briefly linked to Orlando Bloom, further proof that she will be associated with practically every eligible name in Hollywood until she settles into a more long-term relationship again. Much more significant was her enduring friendship with Vince Vaughan. They were no longer an item in Hollywood terms but, in some ways, removing that pressure seemed to suit them better. Occasionally, Vince was sighted in or near Jennifer's company, giving rise to the rumour that they were enjoying a 'friends with benefits' relationship.

Jennifer resumed her film career in late 2007, and while shooting *Management* in Portland, Oregon, phone calls to Vince helped to brighten the lonely evenings away from her close circle of friends in Los Angeles. When she returned home she and Vince met up for drinks at the fashionable Bar Nineteen 12 at the Beverley Hills Hotel. They were both with friends and, according to eye witnesses, spirits were high and, at one point, Jennifer suddenly darted round the table, sat on Vince's lap and gave him a big kiss. The key to their enduring friendship is that they are both amusing and lively company and make each other laugh. It may or may not build up again into something more.

Vince was put in the frame by the *National Enquirer* newspaper when they ran a story just before the New Year suggesting that Jennifer was pregnant. Nothing came of the rumour, although there was some interest in speculating who might be the daddy. It will not be the last time she is the subject of such conjecture. Vince was named as one of three possible fathers, along with Paul Sculfor and actor Jason Lewis, who played the character of Smith in *Sex and the City*. The latter is no doubt just the first in a string of impossibly good-looking men who will be linked to Jennifer in 2008.

Unsurprisingly, however, when the midnight chimes rang in the New Year, Jennifer could be found celebrating in Mexico in the company of Courtney Cox. Boyfriends – even husbands – may come and go but, in Jennifer's world, friends are forever.

Last Thoughts

We all feel we know Jennifer Aniston; that's a huge part of her continuing appeal. I hope anyone reading this book will now know her a bit better. Rachel Green is a character developed by good writers and a talented actress working in unison. Rachel is *not* Jennifer, although they do share universal problems – uncertainty over the future, insecurities over love and career and, of particular importance to Jennifer, an enduring bond with 'friends'. The love and support of friends seems to be the constant theme in Jennifer's life. Her lifelong friends from 'The Hill' are her 'chosen family'; the cast of *Friends* are also her family; former boyfriends like Daniel McDonald were 'dear friends'; Brad Pitt was a 'bud'; Vince Vaughn was a close friend. Andrea, Courteney, Kristin, Kathy, and Mandy: these are the names around which her life has appeared to revolve, but not, it seems, Nancy, her mother.

In my opinion the defining relationships of Jennifer's life are with her mother and father and not with Brad Pitt. Any feelings of rejection, bitterness and anger are rooted in her parental connections and not her high-profile marriage to a very handsome movie star. Jennifer herself said she was not defined by her relationship with Brad, not before, during or after – a view that reflects her position as an empowered woman in today's society. She has never said that she did not want children and to suggest that her marriage foundered on her refusal or inability to produce them on demand is as insulting as it is ridiculous. I believe she and Brad found themselves out of sync, almost inevitably when you consider the amount of time they spent apart. Brad and Angelina Jolie are seeking to avoid that trap by staying together, even if one of them is on location. Brad went along and just hung out with their children when Angelina was filming in Pakistan and subsequently in Prague.

A question I am often asked is: 'Do you think Brad was cheating with Angelina while he was still married to Jennifer?' My reply is that I don't know if they had a physical relationship but my inclination is to believe that they did not. I do, however, believe that they had fallen in love. If that were the case, then the answer to the question would have to depend on one's personal definition of cheating. In any event, Jennifer appears to have given Brad the option of checking out of their marriage and he took it. I also do not see Jennifer as a victim.

Jennifer's relationship with Nancy remains puzzling, although stories of reconciliation have removed that aspect of controversy from Jennifer's life. The attitude seems to be the old favourite of time being the great healer, although Jennifer's decision not to invite Nancy to her wedding or, indeed, to ever introduce her to Brad demonstrates a depth of feeling that no throwaway remark can ever adequately explain. Personally, I won't believe there has been a proper reconciliation until Nancy is seated in the front row at her daughter's second wedding, whenever that may be.

Jennifer's private life will continue to be the subject of intense scrutiny. Every man with whom she shares a margarita will be seen as a potential husband until she finds someone more permanent. I was trying to think of a suitable candidate. Of course the trouble with dating another huge star is that it just doubles the spotlight. She could go for an oldie but goodie like Jack Nicholson but he just seems to have been around the block too many times. She should steer clear of some unsuitable Kevin Federline type because they are never going to be out of the papers. Cries of 'Ditch him Jen,' would inevitably follow. She could go for someone much less famous than herself, following the example of Madonna or Julia Roberts. Perhaps some billionaire who nobody has heard of is the answer?

More seriously, why do we care what happens to Jennifer? I think this is her appeal – she is like a sister or a best friend. She is the one who a million women every day are having lunch with to catch up with the gossip; arranging to go shopping with for shoes; sending notes to on Facebook about something funny that happened on the way in to work; or just gossiping with in the ladies' loo about the boss. She is every woman's best friend. She is also devastatingly attractive with the most beautiful eyes, yet somehow not unobtainable. Of all the many quotes I have heard about Jennifer, the one that sticks most in my mind is the one from movie executive Mary Parent in which she observes that Jennifer appeals equally to men and women and, crucially, that women don't punish her for the fact that men find her so attractive, or 'hot'.

★

I intend to finish this book looking at Jennifer Aniston the actress. There is no reason for her not to celebrate her role as Rachel

Green. Her performance over ten years is a wonderful legacy, even without considering the repeats that net her an estimated $6 million a year. She need never work again as an actress but that would be an enormous pity. Simply, she is very accomplished and, whenever she has been called upon to to stretch herself, she has risen to the challenge. Her performance in *The Good Girl* is the oft-quoted example of that, although I find just as much to praise in her more obvious, romantic-comedy output like *The Object Of My Affection*.

Jennifer's old drama coach Anthony Abeson, who much admires her abilities, recently wrote her an empassioned letter about her future work. He recalls, 'I wrote and asked her, "When was the last time you read Molière? He's a brother of yours; and you must look at *Tartuffe*; the role of Dorine is a part you might want." And I also wanted her to read O'Neill, particularly *Desire Under The Elms*, where the part of the young wife is one she could do.' Anthony firmly believes that Jennifer should return to the theatre. The dilemma is that in the US there is no national theatre so it is not that easy for a star like Jennifer to simply alternate between theatre and film. His sentiment – and one with which I concur – is that the development of talent is increasingly difficult in proportion to the level of success you attain. The desire and pressure to duplicate success magnifies the fear of failure.

Jennifer Aniston is already one of the finest comedy actresses of her generation. I would rank her equal first with Cameron Diaz, but that sort of thing is a matter of opinion. But I also agree with Anthony that she has the potential to be regarded as one of the finest actresses per se and should not be pigeonholed into comedy as if it somehow undermined her talent. Comedy springs from truth and Jennifer is a very truthful actress. Indeed, Anthony ended his letter to Jennifer: 'You deserve the company of giants because just the ability to be both truthful and funny is rare.' I can't say it any better, although the other day I did read a magazine article about Jennifer, giving her advice on how to deal with break-ups. The third suggestion was 'Stay Busty'. This struck me as being just the ticket for Jennifer, until I put my glasses back on and saw that the actual advice was 'Stay Busy'. Oh well.

Sean Smith
July 2007

Jennifer Aniston Natal Chart

11 Feb 1969

Los Angeles, California

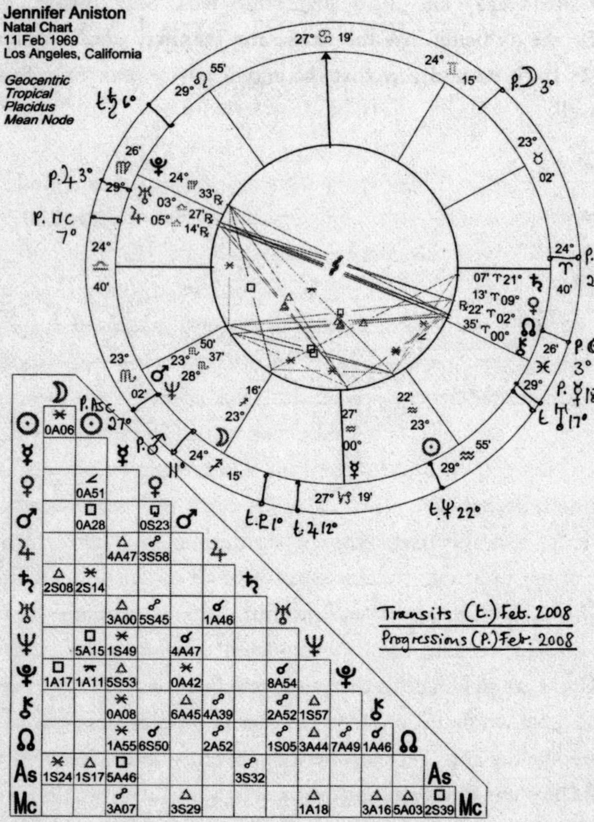

The Jennifer Aniston Birth Chart

Few people could fail to be charmed by this intelligent, tolerant individual, with her exceptional sense of purpose and wise reserve.

As with many people, the birth chart of Jennifer Aniston reveals the conflicting drives which create a complex personality. We notice her Moon, for example, in adventurous Sagittarius and realize she is instinctively a free spirit. Then we see that the planet is shadowed by a significant aspect from Pluto, suggesting at times, perhaps from fear, that she curbs the expression of her feelings, restrains and buries her emotions. So, here there are strengths, and there, weaknesses – like all of us. And yet, somehow less so. Somehow the chart shifts and changes and seems to speak of a woman adept at balancing, at harmonising clashing instincts, at melding together disparate qualities into a strong and admirable whole. And this is Jennifer: a little bit less like us and more like the gods. The girl next door, but shinier. Someone who embodies our times and makes us delight in them.

The key to this alchemy is Mercury, the planet of communication, travel, the rational mind and connections. At the time of

Jennifer's birth, fast moving Mercury had just slipped into Aquarius, a sign where it functions with lightning ease. It endows her with a quick, quirky, questioning mentality, whilst an aspect from Neptune contributes an imaginative, creative dimension. From this position of strength, at the base of her chart, Mercury aspects five other planets, including conjunct Uranus and Jupiter, revealing her role as a communicator for her generation, a role which at present may be pursued through acting. Jennifer may think she has chosen to seek fame in her lifetime. Astrologers would consider that it is her destiny to live out, in public, issues which are pertinent to her peers.

With pivotal Mercury making fine aspects to Uranus and Jupiter, Jennifer will have an innate understanding of the way open education and the cultivation of free thinking liberates people. Her own early education would have encouraged a questioning mind. As a representative of the generation born between 1968 and 1975, when Uranus was positioned in Libra, she will carry the flag, in her personal life and work, for honest relationships based upon equality and fair-minded communication. She is the graceful and intelligent embodiment of liberal western values which stress the importance of unrestricted thought and the right to choose our own associates and lifestyles.

Mercury placed in the fourth house (associated with heritage) tells us much about Jennifer's family life and roots. As a planet which symbolizes mental curiosity and restlessness, her family would have embodied these qualities. She would have been conditioned to adaptability. She would have been a natural go-between. In Aquarius it does not suggest an overly warm emotional environment. Instead, home life would have been driven by social communication, reason-based family decisions and elements of unpredictability; it was a household that made its own rules. Some aspects of tradition, most likely those associated with the father, would have been valued within the home and the young Jennifer's early ambitions may have benefited from a down-to-earth parental attitude.

In her early years, Jennifer would have perceived her father as nomadic, ambitious and self-motivated. Neptune touching the Sun indicates he may not always have been easily available to her, contributing to her early development of emotional self-sufficiency. The planet is conjunct Mars, in sexually charismatic Scorpio, conjuring an image of someone with much glamorous appeal. Jennifer may have felt his time for her was limited. Her mother would have been seen as intense, with high standards expected of her daughter, accompanied by an innate faith in her. The placement of the Moon in Sagittarius suggests a woman who was naturally philosophical; for the most part, able to appreciate lessons learned from hard conditions. The challenging aspect between the Moon and Pluto is a sign that her mother may have had a difficult family background. She would have carried scars and struggled with strong emotions as a young adult, leaving her less than happy in a nurturing role. Later, as a natural teacher, she would be able to guide her daughter through hard-won experience. Her mother's strengths would have included ambition and management ability; a neat aspect between the Moon and Saturn enabling her to organize and bring structure to situations easily. Jennifer would have inherited perfectionist traits from her mother, together with a highly developed instinct to guard her emotions. She is not someone who will open up easily – Jennifer's inner life is heavily defended.

Tensions between Jennifer and her parents would have played

out along very traditional lines. They would have desired that their daughter 'fitted in' to whatever conventions they felt were the norm and Jennifer would have attempted some balancing act, keeping divergent or radical views in the closet. This is indicated by Uranus, the ruler of Jennifer's Sun, in the Libran twelfth house of the horoscope, where it conjuncts Jupiter. The twelfth house is known as the house of secret enemies. Jennifer would have felt driven by the need to find her own truths but might not have felt able to express these freely; a common enough generational issue. The trouble with this is that later in life Jennifer would be likely to replay this dynamic. She will appear to acquiesce to situations that she will unconsciously oppose. Thus she might feel trapped by aspects of her employment or a partnership, failing to initiate changes to become free yet inwardly rebellious. These situations usually force others to enact the needed change, placing them in the role of enemy. And yet, the secret enemy is no other than the person who hides their true needs from themself.

This inclination to self-sabotage is born out by other signs in the chart – the symbols clearly indicating the pull between Jennifer's instinct to be part of a union and her extraordinary drive towards developing her separate individual identity. The Ascendant and Descendent are points which lie across from each other in the birth chart and reveal a great deal about the individual's relationship needs. Jennifer's Libra Ascendant, ruled by decorous Venus, suggests a woman who might seem the embodiment of charm, diplomacy and sweet reasonableness, someone for whom partnership is as natural as the need to breathe. However, Venus is placed in its opposite sign of Aries where it forms a jarring link to Mars. Whilst unquestionably bequeathing allure and popularity – a seductiveness based upon directness – beneath the graciousness lies a competitive and uncompromising spirit. Adding to this tense combination is the uncooperative influence of Uranus, the planet of independence, whilst Mars lies with mystical and enveloping Neptune. Considering this interesting mix, it is fair to say that Jennifer's relationships will be formidable – genuine lessons in the art of give and take, intimacy and freedom, love and loss. She will be drawn to merge, to find closeness of mind and spirit, and driven back, frightened of becoming completely immersed with another. Scared of the vulnerability love can bring, there will be great sensitivity to rejection hidden behind a bright and airy front.

But all's well that ends well, and this we may reasonably predict for Jennifer. With Saturn, the planet associated with perseverance and time-gained wisdom, linked to the partnership area of her chart, Jennifer will achieve greater happiness in her relationships in the second half of her life. Saturn here, opposite her Venus-ruled Ascendant, suggests issues of control will have dominated her partnerships. Her evangelical Moon in Sagittarius, linked to her humane and tolerant Aquarian Sun, reveal she is genuinely driven by the desire to make life more meaningful for others. But with growing insight she will increasingly understand the necessity of reigning in the impulse to impose her principles and ideas on others. She must let them make their own mistakes.

By its placement, beautifully aspected, ever-curious Mercury dominates this chart. It emphasizes how much the bedrock of her family heritage has catalysed her starry flight, and it reveals how much she has learned from the initial relationships formed there. That the family dynamics formed the psychological foundations that she will continue to explore and possibly replicate, is stressed by the positioning of her Sun near the base of her chart; she will be drawn back to her roots, eventually content to honour them.

But Jennifer is more than just a sophisticated human-interactions guru. This horoscope reveals an individual driven to lead a productive and worthwhile life. Many of the planets are placed in cardinal signs – indicative of someone who gets things done – and a strong, action-orientated Mars provides the passion to initiate projects and fight for what she believes in. And undoubtedly, one of the principle things she believes in is money. Energetic Mars makes a positive link to Pluto, traditionally the God of Wealth, revealing an instinctive appreciation of the power of riches. Jennifer can be decisive about investments and has unquestionably known the heady delights of impulse spending. It is appropriate that Mars is joined with Neptune, the planet which rules film, the vehicle which has generated her income. However this combination is significant in other respects. Neptune can be idealistic and spiritually refining in its influence. It is the planet of compassion, sacrifice and atonement. There is a definite feel from this link, together with the stellium of planets in the chart area associated with service, that within this individual lurks a potential spiritual warrior, an 'old soul' whose values lie beyond material pleasures and inclusive relationships.

The sign of moon-ruled Cancer is found at the very top of this birth chart. It informs us that Jennifer has a nurturing, protective side to her personality which will come to the fore in her public life. This could be as simple as becoming a mother in the most conventional manner, a role in which she would shine. However, this birth chart suggests something on a greater scale – a consequence of planets stressing humanitarian instincts and strong desires for fairness. It is likely that Jennifer may use her resources to support projects which provide education for those in need, most likely abroad. This is someone who truly values learning, appreciates the freedom it endows and is sensitive to issues of gender equality. Who could doubt, noting the Jupiter-Uranus combination so powerfully placed, that whatever she instigated would have very great impact.

Between February 2005 and November 2006 Jennifer will have experienced the effects of transiting Pluto, the planet of death and regeneration, forming a difficult aspect to her natal Pluto. This is never a comfortable time as issues are forced to the surfaces which have been buried, demanding recognition. The energy of a Pluto transit can seem unforgiving; the more change is resisted, the harsher is the battering. The inevitable destruction of attachments which may no longer be beneficial to the individual is completely non-negotiable. Anything that forms a barrier to future growth can be ruthlessly swept away. In Jennifer's chart, Pluto rules the area associated with finances and personal values. By placement, it would have affected friends, hopes and dreams, whilst indirectly it influences the chart point connected with legal partnerships. All of these concerns will have undergone transformative change during this time, enabling rebirth and progression.

This planetary energy is one of a number of significant transits which span, for everyone, the mid-life years; its shocking nature felt most by those who are used to controlling situations. But there is no question that Jennifer will be stronger from this experience – rigid values and approaches will have softened and clearer life priorities will have emerged. The remaining outer-planet transits occur during 2011 for Jennifer, stripping away whatever belongs to youth, strengthening her spirit and repositioning her towards her chosen life's direction.

In the meantime 2008 will be a year of strong attachments which will prompt greater self expression and vision. Between February 2008 and January 2009 Neptune joins the Sun in the birth chart stressing much greater sensitivity and compassion. Jennifer may use this energy to change her creative work in subtle ways. Her ambition will alter and broaden. If she remains in film, she is likely, over the next few years, as transiting Pluto moves to aspect Uranus, to explore darker, more intense subjects. The indications are that she will find her true power as a communicator or go-between, although this may be carried on behind the scenes.

Jennifer must guard against the draining of emotion and energy, protecting herself from those who demand too much of her. Advising someone who must already be finely tuned to health issues to maintain this awareness might seem unnecessary but 2009 will bring some challenges which may undermine her vitality. During these years, Jupiter, the great benefic, will be at the bottom of Jennifer's chart. She will be strongly motivated by the need to ensure her personal life is secure and contented, realizing that the inner growth she is seeking now comes from this private stability and that this is essential for future success in the world. She may move; essentially this is the perfect time to establish a base where she feels comfortable and at peace.

Madeleine Moore

July 2007

Acknowledgements

One of the joys of writing a book about an American star is that it gives me the opportunity to cross the Atlantic and spend some time in a country I love. This time, I was lucky enough to be based in both New York and Los Angeles. I would like to thank everyone I met in these two great and very different cities who helped make *Jennifer* such an enjoyable project.

Firstly, my thanks to Cliff Renfrew for putting up with me as a house guest in Santa Monica for far too long. It was great to see my old friends Richard Mineards and Gill Pringle who have always been so helpful with my books. Bob Smith and Bev Ecker also gave me excellent advice. I am grateful to everyone who shared their thoughts and memories of Jennifer Aniston and enabled me to build a picture of the real person behind the image. Some wished to remain anonymous because of the very small-world nature of Hollywood and I have respected their wishes. Others included Anthony Abeson, Michael Baroni, Martin Grimes, Steve Levy, Ed McCarthy, Raven Metzner, D. David Moran, Bellina Logan, Lauren Pratt, Laila Robins and Thor Wasbotten.

I strongly recommend *Friends . . .'Til the End* by David Wild, filled with excellent pictures and memories of a great TV series. Guiltily, I enjoyed Nancy Aniston's book *From Mother and Daughter to Friends: A Memoir*. Jennifer has given a number of illuminating interviews over the years, in particular to Leslie Bennetts in *Vanity Fair*, but also, among others, to *Rolling Stone*, *Vogue*, *People* magazine and *W* magazine. My favourite Jennifer website is www.anistonavenue.com. I was hoping to find The Holy Tabernacle of Aniston the Divine but this brilliant sounding website seems to have disappeared.

In London, the enthusiasm and good advice of my agent, Gordon Wise at Curtis Brown, has been invaluable. I would like to thank Lizzie Clachan and Alison Sims for doing such outstanding research. Lizzie, who has been my principal researcher on six books, is a very talented artist and I hope you caught the installation she designed in front of the Royal Festival Hall this summer. Adele's Typing Works were as dependable and speedy as ever in transcribing all my tapes.

At Pan Macmillan, my thanks to Ingrid Connell for commissioning this biography and overseeing its progress, project editor Lorraine Baxter for looking after the book so well, Georgina Difford for editorial management, Neil Lang for designing the cover, Rafi Romaya for text design, Linda Sima for production, Helen Guthrie for publicity and Stephen Dumughn for marketing.

Once again, the incomparable Madeleine Moore has produced a fascinating birth chart. She never sees the manuscript before compiling the chart and brings a fresh, open mind to all her subjects. Finally, thank you to Zoë Lawrence for her help and support with all my books.

Index

INDEX

INDEX